# FORD DIAMOND JUBILEE
# RECIPE COLLECTION

Favorite Recipes and Selected
Food Articles from Thirty Years
of Ford Publications

Recipes compiled and tested
by Nancy Kennedy
Food Editor, Ford Times and
Continental Magazines

# FOREWORD

Dear Reader:

The material in this Diamond Jubilee Recipe Collection is a culinary summation of Ford Motor Company Publications. The recipes and articles were selected from *Ford Times*, from the six cookbooks we have published and from the Lincoln-Mercury Times. To a considerable degree, the book is the result of a popularity contest, because the recipes are the ones most often requested by readers who had seen them, remembered them, lost the publication in which they appeared and written to us to get them again.

Although our magazines, especially *Ford Times*, are best classified as being in the field of travel, they are to some extent also food magazines, because food and travel have been and always will be inseparable. For this reason, the most popular single feature of *Ford Times* is "Favorite Recipes from Famous Restaurants," in which each month we show a picture of each of three or four restaurants, with a brief description and one or two recipes from each. Over the years we have published about 3,000 recipes.

This feature has been of particular help to motoring Americans looking for something a little better than the ordinary at mealtimes during a journey by car. And we pride ourselves that the feature has taught many of our readers a lot about the various foods of America — the blueberry griddle cakes of Maine, the she-crab soup of South Carolina, the Olympia oysters of the Pacific Northwest, the pecan pies of Georgia, the fried perch of Michigan — that whole long and delectable list of native and ethnic dishes that make American food the delight it is.

In addition to recipes we have included a number of Ford Times food stories published throughout the years. These include stories about cooking in camp and cooking along the road, about regional food festivals, and about the variety of cooking equipment available to travelers.

We take special pleasure in offering this one-volume summation of foods in Ford publications on the occasion of Ford Motor Company's 75th anniversary. We believe you will find it pleasant to read and feel confident that it will add to your enjoyment in the dining room.

Nancy Kennedy

Book designed by Patrick W. Barney

Cover illustration by Mike Mikos

Book illustrations by Mary Haddad, Sue Georges,
Louise Clark, (Students at the Center for Creative Studies,
Detroit, Michigan) and April van der Herchen.

Editorial assistance by Kay Savage and Mary Zimmer

# TABLE OF CONTENTS

# APPETIZERS

## DANISH LIVER PASTE LOAF

1½ pounds pork liver
¾ pound pork fatback
1 large onion, minced
2 cups rich white sauce
4 eggs
2½ teaspoons salt
½ teaspoon pepper
4 ounces anchovy paste
Dash of mixed spices

Grind liver and pork separately 3 times, then together, adding the onion. Combine with the white sauce. Beat well; add eggs one at a time; then seasonings. Turn into a well-greased pan and set in a pan of water. Grease a piece of brown paper fitted to the pan and tie over the top. Bake about 2 hours or until firm in a moderate oven.

## FRENCH-FRIED DEVILED EGGS

Cut 6 hard-boiled eggs lengthwise and remove yolks. Season yolks to taste with Worcestershire sauce, mustard, salt, black pepper, oil and vinegar. Pack back into whites and hold together with toothpicks. Dip eggs into 2 beaten egg yolks, then flour and bread crumbs. Fry in deep fat until golden brown. Drain eggs on brown paper to rid them of excess grease; remove toothpicks. Serve these deviled eggs in creole sauce, or serve them on spinach or other cooked greens.

## STUFFED MUSHROOMS

12 large mushrooms
1 tablespoon lemon juice
4 tablespoons butter
1 cup minced white meat of chicken
1 cup fresh bread crumbs
Chicken broth
1 egg
1 teaspoon minced parsley
1 tablespoon grated onion
1 teaspoon salt
¼ teaspoon pepper

Remove mushroom stems; place caps in cold water to which lemon juice has been added to prevent discoloration. Chop stems into fine pieces; sauté in butter. Add chicken, stirring to prevent burning. Moisten some bread crumbs with chicken broth and egg; add to mixture. Stir in parsley, grated onion, salt and pepper. Stuff mushroom caps and sprinkle with buttered crumbs. Bake 30 to 45 minutes in shallow pan with a little water. Serves 6.

## FINGER CUCUMBER SANDWICHES

Slice cucumbers very thin, salt down, and let stand ½ hour. Squeeze out the juice; add lemon juice, finely cut onion, and a little thick cream. Spread between bread, cut into finger shapes.

## CHEESE SPREAD

- 1 pound Roquefort or blue cheese
- 5 tablespoons lemon juice
- 5 tablespoons Worcestershire sauce
- 2 tablespoons A-1 sauce
- 1 teaspoon dry mustard
- 1 teaspoon pepper
- 4 cakes cream cheese
    or 1 pound cottage cheese

Cut Roquefort cheese in small pieces. Place in electric mixer bowl. Add lemon juice, sauces, mustard and pepper. Beat, using low speed, till light and smooth. Add cottage or cream cheese. Beat again to the consistency of heavy, whipped cream. This spread can be kept for weeks in the refrigerator in a tightly covered jar.

## CHINESE-HAWAIIAN BARBECUED RIBS

- 1 inch of green ginger root
- ½ clove garlic
- ½ cup soya sauce
- ¾ cup sugar
- ½ cup catsup
- 2 ounces sherry
- 1 teaspoon salt

Crush ginger root and garlic. Place in pan. Add remaining ingredients. Rub it into a section of young pork loin back ribs and marinate for 3 hours. Place ribs on rack in a 325° oven and cook ¾ hour. Place a shallow pan of water under ribs to catch falling juices. Use balance of sauce for basting. Remove from oven, cut ribs apart, and serve hot as a delectable appetizer.

## LINDSEY CLUB CHEESE

- 1 ounce stuffed Spanish olives
- 1 medium green pepper
- 1 ounce parsley, chopped
- 6 ounces imported Roquefort cheese
- ½ pound sweet butter
- 1 pound cream cheese
- 1 teaspoon Spanish paprika
- 2 drops Tabasco sauce
- 1 teaspoon Lea and Perrins sauce

Run olives, green pepper and parsley through a fine meat grinder or blender. Press moisture from this mixture. Run Roquefort through grinder. Melt butter, then place all ingredients in a bowl and blend. Serve in loaf form with crackers. Serves 12.

## SEAFOOD COCKTAIL

- 1 lobster, boiled
- ½ pound each: blanched scallops, shrimp, crab meat and salmon
- 4 stalks celery, diced
- 3 tablespoons vinegar
- 6 tablespoons salad oil
    Salt and pepper, to taste

Dice all seafood ingredients and mix together lightly with other ingredients. Serve on a lettuce leaf with sauce.

**Sauce:**

Into 1 pint of mayonnaise, blend 3 ounces of capers, 1 medium-size onion, chopped; 3 small gherkins, chopped; stalk of parsley, chopped; a pinch of summer savory, marjoram and thyme, and 5 tablespoons of chili sauce.

## COCKTAIL SANDWICHES

- 3 hard-boiled eggs
- 18 small stuffed olives
- 2 thin slices Bermuda onion
- 1 heaping tablespoon mustard
    Salt and pepper, to taste
    Thin bread or crackers

Chop and then grind into paste the eggs, olives and onion. Blend in mustard and salt and pepper to taste. Spread on very thin bread slices or crackers. Also makes a good filling for a closed sandwich garnished with lettuce.

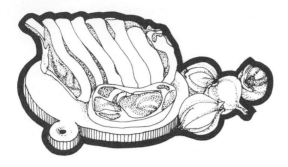

## MARINATED BEEF SLICES
1 pound sirloin steak, cooked
1 onion, sliced
  Salt and pepper
1 ounce lemon juice
1 cup sour cream
  Lettuce

Slice cooked sirloin into julienne strips. Add sliced onion and salt and pepper, to taste. Sprinkle lemon juice over meat mixture and blend in sour cream. Mix well and serve on lettuce leaf. This is a popular appetizer.

## VILLAGE CHEESE DIP

Have ½ pound cream cheese and ½ pound Roquefort cheese at room temperature. Mix with 1 cup sour cream and 1 tablespoon pure garlic powder until mixture is creamy. Serve as dip with potato chips, Fritos, celery and carrot sticks.

## MOCK PÂTÉ DE FOIE GRAS
1 cup chicken livers
4 tablespoons chicken fat
6 hard-boiled eggs
  Salt and pepper, to taste
¼ teaspoon paprika
1 teaspoon onion, grated

Sauté chicken livers in fat until tender. Mash into a paste with eggs, then add salt, pepper, paprika and onion. If too stiff add additional chicken fat. Spread on toast or lettuce leaf. Makes 1 cup.

## COTTAGE CHEESE SPREAD

Whip following ingredients in electric mixer: 1 pound cottage cheese; 1 tablespoon green pepper, finely chopped; 1 tablespoon carrot, finely chopped; 1 teaspoon onion, finely chopped; and garlic salt, to taste. Spread on crackers or Melba toast.

## CHICKEN LIVER PASTE
2 pounds chicken livers
1 pound fat pork
1 medium-size onion
½ teaspoon sage
½ teaspoon allspice
¼ teaspoon mace
¼ teaspoon nutmeg
½ teaspoon ground cloves
2 teaspoons salt
½ teaspoon black pepper
2 tablespoons flour
3 tablespoons cream
4 tablespoons brandy
2 eggs, slightly beaten

Put meat portions through medium food chopper three times. Add remaining ingredients and put through chopper again, using fine cutter.

Rub baking pan with clove of garlic around sides before filling with mixture. Place baking pan in a larger pan filled with water to the level of meat. Bake in water pan bath at 300° for 3 hours. If crust forms at top of liver paste before 1½ hours, cover with greased paper for rest of time. Cool in baking pan until room temperature, then cover and refrigerate until serving time. Excellent for appetizers or open-face sandwiches.

## SCOTCH EGGS

Divide 1 pound of lean, ground pork into 6 portions. Shell 6 hardboiled eggs. Enclose each egg in a coating of ground pork. Beat 2 raw eggs lightly, coat each egg in beaten, raw eggs and roll in bread crumbs. Fry in 350° deep fat until pork is cooked and each egg is golden brown. Place on bed of parsley; serve with tomato relish. Serves 6.

## SAUERKRAUT BALLS

- 4 ounces cooked pork
- 4 ounces corned beef
- 4 ounces ham
- 1 small onion, chopped fine
  Pinch of chopped parsley
- 1 cup flour
- ½ teaspoon dry mustard
- ½ teaspoon salt
- 1 cup milk
- 1 pound sauerkraut
- 2 eggs, beaten
- 1 cup bread crumbs
  Deep fat for frying

Run meats through a grinder on medium or fine; add onion and parsley. Fry this mixture until brown. Combine flour, mustard and salt; sift once. Add to meat, then add milk. Cook until fluffy. Cool, then add to sauerkraut.

Put entire meat mixture through a grinder twice, mixing thoroughly. Roll into 1½-inch balls, dredge in flour, dip in egg, roll in bread crumbs and fry in deep fat. Serve hot as an appetizer.

# BREADS & MUFFINS

## BOSTON BROWN BREAD

- 3 cups bread flour
- 3 cups yellow corn meal
- 3 cups whole wheat flour
- 1 tablespoon baking soda
- 2 cups raisins
- 1 tablespoon cinnamon
- 1 tablespoon ginger
- 3 eggs, beaten slightly
- 3 cups molasses
- 3 cups sour milk

Mix dry ingredients together first; then combine remaining items in a separate bowl. Add dry mix to this liquid and stir well. Spoon equal parts into 4 well-greased, tall No. 5 tins. Cover with lids or waxed paper tied on firmly and steam for 3 hours. Makes 4 loaves.

## BANANA BREAD

- 3 very ripe bananas
- ¾ cup sugar
  Pinch of salt
- 1 egg
- ¼ cup butter
- 1 teaspoon soda
- 1 tablespoon water
- 2 cups pastry flour

Mash bananas with a fork. Blend in sugar, salt and beaten egg. Melt butter and stir into banana mixture. Dissolve soda in water and add with sifted flour. Mix and bake in loaf pan for 45 minutes in 350° oven. Makes 1 loaf.

## POPOVERS

    2 eggs
    2 cups sifted flour
    2 teaspoons salt
    2 cups milk

Beat eggs until frothy; add flour sifted with salt; then add 1 cup of milk. Beat mixture well, then add remaining milk and beat again until smooth. Chill batter in the refrigerator. Grease iron muffin pan with unsalted vegetable fat and heat to sizzling point. Pour in batter and bake 15 minutes in a 450° oven and 20 minutes at 350°.

## BUTTERMILK BISCUITS

    ½ cup lard
    3 cups flour, sifted
    ½ level teaspoon salt
    ½ level teaspoon soda
    3 level teaspoons baking powder
    1¼ cups buttermilk

Cut lard into mixture of dry ingredients. Slowly add buttermilk. Roll onto floured board and cut. Bake in 425° oven 15 minutes.

## SPOON BREAD

    1 cup white corn meal
    1½ cups boiling water
    1 egg
    1 tablespoon butter
    1 cup buttermilk
    1 teaspoon baking soda
    ¾ teaspoon salt
    ½ cup milk or light cream,
        sour or sweet

Pour boiling water over corn meal; beat well, then let cool slightly. Mix in remaining ingredients (except ½ cup milk or cream). Pour batter into hot, greased 7-inch baking dish. Bake in 350° oven for 30 to 40 minutes. If soft top is desired, add a few spoonfuls milk or cream from time to time while bread is baking, and bake 1 hour altogether.

## ORANGE BREAD

    1 egg
    1 cup milk
    1 tablespoon fat
    2½ cups flour
    1 teaspoon salt
    3 rounded tablespoons sugar
    4 teaspoons baking powder
    1 heaping cup candied orange peel,
        grated

Beat the egg thoroughly and add to milk. Cut fat into the flour. Add salt, sugar and baking powder. Stir in milk-and-egg mixture slowly. Add orange peel, put into a greased loaf pan and bake in a medium oven. This delicious bread will go with fruit and gelatin salads, add variety to the bread tray at dinner or make a party sandwich with a filling of cream cheese.

## CORNY BISCUITS AU GRATIN

    4 cups Bisquick
    1 teaspoon sugar
    ½ teaspoon salt
    1 heaping tablespoon shortening
        Cheddar cheese (to individual taste)
    ½ cup cream-style corn
        Water enough for a soft dough
        Bran

Mix dry ingredients, then work in shortening as for pie crust. Grate cheese into the corn, add ½ cup of water, and mix together. Add corn-cheese mixture to dry ingredients and mix fast, adding more water as necessary to make a very soft biscuit dough. "Flour" the board with bran and pat out dough about

¾ inch thick on top of it. Cut into biscuits and bake in a moderately hot oven.

## SWEDISH RYE BREAD

2½ cups lukewarm water
2 cakes compressed yeast
2 cups dark rye flour
10 cups white flour
1 cup molasses
1 cup brown sugar
2 tablespoons salt

Crumble yeast into water; stir until dissolved. Combine yeast with molasses, sugar and salt. Work in flour, knead, cover and let rise. Shape into 6 loaves. Let rise until double in bulk. Bake 45 minutes at 375°.

## HUCKLEBERRY MUFFINS

1 cup huckleberries
2 cups flour
¼ teaspoon salt
⅓ cup shortening
4 teaspoons baking powder
1 cup milk
1 egg

Wash and drain huckleberries and sprinkle with ½ teaspoon flour. Sift dry ingredients and cut in shortening. To this add milk and beaten egg. Stir floured berries in quickly; don't mash them. Bake in hot greased muffin pans for 20 minutes in a moderate oven. (Blueberries can be substituted.) Pop a batch into the oven for a Sunday morning breakfast surprise.

## BROWN BREAD

1 cup flour
½ teaspoon baking powder
½ teaspoon baking soda
½ teaspoon salt
⅓ cup yellow corn meal
⅔ cup whole wheat flour
½ cup brown sugar (packed)
⅔ cup raisins
⅓ cup molasses
1⅓ cups buttermilk

Sift flour, baking powder, baking soda and salt together. Blend and add corn meal, wheat flour, brown sugar, raisins and molasses. Blend in buttermilk, mix well, and pour into greased bread tin. Bake 2 to 2½ hours at 325° (until bread springs back to touch). Turn on side and let cool before turning out.

## HONEY BUNS

Combine 4½ tablespoons white sugar, 2 egg yolks, pinch of salt, 4½ tablespoons melted shortening, and ½ cup milk. Crumble 1 yeast cake in ¼ cup warm water and add ½ teaspoon white sugar. Dissolve yeast and sugar and let rise a little; then combine with first mixture. Gradually add flour—3½ to 4 cups—until dough is stiff. Knead dough for 10 minutes. Place in greased bowl, cover and set in warm spot until dough doubles in bulk. Roll dough out into oblong shape and brush with melted butter. Sprinkle thickly with brown sugar and cinnamon. Roll up like a jelly roll and cut in 1-inch slices. Place in buttered muffin pans that have brown sugar and butter in the bottom of each cup. Let rise for about ¾ hour. Bake in moderate oven for 20 to 30 minutes until brown on bottom. Remove from pans as soon as taken from oven. Makes about 2½ dozen buns.

## NUT BREAD
   1 cup brown sugar
   1 egg
   1 cup milk
3¼ cups flour
   4 teaspoons baking powder
   ½ teaspoon salt
   1 cup chopped walnuts, floured

Mix sugar, egg and milk; add sifted flour, baking powder and salt. Stir in floured nuts and pour into greased loaf pan. Bake in very slow oven—barely warm—for first 15 minutes. Then bake 45 minutes at 325°.

## BLUEBERRY MUFFINS
14 ounces sugar
12 ounces shortening
   8 eggs
   ½ teaspoon vanilla
7½ cups flour
   ¼ teaspoon salt
   3 teaspoons baking powder
   1 quart milk
   2 cups blueberries, washed

Blend sugar and shortening well before adding eggs and vanilla. Stir in flour, salt, baking powder and milk, mixing until batter is smooth. Add blueberries and stir lightly. Bake in lightly greased muffin tins in a 350° oven for about 20 minutes. This recipe makes 4 dozen muffins.

## SPOON BREAD
   2 cups milk
   ¼ pound butter
   4 eggs
   ½ cup corn meal
   2 tablespoons baking powder
   2 tablespoons sugar
   ½ tablespoon salt

Bring milk and butter to boil. Beat yolks and whites separately. Pour boiling milk and butter into dry ingredients and mix well. Blend in yolks and fold in whites. Pour mixture into a well-greased pan. Bake in 450° oven until brown, about 30 minutes.

## HUSHPUPPIES
   1 cup corn meal
   1 tablespoon flour
   1 teaspoon baking powder
   ½ teaspoon salt
   1 tablespoon grated onion
   1 egg, unbeaten
   ½ cup milk (approx.)
      Deep fat

Blend dry ingredients together; then add onion, egg and milk—just enough milk should be added to make a stiff batter. Form mixture into balls about the size of English walnuts and fry in deep fat.

## HUSHPUPPIES
   1 teaspoon soda
   3 cups buttermilk
   3 cups white corn meal
   ½ cup plain flour
      Pinch of salt
      Deep fat

Mix soda with buttermilk. Add this mixture to corn meal and flour to form a stiff batter. Add salt. Cut dough into balls with a tablespoon and fry in 350° fat about 4 or 5 minutes. Serves 6.

12

## LITTLE RICE CAKES

   3  whole eggs
   1  cup cold boiled rice
   ½  cup granulated sugar
   ½  teaspoon salt
      Pinch of nutmeg
   1  cup flour
   3  teaspoons baking powder
      Hot fat for frying
      Powdered sugar and cinnamon

Beat eggs until fluffy; add other
ingredients (except fat and cinnamon
mixture). Beat well. Drop by
tablespoonfuls into hot fat, and fry to a
golden brown. Drain on brown paper
and sprinkle with powdered sugar and
cinnamon. These cakes can be served
with apple jelly or orange marmalade as
an added treat with a chicken or ham
dinner. Serves 6.

## ORANGE-DATE-NUT BREAD

   1  whole orange
   6  ounces dates
   2  tablespoons butter
   1  egg
   1  cup sugar
   2  cups flour, sifted
   ½  teaspoon soda
   1  teaspoon baking powder
   ¾  teaspoon salt
   ¾  cup nuts, chopped

Grind whole orange and dates. Strain
juice from orange into a cup. Add hot
water to it until there is 1 cup liquid.
Add butter and 1 egg and set aside to
cool. Put ground orange and dates in a
bowl, stir in liquid mixture. Blend in dry
ingredients and add nuts. Pour into a
well-greased 3x9-inch pan. Bake 1 hour
in a 350° oven.

## MAPLE NUT MUFFINS

Sift together into a bowl 2 cups sifted
all-purpose flour; 4 teaspoons baking
powder and ½ teaspoon salt. Combine 1
egg; ½ cup milk; ½ cup maple syrup and
¼ cup melted shortening, then add to dry
ingredients, mixing until all flour is
moistened. Stir in 1 cup chopped nuts.
Fill 12 greased muffin tins ⅔ full and
bake in 400° oven 18-20 minutes.

## IRISH CHRISTMAS BREAD

   ⅓  cup butter
   ⅓  cup sugar
   2  eggs
   1  yeast cake
   ½  cup raisins, cut
   ½  cup currants
   3  ounces candied fruit and
         peel, mixed
   2  cups flour
   ¼  teaspoon salt

Cream butter and sugar. Beat in eggs.
Dissolve yeast in 2 tablespoons warm
water and add to butter mixture. Stir in
raisins, currants and candied fruit. Beat
in flour and salt. Let dough stand at
room temperature for 2 hours. Pour into
a well-greased 5x9-inch loaf pan. Let
stand in warm place for 2 hours. Bake
one hour in a 325° oven.

## GARLIC ROLLS

Split 3 rolls in half. Rub split section of
roll with garlic clove. Heat rolls in oven,
until hot, remove and spread with butter.
Sprinkle liberally with grated Parmesan
cheese and lightly with paprika. Put
under broiler and toast until brown.
Serves 6.

## RAISED DOUGHNUTS
1 cup milk, scalded
¼ cake yeast
¼ cup lukewarm water
1 teaspoon salt
2 cups flour
⅓ cup butter, melted
1 cup light brown sugar
2 eggs, well beaten
½ teaspoon nutmeg

Cool milk to lukewarm. Dissolve yeast in lukewarm water. Combine dissolved yeast with salt and about half the flour or flour enough for a stiff batter. Let rise an hour. Add melted shortening, sugar, eggs, nutmeg and remaining flour. Let rise again; if too soft to handle, add more flour. Turn on floured board, pat and roll ¾ inch thick. Cut out with biscuit cutter and shape into balls between hands. Fry in deep hot fat (375°). Makes about two dozen doughnuts.

## ORANGE ROLLS
2 eggs
¾ cup sugar
1 teaspoon salt
1 cup lukewarm milk
1 yeast cake
1 cup warm water
   Flour for soft dough (7-8 cups)

Beat eggs, add sugar and salt. Add milk and yeast dissolved in water. Add flour a little at a time. Stir until dough does not stick to greased hands. Let rise for 30 minutes. Roll a portion of dough into an oblong shape on floured board.

**Orange Mixture:**

Melt ¼ pound butter and combine with 1 cup sugar and grated rind from 2 oranges. Cook in a skillet until mixture thickens slightly.

Spread half of dough with half of orange mixture. Roll up dough lengthwise and cut into 1½-inch slices. Prepare remaining dough the same way. Lay rolls in greased pan, let rise for 20 minutes and bake in 350° oven for 20 minutes. Makes 3 dozen.

## SWEDISH BREAD
2 packages dry yeast
1 teaspoon sugar
7-8 cups white flour
1½ tablespoons salt
1 cup brown sugar
5 tablespoons heated molasses
   (add pinch of soda)
5 tablespoons melted shortening
1½ cups rye flour
1½ cups wheat flour
1 orange, grated rind only
1 teaspoon caraway seed

Dissolve yeast in ¼ cup water and a teaspoon of sugar. Let stand 5 minutes. Add to 4 cups water and enough white flour to make soft sponge, about 4 cups. Let stand in warm place until it becomes bubbly. Add remaining ingredients, beating well with enough white flour to make stiff dough. Let rise in greased bowl. When double in bulk, knead and let rise again. Shape into 4 loaves and let rise in greased loaf pans. Bake in moderate oven 40 minutes.

## DATE AND PINEAPPLE BREAD
Combine ⅓ cup milk, 1 well-beaten egg, ⅓ cup melted shortening, 1 cup chopped dates, a 9-ounce can crushed pineapple and 1 cup chopped walnuts. Sift together 3 cups sifted flour, ¾ cup sugar, 3 teaspoons baking powder, ¼ teaspoon soda and ¾ teaspoon salt. Add to first mixture and blend only to moisten. Bake

in a greased 1-pound loaf pan at 350°
50-55 minutes.

## HOT EGG BREAD

   2 **cups water-ground white corn meal**
   ¼ **teaspoon soda**
   2 **teaspoons baking powder**
   1 **teaspoon salt**
   2 **eggs, beaten**
   2 **cups sour milk or buttermilk**
   2 **tablespoons melted fat or oil**

Sift dry ingredients together. Add eggs
and milk into dry ingredients, then fat.
Pour into greased 8-inch-square pan and
bake in 425° oven 20-30 minutes. Serve
hot. Makes 8 portions.

## PELL'S BREAD

Heat 2¼ cups homogenized milk to 180°;
cool to 110-112°. Dissolve 1 ounce dry
yeast, 1 ounce salt, 1½ tablespoons honey
or sugar, 2 well-beaten eggs and ¼ cup
melted shortening into cooled milk. Mix
into 2 pounds hard wheat flour with
electric mixer at low speed 5-8 minutes.
Knead dough, then let rise at room
temperature until double in size. Shape
into 2 loaves and place on a greased
baking sheet, allowing to rise a second
time until double in size. Bake at 340°
for 30 minutes, remove and brush loaves
with butter. Slice an inch thick or more
and serve very hot. Yields two 27-ounce
loaves.

## RAISIN BREAD

   1 **package dry yeast, dissolved in**
      ¼ **cup warm water**
   1 **quart warm milk**
   ½ **cup sugar**
      **Flour**
   2 **cups raisins**
   1 **cup walnut meats, broken**
   1 **tablespoon cinnamon**
   1 **tablespoon salt**
   2 **tablespoons shortening**

Add dissolved yeast to warm milk and
sugar. Add flour until mixture forms a
sponge dough. Place in a greased bowl
and let rise in a warm place for 1 hour.
Mix raisins, nuts, cinnamon, salt and
shortening, and enough more flour for a
stiff dough; knead into a raised dough.
Knead again and place in 4 or 5 greased
loaf pans to rise again. Bake in 400°
oven for 45 minutes. Cover with
powdered sugar icing and sprinkle with
chopped walnuts while bread is warm.

## DATE NUT BREAD

   ½ **cup butter, melted**
   2 **yeast cakes**
   5 **cups flour**
   2 **eggs**
   1 **tablespoon salt**
   1 **tablespoon cinnamon**
   2 **cups dates, chopped**
   1½ **cups walnuts, chopped**
   1 **cup sugar**

Put 2 cups lukewarm water in a mixing
bowl; add butter, yeast and 2 cups flour.
Make a sponge by mixing and let stand
in warm place until dough doubles in
size. Add remaining ingredients, mixing
well, and then knead; again let mixture
double in size. Shape into 3 loaves
4½x8x2½ inches; let rise again and bake
at 350° for 1 hour. Makes three 8-ounce
loaves.

## NUT BREAD

Cream together 2 tablespoons butter; 3 tablespoons vegetable shortening and 1 cup sugar. Then add 2 eggs, 3 tablespoons orange marmalade and 1 small cooked potato, mashed. To 4½ cups sifted flour add 4½ teaspoons baking powder, 1 teaspoon soda and 1 teaspoon salt. Sift flour alternately into batter with 2 cups orange juice. Slowly beat after each addition. Stir in 1 cup coarsely chopped pecans. Half-fill 2 or 3 greased loaf tins and bake covered in 350° oven for 20 minutes. Uncover and bake for 35 minutes. This is especially good sliced thin and toasted.

## CINNAMON ROLLS OR BREAD

Scald 1½ cups of milk. Add 2 tablespoons sugar, 1 teaspoon salt and ⅓ cup melted butter. Cool to lukewarm. Soften 3 yeast cakes (or 3 envelopes of dry yeast) according to package directions. Stir well and add to milk. Add 1 well-beaten egg. Mix in about 5 cups of all-purpose flour to make dough that is easy to handle but not too stiff. Brush dough with melted butter and put in a warm place until it rises to twice its bulk.

Roll out dough to ¼-inch thickness. Brush with melted butter. Sprinkle with 1 cup of brown sugar and ¼ cup cinnamon. Roll up like a jelly roll and cut into 36 slices.

For bread, divide roll into 3 parts. Place on greased baking tin. Let rise again to twice its bulk. Bake rolls in 375° to 400° oven for 10 minutes. Bake loaves at same temperature, but for 30 to 35 minutes. Brush them with butter as they come from oven.

# CAKES

## DATE TORTE

- 2 eggs, well beaten
- 1 cup powdered sugar
- 1 cup chopped dates
- 1 cup chopped nut meats
- 1 teaspoon baking powder
- 2 tablespoons flour

Mix the above ingredients in the order listed and bake in a shallow pan (about 7 inches by 11) for 20 minutes in a moderate oven. When cold, crumble and serve with whipped cream. Ice cream or custard may be substituted for the whipped cream. The torte keeps well if the correct amount of flour is used.

## DUTCH FAMILIE CAKE

- ½ cup shortening
- 2 squares bitter chocolate
- 1 cup sugar
- 2 eggs, well beaten
- 1 cup applesauce

1 teaspoon vanilla
½ cup pecans, chopped
1 cup flour
½ teaspoon baking powder
¼ teaspoon baking soda
¼ teaspoon salt

Melt and blend shortening and chocolate. Cool; then stir in sugar, eggs, apple sauce, vanilla and pecans. Sift flour, baking powder, soda and salt together; then stir into chocolate mixture. Pour into greased, 8-inch square pan and bake for 35 to 40 minutes in 350° oven. Cut into portion squares. Serves 8 to 10. This recipe is from Haarlem, Holland.

## BLITZ TORTE

¾ cup butter
¾ cup sugar
6 egg yolks
1½ cups cake flour
1½ teaspoons baking powder
½ cup milk

Cream butter and sugar together thoroughly; add beaten egg yolks. Sift cake flour and baking powder into mixture alternately with milk. Pour into two 9-inch layer-cake pans and spread following mixture on each:

6 beaten egg whites
1½ cups sifted sugar
1 cup walnuts, chopped

Bake for 45 minutes in 350° oven.

Filling:

2 eggs, beaten
1½ cups milk
1½ teaspoons cornstarch
1¾ tablespoons sugar
1 teaspoon vanilla

Stir over medium fire until mixture thickens and boils. Place bottom layer meringue-side down, top layer meringue-side up; spread filling between.

## ORANGE RAISIN CAKE

1 cup brown sugar
1 egg

½ cup butter
1 cup buttermilk
2 cups flour
1 teaspoon soda
1 teaspoon baking powder
 Pinch of salt
1 orange, juice and rind
½ cup raisins
½ cup nuts

Beat sugar, egg, butter and buttermilk together. Add flour, soda, baking powder and salt. Grind together orange rind, raisins and nuts. Add half of ground mixture to batter. Mix, pour into greased cake tin, and bake 40 minutes at 350°. Pour juice of orange over cake as soon as cake is removed from oven. Add remaining ground mixture to a powdered sugar icing and spread over cake.

## JAM CAKE

1 cup sugar
½ cup butter
½ cup sweet milk
2 cups flour
1 teaspoon baking soda
3 eggs, beaten
2 cups jam
2 glasses jelly
1 teaspoon cinnamon
1 teaspoon allspice
1 teaspoon nutmeg
1 teaspoon cloves
1 teaspoon ginger

Cream sugar and butter. Add milk alternately with flour, which has been sifted with soda. Add all other ingredients and combine, being careful not to break jam and jelly into too-small pieces. Bake in two greased, 9-inch layers at 350° and fill with pecan whip.

Pecan Whip:

3 cups sugar
1 cup whipping cream
1 tablespoon butter
1½ cups pecans

Combine 2 cups sugar, cream and butter. Melt remaining sugar in a warm skillet, until brown, but do not burn. When sugar is melted, add other mixture and cook until heavy. Remove from fire and beat until creamy. Add pecans and spread between layers of cake.

## PINEAPPLE UPSIDE-DOWN CAKE

Melt 2 tablespoons butter in baking pan; sprinkle ¾ cup brown sugar over it. Arrange pineapple slices (or apricot halves) with maraschino cherries to garnish. Add sprinkling of pecans or walnuts and cover with the following batter:

3 egg yolks, beaten well
1½ cups sugar
1½ cups cake flour, sifted
1 teaspoon baking powder
½ teaspoon salt
½ cup boiling water
3 egg whites, beaten stiff

Bake about 45 minutes at 350°. Serve with whipped cream or a small scoop of vanilla ice cream.

## FUDGE UPSIDE-DOWN CAKE
**Cake:**

1 tablespoon shortening
¾ cup sugar
½ cup milk
1 teaspoon vanilla
1 cup flour
1 teaspoon baking powder
½ teaspoon salt
1½ tablespoons cocoa

Cream sugar and shortening. Add milk and vanilla. Sift flour, baking powder, salt, cocoa into mixture. Pour into greased, 8-inch-square cake pan.

**Topping:**

Combine ¼ cup cocoa, ½ cup each white and brown sugar. Spread ½ cup chopped nuts over batter and cover with cocoa-sugar mixture. Pour 1¼ cups boiling water over topping and batter. Bake 35 minutes in a 350° oven. When cool cut into squares and serve topped with whipped cream. Yields 8 to 10 portions.

## MARBLE CAKE (1800)
**Light Mixture:**

1½ cups sugar
½ cup butter
2½ cups flour
1 teaspoon cream of tartar
½ teaspoon soda
½ cup milk
4 egg whites, beaten

Blend sugar and butter. Sift flour with cream of tartar and soda and add to sugar-butter mixture, alternating with the milk. Fold in egg whites.

**Dark Mixture:**

1 cup brown sugar
½ cup each of molasses and butter
1½ cups flour
½ teaspoon soda
1 teaspoon cream of tartar
½ cup sour milk
4 egg yolks, beaten
Pinch of clove, cinnamon and nutmeg

Blend in same order as for light mixture. Butter two bread loaf pans and alternately spoon in light and dark mixtures. Bake in 350° oven for 1 hour.

## OLGA'S FAMOUS CHOCOLATE CAKE

  2 cups cake flour, sifted
  1 teaspoon soda
  ½ teaspoon salt
  ⅓ cup butter
  1¼ cups sugar
  1 egg
  3 squares unsweetened chocolate, melted
  1 teaspoon vanilla
  ½ cup thick sour cream
  ¾ cup sweet milk

Sift flour, soda and salt 3 times. Cream butter and sugar thoroughly. Beat egg into mixture; then blend in chocolate and vanilla. Add about a quarter of the flour and beat well, then add sour cream and beat. Add remaining flour alternately with milk. Beat after each addition. Bake in two greased, 9-inch layer pans in 350° oven for about 30 minutes. Frost with chocolate butter cream icing.

## CHEESE CAKE

  2 tablespoons butter
  4 crumbled zwieback
  1½ pounds cream cheese
  6 eggs (separated)
  1 cup sugar
  1 tablespoon lemon juice
  1 teaspoon vanilla
  ½ pint heavy cream

Combine butter and zwieback and sprinkle over bottom of spring mold pan. Cream cheese and add each egg yolk separately. Cream after each addition. Blend in sugar, lemon juice, vanilla and cream. Fold in beaten egg whites which are dry and stiff. Pour mixture over zwieback and bake in 310° oven for 1 hour. Turn oven down to 250° and leave cake in for additional hour.

## SWISS CHALET NUT CAKE

  8 eggs
  1 cup sugar
  ½ pound hazelnuts, ground

  2 ounces flour
  1 ounce vanilla
  2 ounces kirschwasser

Beat eggs and sugar together until they foam. Then slowly stir in nuts, flour, vanilla and kirschwasser. Pour batter into 8-inch round cake pan lined with waxed paper. Bake in 250° oven for 45 minutes. Cool cake.

### Icing:

  ½ cup sugar
  ¼ pound hazelnuts, chopped or ground
  5 ounces water
  1 ounce kirschwasser

Cook sugar, nuts and water together until syrup spins a thread. Add kirschwasser. While hot, spread on cake.

## WILLIAMSBURG ORANGE WINE CAKE

  ½ cup butter
  1 cup sugar
  2 eggs, beaten
  1 teaspoon vanilla
  1 orange rind, grated
  1 cup whole seedless raisins
  ½ cup English walnuts, chopped
  2 cups sifted pastry flour
  1 teaspoon soda, sifted
  ½ teaspoon salt, sifted
  1 cup sour milk

Cream butter and 1 cup sugar. Add eggs, vanilla, rind, whole raisins and walnuts. Sift flour with soda and salt; add to mixture alternately with sour milk. Bake in greased square cake pan in moderate oven for 30 to 40 minutes.

### Wine Icing:

Mix ⅓ cup sweet, soft butter with 2 cups confectioners' sugar. Add sherry wine slowly, beating well. When desired consistency, spread on cooled cake.

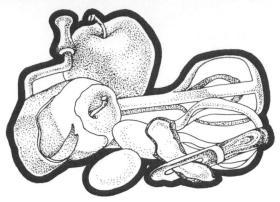

## CEDRIC ADAMS CAKE
    4 squares chocolate, melted
    4 tablespoons butter, melted
    2 cups sugar
    2 teaspoons soda
    2 cups rich milk
    3 cups flour, sifted
    ¼ teaspoon cream of tartar
    ¼ teaspoon salt
    2 teaspoons vanilla
    4 egg whites, beaten stiff

Add sugar to combined chocolate and butter. Dissolve soda in milk, then add dry ingredients and milk alternately to the chocolate mixture. Add vanilla and fold in egg whites. Pour batter into three 9-inch greased layer pans. Bake in 350° oven for 20 to 25 minutes. When cool, frost lavishly with 7-minute icing and drip melted chocolate over frosting after it is set.

## DATE-NUT TORTE
    4 eggs, beaten
    1 cup sugar
    1 cup bread crumbs, dry
    1 teaspoon baking powder
    ½ teaspoon salt
    1 teaspoon vanilla
   12 ounces dates, chopped
    1 cup walnuts, chopped
      Whipped cream

Slowly add sugar to eggs and beat until thick and lemon-colored. Mix bread crumbs with baking powder and salt and fold carefully into egg mixture. Add vanilla and spread in a well-greased and floured pan. Sprinkle with dates and

walnuts. Bake in a 325° oven for 45 to 60 minutes. Serve in squares topped with whipped cream.

## APPLE TORTE
    1 egg
    ¾ cup sugar
    ¾ cup apples, sliced
    1 teaspoon baking powder
    ½ cup flour
      Pinch of salt
    ¼ teaspoon almond extract
    ¼ cup walnut meats, chopped
      Whipped cream

Beat egg slightly, add sugar and apple slices. Then stir in remaining ingredients (except cream). Mix well. Pour into greased pie tin and bake in 325° oven for 25 minutes. Serve topped with whipped cream.

## OZARK BLACK WALNUT CHOCOLATE TORTE
    ½ cup black walnuts, chopped
    ½ cup chocolate cookie crumbs
    1 envelope plain gelatin
    ¼ cup cold water
    1 package semi-sweet chocolate
    ½ cup sugar
    ¼ teaspoon salt
    ½ cup milk
    3 eggs, separated
    1 cup cream, whipped

Combine crumbs and nuts. Rinse out one 8-inch spring form pan with cold water. Line with wax paper. Cover bottom with half of crumb mixture. Soften gelatin in water. Cook chocolate, ¼ cup sugar, salt and milk in a double boiler until blended. Beat egg yolks and add hot mixture slowly, stirring rapidly. Return to double boiler; cook, stirring, till thickened. Remove; add gelatin, stir until dissolved. Chill until nearly thickened. Beat egg whites and add ¼ cup sugar. Fold in chocolate mixture and cream. Turn into pan. Top with remaining crumb mixture. Chill till firm.

## MOLASSES BLUEBERRY SPONGE CAKE

Cream ½ cup sugar and ½ cup shortening (some butter). Blend in 1 cup molasses. Beat in 1 egg. Sift together 1 tablespoon soda, 1 teaspoon each: salt, ground cloves, cinnamon and nutmeg, ½ teaspoon ginger, and 2½ cups of flour. Beat all together then add 1 cup boiling water and beat thoroughly. Fold in 1 cup blueberries and bake in 9-inch square pan in 350° oven for 40 minutes. Serve hot with blueberry sauce, topped with whipped cream. Serves 12.

**Blueberry Sauce:**

Bring to a boil 1 pint blueberries, 1 cup water, ½ cup sugar, 1 teaspoon vinegar and a dash of nutmeg. Add 2 tablespoons cornstarch mixed with ¼ cup cold water. Cook until clear.

## NO-BAKE FRUIT CAKE

- ¾ cup milk
- 1 pound marshmallows
- 1 pound graham crackers, crushed
- 1 pound seedless raisins
- 1 pint jar mixed candied fruit
- 4 cups walnuts or pecans
  Candied cherry and pineapple
  Blanched almonds
  Sherry

Scald milk over low heat. Add marshmallows, stir constantly and cook until smooth. Remove from heat. Mix graham cracker crumbs with raisins, mixed candied fruits and nuts. Blend marshmallow mixture into this. Line a 2-quart casserole or mold with waxed paper. Add fruit cake mixture. Press down firmly, so it takes the shape of the container. Decorate top with candied pineapple and almonds. Let age at least a month. Sprinkle sherry over cake about twice a week while aging.

## BLUEBERRY UPSIDE-DOWN CAKE

Arrange 1 pint fresh or frozen blueberries in a 2x6x8-inch baking pan. Sprinkle 1 cup sugar and ⅛ teaspoon nutmeg over them. Sift together three times: 1 cup all-purpose flour; ¾ cup sugar, 2 teaspoons baking powder and ¼ teaspoon salt. To sifted flour mixture add 2 unbeaten eggs; ⅓ cup milk; ¼ cup shortening and 1 teaspoon vanilla. Beat them all together and place dough mixture on top of berries. Bake in 350° oven — 30 minutes for fresh berries or 50 minutes for frozen. Cut in squares with whipped cream or ice cream. Makes 6 portions.

## MAPLE HICKORY CAKE

- ¾ cup butter
- ½ cup sugar
- ½ cup maple syrup
- 1 teaspoon vanilla
- 3 eggs, beaten
- 2 cups flour
- 1 teaspoon salt
- 2½ teaspoons baking powder
- ¼ cup milk
- ½ cup hickory nuts, chopped

Cream butter and sugar, add maple syrup slowly beating all the while. Add vanilla and eggs. Beat mixture until smooth. Sift flour, salt, baking powder together. Add flour mixture to first mixture alternately with milk. Fold in nuts. Pour into 2 greased and floured 8-inch round cake pans. Bake 35 minutes in 375° oven.

**Frosting:**

Cook 1 cup maple syrup until a sample of it forms a soft ball in cold water. Slowly drip syrup into 2 egg whites stiffly beaten, beating all the time. Blend in 1 teaspoon vanilla and pinch of salt, continuing to beat until frosting is of desired consistency. Use for filling and frosting.

21

## GRIPSHOLM APPLE CAKE

- 4 cups tart apples, sliced
- 3 cups bread crumbs
- ¾ cup butter
- 1 teaspoon cinnamon
- 1 cup sugar
  Pinch of salt
  Grated rind of ½ lemon

Peel and cut apples into thin slices. In a well-buttered baking dish arrange a layer of apple sections. Sprinkle with a mixture of sugar, cinnamon and crumbs. Add a few dots of butter to each layer. Fill dish with alternate layers of apples and crumbs, with crumbs on top. Bake in 350° oven until apples are tender, about 45 minutes. Cool. Serve with vanilla sauce, whipped cream or ice cream. Makes 8 portions.

### Vanilla Sauce:

Mix together 1 cup milk, 1 cup light cream, 2 tablespoons sugar, ½ teaspoon vanilla and pinch of salt. Bring to a boil. Thicken by slowly adding 4 egg yolks over medium flame.

## LITTLE HOUSE QUICK COFFEE CAKE

- ½ cup sugar
- 3 tablespoons shortening
- 2 eggs
- 1¼ cups milk
- 2½ cups flour
- 4 teaspoons baking powder
- 1½ teaspoons salt

Cream sugar and shortening. Add eggs, beat well. Stir in milk and dry ingredients. Spread in oblong, 9x12-inch cake pan and sprinkle with sugar, cinnamon and chopped nuts. Bake in moderate oven about 40 minutes. Serve warm with butter. Makes 12 portions.

## ORANGE CREAM ANGELFOOD CAKE

Beat 1 pint egg whites until stiff, not dry. Add 2 teaspoons cream of tartar, 1½ teaspoons salt and 2 cups confectioners' sugar, sifted three times. Beat again until you can draw a spatula through whites and the opening will remain. Sift cake flour and confectioners' sugar 3 times, then measure out 1½ cups of flour and 2 cups more of sugar. Fold sugar and flour into egg whites lightly by hand. Add 1 teaspoon vanilla and ½ teaspoon almond extract. Pour into ungreased 10-inch tube pan. Bake at 300° for 50 minutes. Turn off oven and let cake remain for 10 minutes. Invert tin and let stand 1 hour before filling and frosting.

### Filling:

Combine in top of double boiler: 1 cup sugar, 2 whole eggs, 4 tablespoons flour and grated rind and juice of 2 oranges. Boil, stirring constantly. When thick, remove and cool. Add 2 cups whipped cream. Slice cake in several layers and spread filling. Frost with an orange butter cream icing.

## PINEAPPLE CASHEW CAKE

- ¾ cup butter
- 1¼ cups sugar
- ½ teaspoon salt
- 1 teaspoon vanilla
- 3 egg yolks
- 2½ cups cake flour
- 1 tablespoon baking powder
- ¾ cup milk
- 5 ounces crushed pineapple
- 3 egg whites

Cream butter, sugar, salt and vanilla well. Add egg yolks in three portions and continue creaming until light and fluffy. Sift flour and baking powder three times. Add alternately with milk. Drain pineapple slightly. Chop crushed pineapple and add to batter, mixing until smooth. Whip egg whites stiff but not dry. Fold in lightly, but thoroughly. Divide into two greased 10-inch cake pans. Bake at 330° for 25 to 30 minutes.

### Icing:

Cream ¾ cup butter, 3 cups confectioners' sugar and ½ teaspoon salt. Add 1 egg yolk and continue creaming until light and fluffy. Add 4 ounces chopped, crushed pineapple (do not drain); mix well. Fill and ice cake and sprinkle with about 4 ounces coarsely chopped and toasted cashew nuts.

## APPLE GINGERBREAD

Place 4 cups peeled and sliced apples in a 12x18-inch pan. Sprinkle with 1 cup sugar and simmer for about 5 minutes.

### Cake:

- 1 cup sugar
- 1 cup molasses
- ½ cup butter
- 1 teaspoon cinnamon
- 1 teaspoon ground cloves
- ½ teaspoon salt
- 1 teaspoon ginger
- 1 cup boiling water
- 1 scant teaspoon soda
- 2½ cups flour
- 2 eggs, beaten

Combine ingredients in order listed and pour batter over apples. Bake in 350° oven for 30 minutes, or until done. Serve topped with whipped cream.

## MOCK CHEESE CAKE

- 3 egg yolks, beaten well
- 1 can Eagle brand milk
- ½ cup lemon juice
- 2 cups applesauce
- 3 egg whites

- ½ cup sugar
- 1 graham cracker crust

Beat egg yolks well and add milk, then the lemon juice very slowly. Beat at high speed with an electric mixer until thick and creamy. Remove beater and fold in applesauce by hand. Beat egg whites until they peak, and gradually add sugar. Fold into the egg mixture. Pour mixture into crust in 9x9-inch spring form pan, and bake in 450° oven for 15 minutes, then at 350° for 1 hour or until mixture is well set and brown. Serves 6-8.

## GRADY CAKE

Cream 1 cup butter with 2 cups sugar. Add 4 egg yolks. Alternately sift in 2 cups cake flour and 1 cup milk. Mix thoroughly. Add 2 squares melted chocolate and ¼ teaspoon salt. Fold in 4 stiffly beaten egg whites, gently but thoroughly. Stir in 1 teaspoon vanilla and 1 cup chopped walnuts. Bake in two 9-inch greased pans in a 325° oven for 45 minutes. When cool, ice with chocolate fudge frosting.

This recipe requires no baking powder or soda.

### Chocolate Fudge Frosting:

Melt 2 squares unsweetened chocolate in a double boiler, add ¼ pound butter and melt. Add 3 cups powdered sugar and 5 tablespoons boiling water. Stir until thoroughly mixed. Remove from heat. Add 1 teaspoon vanilla and whip until frosting cools to spreading consistency.

## RICH FRUIT CUPCAKES

½ cup butter
1⅓ cups sugar
3 eggs, separated
¼ teaspoon mace
2¼ cups flour
¼ teaspoon salt
3 teaspoons baking powder
¼ cup each: currants, raisins, citron,
    candied pineapple and candied
    cherries
⅓ cup milk

Cream butter, add sugar and egg yolks. Sift dry ingredients together and combine with finely chopped fruit. Stir alternately into first mixture with the milk. Beat thoroughly. Beat egg whites and fold into mixture. Drop batter into small greased cupcake pans. Dust top with granulated sugar and bake in 350-375° oven about 25 minutes. Do not ice. Serves 6.

## MAPLE SPONGE CAKE WITH MAPLE ICING

Make your favorite sponge cake, substituting maple syrup for the flavoring and part of the liquid, if your recipe calls for any.

### Maple Icing:

Boil ¾ cup maple syrup with 1 tablespoon light corn syrup to the stage where a teaspoonful of it forms a soft ball in water. Add a few grains salt to 1 egg white and beat until stiff but not dry. Pour syrup in a thin stream onto egg whites, beating constantly. Continue beating until icing reaches spreading consistency. This is enough to frost one 9-inch tube cake. The subtlety of the maple taste, which is easily lost in cooking, comes through exceptionally well in this recipe. Also, if made one day and kept covered until the next, icing stays moist and soft.

## VALLEY GREEN POUND CAKE

1 pound butter (2 cups)
1 pound sugar (2 cups)

1 pound eggs, separated (about 10)
1 tablespoon vanilla
2 teaspoons orange extract
1 pound all-purpose flour, sifted
    (3¾ cups)

Cream butter and beat in sugar gradually; cream well. Add egg yolks slowly and continue beating until thoroughly blended. Add vanilla and orange extract, then lightly fold in sifted flour. Beat egg whites until barely stiff. Fold gently into batter. Pour into two 8x4x3-inch loaf pans which have been lined with heavy waxed paper and buttered. Bake 1½ hours in 325° oven.

## OBST KUCHEN (Fruit Cake)

**Dough:**

1 cup milk
½ cup sugar
1 tablespoon salt
1 cake compressed yeast
1 cup lukewarm water
6 cups sifted all-purpose flour
6 tablespoons shortening, melted

**For Each Kuchen:**

3 tablespoons butter, melted
1 cup sugar
2 cups sliced apples, rhubarb,
    pitted cherries or sliced peaches
2 tablespoons flour
1 egg, beaten
2 tablespoons cream

Scald milk, ½ cup sugar and salt together. Cool until lukewarm. Dissolve yeast in lukewarm water and add to cooled milk. Add 3 cups of flour and beat until smooth. Add melted shortening and remaining flour. Knead well. Place in greased bowl, cover and set in warm place away from drafts. Let rise until double in bulk or about three hours. This makes enough dough for five 9-inch kuchens. Store extra dough in refrigerator. For each kuchen, roll out ⅕ of quantity and place in greased 9-inch pie plate; make a high rim of dough around outside. Brush with butter and sprinkle with ¼ cup sugar. Let rise. Press prepared fruit into dough close together. Sprinkle remaining sugar and flour over fruit. Before baking, combine beaten egg and cream and spoon over fruit. Cover cake with pan and bake for 10 minutes at 425°, then remove pan and continue baking for about 25 minutes more.

## CHOCOLATE CAKE

½ **cup butter**
2 **cups sugar**
2 **eggs, well beaten**
2 **cups cake flour**
2 **teaspoons baking powder**
½ **teaspoon salt**
4 **squares chocolate, melted**
1½ **cups milk**
1 **teaspoon vanilla**
1 **cup nut meats, chopped**

Cream butter and sugar together; add eggs and mix well. Sift flour, baking powder and salt together. Add chocolate to batter and alternate adding dry ingredients with milk and vanilla (about three parts of each). Add nut meats. Bake in three 9-inch tins at 350° about 30 minutes or until done.

### Frosting:

Cream together ½ cup butter and 1½ cups confectioners' sugar. Add 1 well-beaten egg, blend well. Stir in 2 squares melted, unsweetened chocolate, ½ teaspoon salt, 1 teaspoon vanilla, 1 teaspoon lemon juice and 1 cup chopped nut meats. Blend, fill and frost cooled cake layers.

## DUTCH COCOA CAKE

1½ **cups cake flour, sifted**
1¼ **cups sugar**
3 **teaspoons baking powder**
1 **teaspoon salt**
¼ **cup cocoa**
½ **cup vegetable shortening,**
    **unmelted**
1 **teaspoon vanilla**
1 **cup evaporated milk**
2 **eggs**

Sift together flour, sugar, baking powder, salt and cocoa. Add shortening, vanilla and ⅔ cup of evaporated milk. Beat two minutes at high speed. Add remaining milk. Beat well, then add eggs and beat 2 minutes more at high speed. Pour into two 9-inch greased layer cake pans and bake in 350° oven for 35 minutes. Cool, split with sharp knife to make 4 layers. Fill with Whipped Cream Filling, then frost with Chocolate Icing.

### Whipped Cream Filling:

Dissolve 1 teaspoon gelatin in 4 teaspoons of cold water. Begin to whip 1½ cups whipping cream in a chilled bowl; when half whipped add gelatin mixture. Beat 3 to 4 minutes longer. This filling holds its shape well.

### Chocolate Icing:

Melt ¼ cup butter or vegetable shortening mixed with ⅓ cup cocoa. Pour in 5 tablespoons scalded milk and 2 teaspoons vanilla; blend with 2 cups confectioners' sugar and ¼ teaspoon salt. Beat at high speed until stiff. Frosting will be thin at first.

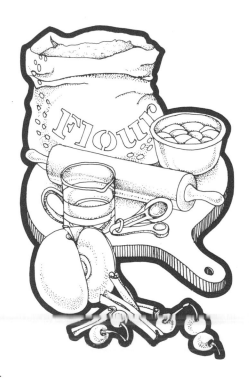

## GRINTER HOUSE PRUNE CAKE

- 1 cup sugar
- ¾ cup vegetable shortening
- 2 eggs
- 2 teaspoons cinnamon
- ¼ teaspoon ground cloves
- ¼ teaspoon salt
- 1 cup pitted, stewed prunes, chopped warm
- 2½ cups all-purpose flour
- 3 teaspoons baking powder
- ¾ teaspoon soda, dissolved in
- 1 cup hot prune juice

Cream sugar and shortening together by hand; add eggs, beat well. Stir in spices and prunes, beat batter again. Sift flour and baking powder together; combine soda and prune juice. Add these two mixtures alternately while continuing to beat. Pour batter into greased 12-inch sheet pan or two greased 8-inch layer pans. Bake 45 minutes at 350°. Spread with Orange Topping.

### Orange Topping:

Cream 2 teaspoons butter with 1 cup sugar; beat in 1 egg. Add 2 tablespoons flour, beating until smooth. Stir in ¾ cup prune juice and cook over medium heat until thick. Beat in 1 tablespoon orange juice and 1 tablespoon grated orange rind. Spread over cooled cake. This prune cake is often topped with whipped cream or vanilla ice cream.

## LEMON CHEESE CAKE

**Crust:**

Mix 1 box finely rolled zwieback, 1 cup granulated sugar, 6 tablespoons melted butter and 1 teaspoon cinnamon. Press firmly into the bottom and sides of a well-buttered spring form (6½ to 7-inch pan 3 inches deep).

**Filling:**

Rub 2 cups dry cottage cheese through a sieve; add 4 beaten egg yolks, 1 cup sugar, ¼ teaspoon salt, 3 tablespoons lemon juice and grated rind of 1 lemon. Cook mixture in double boiler until thoroughly heated. Don't overcook. Dissolve 2 envelopes of gelatin in ½ cup water, add to mixture. Whip 1 cup whipping cream flavored with ½ teaspoon vanilla; beat four egg whites sweetened with ¼ cup sugar. Fold into cooled cheese filling. Pour into crust. Chill in refrigerator for six hours.

## AUNT MARGARET'S APPLESAUCE CAKE

- ½ cup butter
- 1 cup sugar
- 2 cups all-purpose flour, sifted
- 1½ cups canned applesauce
- 1 teaspoon ground cloves
- 1 teaspoon cinnamon
- 2 teaspoons soda
- 1 cup seedless raisins

Cream butter and sugar together. Beat in flour and applesauce alternately. Stir in clove and cinnamon. Dissolve soda in 1 tablespoon hot water and combine with mixture. Mix in raisins thoroughly. Pour into 2 greased 9-inch layer pans and bake in 350° oven 30 minutes. Test with toothpick. Cool. Use filling as directed.

**Filling:**

Mix together 1 cup sugar; 1 cup whipping or sour cream; 1 cup mixed nuts, raisins, figs and dates, cut fine. Place mixture over low fire and cook until thick. Cool and flavor with 3 tablespoons rum, if desired. Place between layers and on top layer.

## TOWN & COUNTRY CHEESE CAKE

- 2 pounds cream cheese
- 9 ounces granulated sugar
- 3 egg yolks
  Vanilla and salt to taste
  Grated rind and juice of one orange
- 3 whole eggs
- 4 ounces sour cream
- 6 ounces Cheshire (or Cheddar) cheese, finely grated
- 1 cup graham cracker crumbs

Mix cream cheese into a smooth paste; add sugar and egg yolks, vanilla, salt, orange rind and juice. Add whole eggs, sour cream, and Cheshire (or Cheddar) cheese. Line a deep cheese cake tin, 9-inch diameter, with graham cracker crumbs. Pour the cheese cake mix into the pan and bake at 350° for 75 to 80 minutes. Let stand in oven. Top with pineapple sauce when serving.

### Pineapple Sauce:

Cut a fresh pineapple in cubes, sprinkle some sugar on it (keep sauce fairly tart), and let the pineapple soak for an hour; then add some lemon juice and keep in refrigerator until serving time.

## BANANA NUT CAKE

- ¾ cup butter
- 2 cups sugar
- 3 large eggs
- 4 medium bananas
- 1 teaspoon baking soda
- ½ cup nuts
- 3 cups flour
- 2 teaspoons baking powder
- ½ teaspoon salt
- ½ cup buttermilk
- 1 teaspoon vanilla

Cream butter and sugar well. Add eggs one by one, beating thoroughly after each addition. Add mashed bananas with baking soda. Add nuts. Sift flour with salt and baking powder and fold into batter, alternating with buttermilk.

Add vanilla. Beat until smooth. Pour into four 8-inch round cake pans which have been greased. Bake 30 minutes at 350°.

### Filling and Icing:

Mix 2 cups sugar and ¼ cup white Karo syrup together, add ½ cup boiling water. When the sugar has completely dissolved, remove from heat, cool, pour slowly into stiffly beaten whites of 4 eggs and continue to beat until icing is stiff enough to spread.

## GERMAN CHOCOLATE CAKE

- ½ cup butter
- 2 cups granulated sugar
- ½ cup vegetable shortening
- 4 eggs
- 1 teaspoon soda
- ¼ teaspoon salt
- 2½ cups flour
- 4 tablespoons cocoa
- 1 cup buttermilk
- 4 tablespoons cold black coffee
- 1 teaspoon vanilla

Cream butter, shortening and sugar together, then add eggs one at a time. Sift all dry ingredients together. Add to the creamed mixture alternately with the buttermilk, half at a time. Finally, add coffee and vanilla. Bake in three 9-inch, greased layers for 35 minutes in a 350° preheated oven.

### Filling and Icing:

- 1 cup cream
- 1 cup sugar
- 3 egg yolks
- 1 teaspoon vanilla
- ¼ pound butter
- 1 cup coconut
- 1 cup pecans, chopped

Place cream, sugar, egg yolks, vanilla and butter in saucepan, and cook together 10 minutes, stirring all the time. Add coconut and pecans. Cool and spread on cool cake.

## RICH APPLE COFFEE CAKE

Mix together like pie crust: 1¼ cups flour, 1 teaspoon sugar, ½ teaspoon salt, 1 teaspoon baking powder and ¼ pound butter. Add 2 teaspoons milk and 1 egg yolk. Put into ungreased, 7x11-inch coffee cake pan. Cover with 8 medium baking apples, quartered and laid in rows. Top with mixture of: 1½ tablespoons flour, ¾ cup sugar, 1 teaspoon cinnamon and 2 tablespoons butter. Bake in 375° oven for 45 to 50 minutes.

## GERMAN'S CHOCOLATE CAKE

Melt 1 package (4 ounces) German's Sweet Chocolate in ½ cup boiling water. Cool. Cream 1 cup butter and 2 cups sugar until fluffy. Add 4 unbeaten egg yolks, one at a time, and beat well after each. Add melted chocolate and 1 teaspoon vanilla. Mix well.

Sift together ½ teaspoon salt, 1 teaspoon baking soda, 2½ cups cake flour. Add alternately with 1 cup buttermilk to chocolate mixture, beating well. Beat until smooth. Fold in 4 stiffly beaten egg whites. Pour into three 8- or 9-inch cake layer pans, lined on bottom with waxed paper. Bake in moderate oven (350°) for 30 to 40 minutes. Cool. Fill layers and frost top with coconut-pecan frosting.

### Coconut-Pecan Frosting:

Combine 1 cup evaporated milk, 1 cup sugar, 3 egg yolks and 1 stick butter. Add 1 teaspoon vanilla. Cook over low heat, stirring constantly, until thickened (about 14 minutes). Add 1⅓ cups coconut and 1 cup chopped pecans. Beat until thick enough to spread.

## PEAR PRESERVE CAKE

2 cups sugar
1 cup butter
4 eggs
2½ cups flour
1 teaspoon soda
1 teaspoon salt
1 teaspoon nutmeg
1 teaspoon cinnamon
1 teaspoon ground cloves
1 cup buttermilk
1 teaspoon vanilla
1 cup pecans, chopped
1 cup raisins
1 cup pear (or peach) preserves

Cream butter and sugar thoroughly. Beat in eggs, one at a time. Reserve ½ cup of flour. Sift remaining dry ingredients together.

Alternately add dry ingredients and buttermilk. Add vanilla. Dredge nuts and raisins in remaining ½ cup of flour, add to batter. Stir in preserves. Pour into 3 paper-lined, deep 9-inch layer pans (or a large sheet cake pan). Bake for about 25 minutes at 350°.

### Topping:

Combine 2 cups sugar, ½ cup cream, 4 tablespoon white Karo syrup and ¼ pound butter. Cook to soft ball stage and pour over cake while both cake and topping are hot to saturate layers or sheet cake.

## CARROT CAKE

Into mixing bowl sift together and mix well:

2⅓ cups cake flour or 2 cups plus 1 tablespoonful regular flour
2 cups granulated sugar
1 teaspoon baking soda
2 teaspoons baking powder
1 teaspoon salt
2 teaspoons ground cinnamon

Add 1¼ cups salad oil. Beat for 2 minutes, starting at medium speed and increasing to fast. Scrape down sides of bowl while mixing. Add 4 eggs and 2 teaspoons vanilla extract; beat for 2 more minutes, scraping down sides. Stir in 2 cups finely grated carrots, 1 cup drained crushed pineapple and 1 cup chopped pecans.

Pour into two 9-inch or three 7- or 8-inch greased and floured cake pans.

Bake at 325° for 45 to 50 minutes. Remove from oven, cool for 15 minutes, then turn out on cake rack.

**Frosting and Filling:**

Soften 6 ounces cream cheese in 3 tablespoons cream and 1½ teaspoons vanilla. Beat for 5 to 7 minutes or until light and fluffy. Add ½ teaspoon salt, then 1 pound confectioners' sugar, one cup at a time, blending well after each addition. Stir in ¾ cup pecans, ½ cup raisins, ½ cup coconut.

# COOKIES

## NEW HAMPSHIRE FRUIT COOKIES

- 1 cup butter
- 1½ cups sugar
- 3 eggs, well beaten
- 1½ tablespoons water
- 3¼ cups flour, sifted
- 1 teaspoon baking soda
- ¼ teaspoon salt
- ½ teaspoon cinnamon
- ½ cup raisins, chopped
- ½ cup currants, chopped
- 1 cup walnuts, chopped

Cream butter and sugar together until light and fluffy. Add eggs and water; beat thoroughly. Sift dry ingredients together and add to mixture with fruits and nuts. Mix well. Drop by teaspoonfuls on a greased cookie sheet and bake in 350° oven 15 minutes. Makes 48 cookies.

## PECAN PUFFS

- ½ cup butter
- 2 tablespoons granulated sugar
- 1 teaspoon vanilla
- 1 cup cake flour
  (sift before measuring)
- 1 cup pecan meats, ground
  Confectioners' sugar

Cream butter until soft and blend in granulated sugar until creamy. Add vanilla. Stir flour and pecans into mixture. Roll dough into small balls and place on a well-greased cookie sheet. Bake in 300° oven for 45 minutes. Roll puffs in confectioners' sugar while hot, and again when cold.

## TOLL HOUSE COOKIES

- ½ cup butter
- 6 tablespoons brown sugar
- 6 tablespoons granulated sugar
- 1 egg, beaten
- ½ teaspoon soda
- ½ teaspoon hot water
- 1⅛ cups flour, sifted
- ½ teaspoon salt
- ½ cup nuts, chopped
- 6 ounces semi-sweet chocolate morsels
- 1 teaspoon vanilla

Cream butter with sugar. Beat egg into mixture. Dissolve soda in hot water before adding to batter. Sift flour and salt together into mixture. Add nuts and chocolate morsels and vanilla. Drop by half teaspoonfuls onto a greased cookie sheet. Bake 10 to 12 minutes in a 375° oven. Makes 50 cookies.

## CHRISTMAS COOKIES

⅔ cup butter
2 cups sugar
3 eggs, beaten
⅔ cup sour milk
2½ cups sifted flour
1 teaspoon each:
    soda, salt, cinnamon and nutmeg
1 cup raisins, chopped
1 cup nuts, chopped
¼ pound citron, chopped

Cream butter and sugar. Add eggs, milk, flour and seasonings. Stir in raisins, nuts and citron. Drop by teaspoonfuls onto a greased tin so that cookies will not touch. Bake in 300° oven until cookies start to brown. Makes about 6 dozen.

## PLANTATION COOKIES

½ cup butter
½ cup brown sugar
½ cup white sugar
1 egg, beaten
1½ cups flour, sifted
½ teaspoon soda
¼ teaspoon salt
2 tablespoons hot water
1 7-ounce bar semi-sweet chocolate
½ cup pecan meats, chopped
½ teaspoon vanilla

Cream butter, add sugar and egg. Sift salt with flour, and dissolve soda in hot water. Mix these alternately with butter mixture. Add nuts and chocolate in small pieces. Flavor with vanilla and drop by teaspoonfuls on a greased cookie sheet. Bake 10-12 minutes in 375° oven. Makes about 4 dozen cookies.

## ALMOND COOKIES

Beat ¾ cup egg whites until stiff and combine with 1 pound almond paste to form a stiff paste. Add 1 cup flour, 1 teaspoon baking powder, ½ cup sugar and ½ teaspoon salt. Drop onto greased cooky sheet. Bake in 350° oven for 10 minutes. Makes 25 cookies.

## BUTTER BALLS

Cream ¾ cup butter with 1 cup brown sugar. Stir in 1 egg. Measure 2 cups sifted flour and re-sift into butter mixture with 1 teaspoon baking powder. Add 1 teaspoon vanilla. Roll dough into long roll, cut off a piece the size of a hazelnut; dip in granulated sugar, roll in hand until round, dip in sugar again, and place on cooky sheet. Bake in 400° oven for 10 minutes; watch carefully because the balls brown quickly. Makes 4 dozen.

## BISHOP'S LODGE LACY COOKIES

2 cups butter
1 cup white sugar
1 cup brown sugar (light or dark)
2 eggs, separated
1 teaspoon baking powder
2½ cups oatmeal, regular uncooked
1 teaspoon vanilla
1 cup walnuts, chopped

Cream butter, add both kinds of sugar and whip. Stir in egg yolks. Mix baking powder and oatmeal together and add to the mixture. Stir in vanilla and fold in nuts. Beat egg whites to form a stiff peak and fold into the batter. Drop by teaspoonfuls 3 inches apart on greased cookie sheet and bake approximately 8 minutes in a 300° oven. Cool 2 minutes and remove from cookie sheet. Yields 3 dozen.

## PINEAPPLE BARS
**Filling:**
- ¼ **cup sugar**
- 1½ **cups crushed pineapple**
- 1½ **teaspoons cornstarch**
- 3 **teaspoons guava jam**

Blend sugar and cornstarch. Stir into pineapple with jam. Cook and stir over low heat until clear and thick. (Allow to cool while making crust.)

**Crust:**
- 1½ **cups sifted all-purpose flour**
- ½ **teaspoon salt**
- ½ **teaspoon soda**
- 1½ **cups uncooked rolled oats**
- 1 **cup brown sugar**
- ¾ **cup shortening**

Sift together flour, soda and salt. Mix with oats and brown sugar. Work in shortening until mixture is crumbly. Put half of this mixture into 9-inch-square pan, then spread and press filling onto this first layer. Use remaining crumbly mix for top crust. Bake at 375° oven for 40 minutes. Cool in refrigerator until firm. Cut into bars or squares.

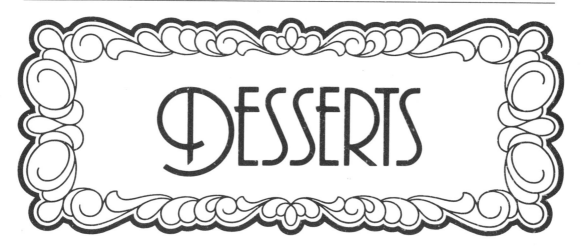

# DESSERTS

## ICE CREAM PRALINE
- 1 **pint cream**
- 6 **ounces granulated sugar**
- 8 **egg yolks**
- 8 **ounces praline paste**
- 1 **pint whipped cream**
- **Fresh strawberries**

Mix cream with the sugar and egg yolks; stir while cooking. Remove from fire before mixture boils, and cool. Then add praline paste, previously prepared by cooking together to the caramel point equal quantities of almonds and sugar which are cooled and reduced to paste. Strain the mixture; add whipped cream and set in a paper-collared mold and freeze for 1½ hours. Remove paper and serve on fancy ice form. Have very ripe fresh strawberries already macerated in "Cordial Medoc Liqueur" or good orange liqueur. Serve as a garnish.

## PINEAPPLE MINTFREEZE

½ cup sugar
½ cup water
½ teaspoon mint extract
 Green food coloring
½ cup lemon juice
½ cup crushed pineapple
1 cup ginger ale

Put sugar, water, mint and food coloring in saucepan and simmer for 10 minutes. Add lemon juice, pineapple and ginger ale, and pour into refrigerator tray. Freeze and serve either as a dinner sherbet or a refreshing dessert. Delicious also as a fruit salad topping.

## BAKED INDIAN PUDDING

1 quart milk
1 tablespoon butter
1 egg
1 cup molasses
1 teaspoon ginger
1 teaspoon cinnamon
¼ teaspoon mace
⅛ teaspoon ground cloves
¼ teaspoon salt
6 tablespoons corn meal
1 cup milk additional

Scald 1 pint milk; mix with other pint of milk. Cook over hot water 20 minutes, then add butter, egg, molasses, spices and corn meal. Pour into buttered baking dish. Bake in 300° oven. After a half hour, pour cup of milk over pudding and continue baking for 2 hours.

## BROOKFIELD INN WINE SPONGES

6 eggs, separated
6 tablespoons sugar
6 tablespoons flour
 Grated rind of 1 lemon

Whip egg yolks; add sugar and mix thoroughly. Sift in flour and mix well. Fold in stiffly beaten egg whites, add lemon rind; then drop batter by teaspoonfuls into deep fat and fry until golden brown. Remove and let drain on brown paper. (They may be kept for several weeks in a tightly lidded jar.)

Sauce:

To 1 quart white wine or cider add a small stick of cinnamon, a few slices of lemon, and sugar to taste. Drop the little sponge cakes in the cold wine or cider and bring to a boil. Simmer slowly for a half hour. Serve hot.

## MERINGUES

2 egg whites
3 drops vinegar
½ teaspoon water
 Pinch of salt
½ cup fine granulated sugar
½ teaspoon vanilla

Beat whites until stiff; add vinegar, water, and salt. Beat a little, then add sugar gradually, and finally add vanilla. Beat until stiff but not dry. Drop spoonfuls of meringue on greased cookie sheet and cook for 1 hour in 250° oven. Cool slowly. Serve filled with vanilla ice cream and topped with strawberry or chocolate sauce. Keep extras in airtight can.

## PEACH ICE CREAM

1 heaping 2-quart basket peaches
5½ cups sugar
½ teaspoon salt
⅓ cup lemon juice
3½ quarts heavy cream

Peel and pit peaches, then grind. Add sugar, salt, lemon juice and cream. Freeze as you would regular ice cream. If your family is small, halve the recipe but don't underestimate anyone's capacity for this delicious summer treat.

## NUT SOUFFLÉ

8 egg whites
2 cups sugar
1 cup chopped pecans
4 cooked prunes, chopped
 Pinch of salt
1 teaspoon vanilla

Beat egg whites till very stiff; then beat in other ingredients in the order listed. Pour the mixture into a pan 10 inches

long, 2 inches deep, and 5 inches wide,
lightly greased with butter. Bake in a
slow oven (300° to 320°) for 45 to 60
minutes on the middle rack. Place a pan
of water under the soufflé to prevent
burning. When soufflé is cold, serve it
with scoops of whipped cream.

## CAROLINA TRIFLE
    1 pint whipped cream
    1 quart boiled custard
       Almond extract, brandy or sherry
    1 lemon-flavored sponge cake

Flavor the cream and custard with either
almond extract, brandy or sherry. Slice
the sponge cake very thin; place a slice
of the cake on a dish and cover it first
with a layer of custard, then a thin layer
of whipped cream. Repeat the process,
using all of the cake slices, and top it off
with a layer of whipped cream. Chill
and serve.

## VIENNESE APPLE STRUDEL
10 apples, peeled
  2 cups bread crumbs
  ⅝ cup sugar
     Basic strudel dough
  ½ cup raisins
  ¼ teaspoon cinnamon
  2 ounces chopped nuts
       (walnuts or almonds)
  ½ cup butter

Slice apples very thin. Fry crumbs
golden brown in butter and add sugar.
On basic strudel dough spread first
apples, then crumbs, raisins, cinnamon
and nuts; then sprinkle with a little extra
sugar and melted butter. Roll the strudel
and place on oiled baking sheet. Dot
with butter and bake in moderate oven
until golden brown — about 45 to 60
minutes.

## BOHEMIAN KOLACKY
    1 cake compressed yeast
    1 cup scalded milk, lukewarm
    1 tablespoon sugar
    ½ cup sugar

    ½ cup softened lard
    2 small eggs, well beaten
    1 teaspoon salt
    3 cups all-purpose flour
    1 cup cooked prune pulp
    2 tablespoons melted margarine
    ¼ teaspoon ground cloves

Combine yeast, milk and tablespoon of
sugar. Let stand while creaming ¼ cup
sugar and softened lard together. Add
eggs and salt to creamed mixture,
blending well. Stir in yeast mixture,
alternating with flour. Beat well, let rise
until doubled in bulk. Shape into small
rolls. Make indentation in center of each
roll and fill with a spoonful of prune
pulp to which margarine, cloves and
remaining sugar have been added. Let
rise until light, about 10 minutes, and
bake in a hot (400°) oven for about 15
minutes, or until done. Makes about 15
tarts.

## ICEBOX CHEESE TORTE
    ⅓ cup cold water
    2 tablespoons gelatin
    2 eggs, separated
    1 cup sugar
    ½ teaspoon salt
    ½ cup milk
    1 pound cottage cheese
    ½ tablespoon vanilla
    ½ pint heavy cream, whipped
Crust:
18 graham crackers, rolled fine
    ⅓ cup sugar
    ⅓ cup melted butter
    ½ teaspoon cinnamon

Pour cold water in mixing bowl and sprinkle with gelatin. Beat egg yolks lightly; add ½ cup sugar, salt, and then milk. Cook over boiling water until custard-like, stirring occasionally while cooking. Add gelatin to hot mixture and stir until well dissolved. Cool until mixture begins to thicken, then add cheese and vanilla. Beat until smooth. Whip cream, egg whites and ½ cup sugar. Fold both into cheese mixture. Line 2-inch-deep pan with crust mixture and pour cheese mixture over it. Set in refrigerator. Serve chilled.

## OZARK BAKELESS PUDDING
- ½ cup butter
- 1 cup sugar
- 2 eggs
- 1 cup chopped nut meats
- 1 small can crushed pineapple
  (peaches may be substituted)
- ½ pound graham crackers

Cream butter and sugar; add well-beaten eggs, nuts and pineapple. Crush crackers; then alternate layers of crackers and mixture in a dish. Set for 12 hours in cooling room or refrigerator. Serve with whipped cream topping or an orange sauce. Serves 6.

## PEAR BEL-AIR
- 4 pears, cooked
- 1 cup strawberries
- ⅓ cup sugar
  Dash of vanilla extract
- 1 quart cream, whipped
- 1 pint English cream

Mash fresh strawberries and add sugar, vanilla, whipped cream and English cream. Place in freezer until solid. To serve, place strawberries in deep dish, follow with pear halves, and cover with Sabayon.

### English Cream:

Mix 3 egg yolks, ¼ cup sugar, and ½ cup sherry and cook till boiling point is reached, stirring constantly. Cool before using.

### Sabayon:

Whip 3 egg yolks, ¼ cup sugar, and ¾ cup milk together in double boiler till fluffy.

## ROQUEFORT CHEESE SPREAD
- ½ pound Roquefort cheese
- 4 small packages cream cheese
  Port (enough wine to form paste)

Blend ingredients and chill thoroughly. Serve with toasted crackers and strawberry jam.

This is an appealing dessert after a seafood dinner.

## GEORGIA PEACH COBBLER
- 1 pound canned peaches
- 1 cup sugar
- 1 tablespoon butter
- 1 teaspoon cornstarch
  Pinch of salt
- ½ cup water
  Pie dough for top strips
  Melted butter

Mix all ingredients (except pie dough and melted butter), and put in a deep pan. Roll out pie dough and cut it in strips. Lay strips on top of fruit mixture in pan, and brush with melted butter.

Bake cobbler 45 minutes in 300° oven.
Makes 6 servings. Delicious with ice
cream.

## ANGEL PIE

Beat 4 egg whites stiff; add ½ teaspoon
cream of tartar and 1 cup sugar. Spread
on a well-greased and floured pie tin
and bake 20 minutes in a 275° oven and
40 minutes at 300°.

**Filling:**

For half the filling, cook the following
ingredients for 8 minutes in a double
boiler:

  **4 egg yolks**
  **½ cup sugar (scant)**
  **1 tablespoon lemon juice**
  **2 tablespoons pineapple juice**
    **Inside rind of pineapple, grated**

For the other half of the filling, whip
together 1 cup whipping cream and 1
tablespoon sugar. Spread half of
whipped cream on cooled pie crust. Add
lemon mixture and remaining whipped
cream. Chill pie in refrigerator and
serve.

## BAKED INDIAN PUDDING

  **4 pints milk**
  **½ cup corn meal**
  **¾ cup maple syrup**
  **½ cup sugar**
  **2 tablespoons butter**
  **½ teaspoon salt**
  **1 teaspoon each:**
    **cinnamon, ginger, nutmeg**
  **2 eggs**

Scald 1 pint milk and mix with corn
meal. Stir until mixture thickens.
Remove from fire and add maple syrup,
sugar, butter and seasonings. Beat eggs
well and stir into remaining 3 pints cold
milk. Add this to hot milk mixture and
pour into buttered baking dish. Bake in
250° oven for 3 to 4 hours. Serve warm,
topped with plain cream or whipped
cream. Makes 8 portions.

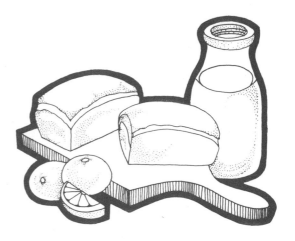

## MERRITT GEMS

  **1 yeast cake dissolved in 1 cup**
    **lukewarm water**
  **1 egg**
  **1 teaspoon salt**
  **¼ cup sugar**
  **1 rounded tablespoon shortening**
  **3 cups flour**
    **Finely chopped citron, to taste**
    **Deep fat**
    **Confectioners' sugar**

Combine ingredients (except fat and
confectioners' sugar); let dough rise to
twice its bulk. Pinch off small pieces or
cut with scissors; fry in fat 3 minutes or
until light brown. Remove, place in
paper bag with confectioners' sugar and
shake. Serve piping hot.

## BREAD PUDDING

  **Rolls or bread slices, 6 cups**
    **when quartered (approx.)**
  **8 eggs, separated**
  **1½ pints cream**
  **½ cup sugar, plus 2 tablespoons**
    **for meringue**
    **Juice of ½ orange**
    **Rind of ½ orange**

Quarter the rolls or bread slices until
you have enough to fill an 8x11-inch
greased baking dish completely. Beat egg
yolks; add cream, ½ cup sugar; mix
thoroughly. Pour mixture over bread.

Combine orange juice and rind; pour over mixture. Bake in preheated 300° oven for 1 hour. Beat egg whites until stiff, then slowly add 2 tablespoons sugar. When bread pudding is done, spread top with egg whites. Bake in preheated 275° oven for about 20 minutes. If desired, sprinkle top with nutmeats. Serves 10 to 12 people.

## CHRISTMAS PLUM PUDDING

½ **pound dry bread crumbs**
1 **cup scalded milk**
1 **cup sugar**
4 **egg yolks, well beaten**
½ **pound seeded raisins**
¼ **pound seedless raisins**
2 **ounces citron, cut fine**
¼ **pound figs, chopped**
½ **pound suet, chopped**
¼ **cup wine, jelly or grape juice**
1 **teaspoon each, nutmeg and**
   **cinnamon**
¼ **teaspoon each, ground cloves and**
   **mace**
1½ **teaspoons salt**
4 **egg whites, beaten stiff**

Soak bread crumbs in milk and cool. Add sugar, egg yolks, raisins, figs and citron. Then add suet, wine, spices, salt and egg whites. Pour into two 2-quart, greased mold pans and cover tightly. Steam 6 hours. Serve with hard sauce.

## NUT AND HONEY TORTE

1 **cup zwieback crumbs, crushed**
1 **cup pecans or walnuts, chopped**
1 **teaspoon baking powder**
¼ **teaspoon cinnamon**
¼ **teaspoon salt**
1 **teaspoon vanilla**
3 **eggs, separated**
½ **cup sugar**

Mix dry ingredients (except sugar). Add vanilla. Beat egg yolks until light, add sugar and beat again until a light lemon color. Add to dry ingredients, mixing thoroughly. Beat egg whites until stiff and fold into mixture. Pour into greased

pan, 8 x 12 inches. Bake in 325° oven for ½ hour.

**Syrup:**

Combine 2 cups water, ½ cup honey and 1 cup sugar and boil for 30 minutes. Pour syrup slowly over hot torte so it will be completely absorbed. Let stand 6 hours. Serves 12.

## MINT PIE

**Filling:**

¼ **pound butter**
1 **cup powdered sugar**
2 **eggs**
2 **squares unsweetened chocolate**
¼ **teaspoon essence of peppermint**

Cream butter and sugar together until smooth. Beat eggs in one at a time until mixture is fluffy. Mix in melted chocolate and peppermint.

**Crust:**

Roll 14 graham crackers very fine and mix with ¼ pound butter. Line pie tin and bake 20 minutes in 350° oven. Cool and fill crust with mint filling. Top with whipped cream before serving.

## LUSCH TORTE

For this recipe you will need: ½ pound vanilla wafers, 1 cup broken pecans, 1 pound confectioners' sugar, ½ pound butter, 6 egg yolks, 4 egg whites, salt and vanilla to taste. Crush wafers into crumbs, save ¼ cup crumbs to top torte. Add to remaining crumbs, 2 tablespoons pecans, 2 tablespoons sugar and enough butter to hold mixture together. Press into the bottom of 1½-inch-deep greased pan, 8 inches square. Bake at 300° until browned, then cool. Save ½ cup sugar for meringue. Then take part of remaining sugar and the butter and put into mixer. Start at slow speed and increase to fast. Add remaining sugar and whip. Add yolks, one at a time, and whip. Add salt and vanilla. Fold in pecans. Make meringue of egg whites and ½ cup sugar and fold into butter mixture. Place over crust and top with crumbs. Cover with wax paper and freeze for 12 hours. Serve with whipped cream. Serves 12.

## PERSIMMON PUDDING

1½ quarts of persimmons
2 eggs, well beaten
¾ cup honey
1 pint milk
½ cup butter
   Ground cinnamon and nutmeg,
      to taste
   Flour

Mash and rub persimmons through a coarse sieve or fine colander. To this add eggs, honey, milk, butter cut in small pieces, seasoning and enough flour to make batter stiff. Bake in 350° oven for 30 minutes.

## FRIED CUSTARD

Put 1 quart milk in double boiler with ¼ teaspoon soda (to keep milk from curdling), and 3 sticks cinnamon. Let come almost to a boil. Take 1 cup warm milk from pan and stir into 2 tablespoons flour and 4 tablespoons cornstarch. Beat till smooth. To this mixture, add another cup warm milk from double boiler, 1 cup sugar, and 6 egg yolks. Beat well; then combine with rest of milk in double boiler. Stir till mixture thickens. Remove from stove, add a pinch of salt, 1 teaspoon vanilla, and 1 tablespoon butter. Beat thoroughly. Pour into greased 8-inch cake pan about ¾ inch thick. Cool and place in refrigerator overnight. Cut into squares. Beat 3 egg whites well. Dip custard into whites, then into finely ground cracker meal. Fry in hot grease, 1 inch deep, till brown. Drain on paper. Serve hot. Serves 8.

## OLD-FASHIONED ICE CREAM

   4 eggs
   2 cups sugar
   ½ teaspoon salt
   3 cups heavy cream
   1 tablespoon vanilla
   2 quarts whole milk

Beat eggs until very light. Gradually add sugar and salt. Beat mixture well. Then add cream and vanilla. Add milk last. Allow about 2½ inches for swelling in freezer can. Freeze in dasher type old-fashioned ice-cream freezer. Makes 1 gallon of delicious vanilla ice cream.

## FIG PUDDING

   7 eggs, separated
   ½ pound sugar
   ¾ pound white bread crumbs
   ½ pound preserved figs
   ½ pound butter, melted
   ½ teaspoon allspice
      Vanilla and brandy to taste

Beat egg yolks and add sugar. Add beaten egg whites. Beat well. Add bread crumbs, figs, butter, allspice, vanilla and brandy to taste. Pour into two-quart mold, and steam 4 to 5 hours. Use a hard sauce for topping. Serves 12.

## MAYFLOWER SPECIAL CREAM PUFFS

Bring ½ cup butter and 1 cup water to a boil in a saucepan. Add 1 cup flour and mix vigorously. Remove from heat and add 4 eggs, one at a time, beating vigorously. Drop by tablespoons onto buttered sheet. Space 1½ inches apart. Shape with handle of spoon into rounds. Bake in 400° oven for 30-35 minutes. Cool. Slit and fill with custard mixture. Makes 18 large puffs.

**Filling:**

Mix ¾ cup confectioners' sugar; 1 tablespoon flour; 3 egg yolks; ½ teaspoon vanilla sugar in a saucepan with a French whip. Then add 1 cup scalded milk. Stir constantly over heat until mixture thickens. Remove from fire, coat with butter and allow to cool. Whip ¾ cup whipping cream and 3 tablespoons confectioners' sugar and fold into cooled custard mixture.

## BLUEBERRY BETTY À LA MODE

- **1 quart blueberries**
- **2 heaping tablespoons cornstarch**
- **1 cup sugar**
- **½ lemon, juice**
- **¼ cup water**
- **Pinch of salt**
- **An 8-inch-square yellow cake**
- **2 quarts vanilla ice cream**

Place berries in heavy saucepan. Add cornstarch, sugar, lemon juice, salt and water. Stir contents gently with wooden spoon until mixed. Cook over moderate flame and stir frequently. When sauce thickens, put aside to cool, reserving 1 cupful for garnish. Slice cooled cake to make 2 layers. Spoon half of berries into cake pan and top with one layer of cake. Pour remaining berries on cake and top with second layer. Cover generously with powdered sugar and sprinkle with nutmeg. Cut portions in 2-inch squares and place a generous scoop of vanilla ice cream on each portion. Top with a teaspoon of sauce. Serves 16.

## APPLE DUMPLINGS

- **6 medium-sized apples**
- **1 cup brown sugar**
- **½ cup granulated sugar**
- **½ teaspoon cinnamon**
- **½ teaspoon nutmeg**
- **⅓ cup butter**
- **1 cup sweetened pineapple juice**
- **Pie crust (enough for 2 double-crust pies)**
- **1 pint heavy cream**

Peel and core the apples. Mix sugars, seasoning and butter. Stuff apples with mixture. Wrap apples individually in pastry and place in baking pan. Pour pineapple juice over dumplings. Start baking in pre-heated 425° oven. After 10 minutes, lower heat to 375° and baste with juice. Continue basting every 10 minutes for 30 minutes or until apples are tender. Serve warm topped with cream. Makes 6 servings.

## COCONUT CREAM TORTE WITH APRICOT

**Crust:**

Beat together 1 egg, ¼ pound soft butter and ½ cup of sugar until foamy. Add 1 teaspoonful of grated lemon peel and a pinch of salt. Then sift in 2 cups pastry flour, slowly mixing the batter. When thoroughly blended, place in refrigerator for 1 hour. Roll into crust and bake in a 9- or 10-inch spring form pan in a 350° oven for 25 minutes.

**Filling:**

Spread baked crust with a generous layer of apricot marmalade, then lay on a thin layer of pound cake or other white cake and moisten this cake with sufficient rum or rum flavoring to give the pastry a rich aroma and full flavor. Make a package of prepared vanilla pudding, then cool it. Whip 1 cup whipping cream and fold into cool pudding. Spread this pudding dome-like over the layers and sprinkle with ground coconut which has been lightly browned in butter. Serve cold. Makes 6-8 portions.

## CHEF MACEROLLO'S PLUM PUDDING

Beat 5 eggs until fluffy, add ⅔ cup brown sugar. Stir in ½ cup of molasses and mix thoroughly. Add 1⅓ cups Sultana raisins; 1⅓ cups currants; 1⅓ cups dark raisins; ¾ cup citron, chopped; ¾ cup candied orange peel, chopped; ⅔ cup candied lemon peel, chopped; 1 cup suet, chopped; ½ cup bread crumbs; 1⅓ pounds apples, peeled and chopped; pinch of salt; 1 tablespoon cinnamon; ½ tablespoon nutmeg; 1 tablespoon ginger; 1 tablespoon allspice; 1 tablespoon caramel; ½ tablespoon orange extract; ½ tablespoon lemon extract; 3 ounces beer; 2½ ounces vermouth and ¾ ounce liquor (brandy, bourbon, rum or triple sec). Mix thoroughly. Place mixture in 3 greased quart molds with covers, or tie on wax paper. Place in pan of water. Steam for approximately 2-2½ hours in 325° oven. After cooling pudding to room temperature, seal over tops with melted paraffin wax and age for at least 2 weeks. Serve resteamed with warm brandy sauce.

## MOLASSES SQUARES

½ cup sugar
¾ cup molasses
5½ ounce package Rice Krispies

Boil sugar and molasses until it forms a soft ball in a glass of water. Butter a 12x18-inch rectangular pan and line with cereal. Pour syrup over it, stir fast and pat down with wet hand. Serve with vanilla ice cream.

## SOUTHERN BREAD PUDDING

6 eggs
½ cup sugar
2 quarts milk
1 tablespoon vanilla
12 slices bread, cut in ½-inch cubes
¼ pound butter
½ cup raisins

Beat eggs and sugar well; add milk and vanilla; fold in bread cubes. Melt butter in 10x12x2-inch pan and pour in mixture. Sprinkle raisins on top. Cook at 350° for 45 minutes. Remove from oven and let cool. Serve with sauce. Yields 20 servings.

**Sauce:**

Beat 1 egg; add 2 tablespoons sugar, 1 pint milk. Cook in double boiler until thick. Remove from heat and add 2 tablespoons sherry; cool. Serve warm or cold on bread pudding.

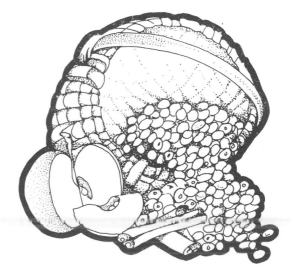

## APPLE PUDDING

2 eggs, beaten
1 cup sugar
1 teaspoon each: soda and cinnamon
¼ teaspoon each: ground cloves and
    salt
1 cup flour
4 tablespoons butter, melted
½ cup nuts
½ cup raisins
3 cups apples, grated

Beat eggs until light, add sugar gradually.
Beat in sifted dry ingredients. Add
butter, grated apples, and floured nuts
and raisins. Spread mixture about 1½-2
inches thick in buttered 8x12-inch pan.
Bake 40 minutes in 375° oven. Serve
with Butterscotch Sauce.

### Butterscotch Sauce:

Mix together 1 cup light brown sugar; 1
cup water; 1 tablespoon cornstarch and 3
tablespoons butter. Cook until thick. Add
½ teaspoon vanilla and serve warm over
pudding.

## CHOCOLATE POTS DE CRÈME

Scald 2 cups cream with 1-inch piece of
vanilla bean, 4 ounces melted sweet
chocolate and ¼ cup sugar; cool slightly.
Beat 6 egg yolks until light and lemon-
colored, then add cream, stirring
constantly. Strain mixture through fine
sieve and pour into 6 small earthenware
pots or custard cups. Set in pan of water,
cover and bake in 250° oven for 15
minutes or until a knife inserted in the
center comes out clean. Serve chilled.
Serves 6.

## CHOCOLATE SOUFFLÉ

2 squares unsweetened chocolate
⅓ cup superfine sugar
3 teaspoons instant coffee
⅓ cup hot water
2 tablespoons flour
4 tablespoons sweet butter
1 cup scalded milk
1 tablespoon vanilla extract

4 egg yolks
7 egg whites
2 tablespoons superfine sugar

Melt chocolate in double boiler, add ⅓
cup sugar and stir, then mix in coffee
mixed with hot water. Make a smooth
white sauce with butter, flour and milk
and combine with chocolate mixture.
Cool until just warm and then stir in the
egg yolks, mix well, and add the vanilla.
Beat the egg whites until stiff, but not
dry, add 2 tablespoons superfine sugar,
beat one more minute and fold in the
chocolate sauce. Pour in a well-greased
2½-quart soufflé dish. Bake 5 minutes in
preheated 375° oven, then reduce heat to
350° and bake 20 minutes longer. Serve
topped with Crème Chantilly. Serves 6.

### Crème Chantilly

½ pint whipping cream
1 teaspoon very fine sugar
1 teaspoon pure vanilla extract
Beat until stiff.

## CASATA À LA ERCULIANI

2 8-inch-square layers of sponge
    cake (each about 1¼ inches thick)
4 teaspoons rum
2 cups thick dark chocolate pudding
4 teaspoons Anisette
2 cups thick vanilla pudding
    Chopped cherries and nuts

Place one cake layer in bottom of pan. Sprinkle with rum. Spread cake with chocolate pudding; cover with second layer of cake. Sprinkle this layer with Anisette and then cover with vanilla pudding. Garnish with chopped cherries and nuts. Chill for at least 2 hours before serving. Cut into squares. Serves 12-16.

## COFFEE RUM PARFAIT

Pour 1 cup very hot coffee over 10 ounces small marshmallows, mix until almost melted. Mix in 1 ounce dark rum, then fold in 1 cup heavy cream, whipped, and pour into 5 parfait glasses. Let stand 30 minutes, then refrigerate or freeze for several hours. Top with whipped cream. Serves 5.

## TORTONI ICE CREAM

- 1 **quart heavy cream**
- 3 **eggs**
- 1 **teaspoon almond extract**
- 1 **ounce light rum**
- 1 **cup sugar, extra fine if possible**
- 6 **macaroons, crushed**
- 8-9 **maraschino cherries, cut in half**
- ½ **cup finely chopped walnuts or pecans**

Place mixing bowl and beaters in refrigerator or freezer until cold. Pour heavy cream in bowl and beat at medium speed until it starts to thicken. Add all the other ingredients except cherries and nuts and beat at high speed until batter forms peaks. Spoon into 4-ounce paper cups. Pour cherry juice over top for color (if desired), sprinkle with chopped nuts and top with cherry half. Place in freezer until firm and serve. Tortoni may be stored for a long period of time in a freezer. When ready to serve, remove from freezer for 10-15 minutes. Serves 16-18.

## LOTUS ICE CREAM

- 2⅓ **quarts light cream**
- 3 **cups sugar**
  **Grated rind of 5 lemons**
- ¼ **cup toasted almonds, chopped**
- 2 **teaspoons almond extract**
- 1 **cup lemon juice**

Combine ingredients in order listed and mix well together. Freeze either by hand or electric freezer, or by the refrigerator method. Makes about 4 quarts of ice cream. A refreshing and unusual dessert for a holiday party.

## ZWETSCHKENKNOEDEL

- 2 **pounds potatoes**
- ½ **pound flour**
- 2 **tablespoons butter**
- ¼ **tablespoon salt**
- 12 **small blue plums**

Boil potatoes and mash them. Then while they are still warm, work them together with the flour, butter and salt. With fingers dusted with flour, flatten dough out to thickness of about ¼ inch and cut into 5-inch squares. Place a whole plum in center of each and fold dough over to form a sealed ball. Place these plum dumplings in boiling salt water. They will rise to the top when finished. Remove from water, roll in additional melted butter, then in sweet bread crumbs (made by putting ¾ cup bread crumbs in ¼ cup butter mixed with 1 teaspoon sugar and 1 teaspoon cinnamon) and serve hot. Serves 4-6.

## ICE CREAM TROPICANA

**Crumb Mixture:**

1 cup graham-cracker crumbs
¼ cup flaked coconut
¼ cup pecans, coarsely chopped
1½ tablespoons sugar
¼ teaspoon ground cinnamon
¼ teaspoon ground mace
¼ cup melted butter

Place first 6 ingredients in a bowl. Add melted butter; toss lightly with a fork. Cover and set aside at room temperature.

**Fruit Mixture:**

1 cup strawberries, sliced
1 cup seeded or seedless grapes, sliced
1 cup pineapple chunks
⅓ cup sugar
1 lemon, juice and grated rind

Place fruits in bowl. Thoroughly blend sugar with lemon rind; add, with juice, to fruits and toss so that fruit is thoroughly coated. Cover and chill.

Divide 1 quart of vanilla ice cream into 6-8 portions. Top each portion with fruit mixture and then sprinkle each with portion of crumb mixture.

## ALMENDRADO

2 envelopes gelatin
1 cup cold water
9 egg whites, room temperature
1¾ cups sugar
   Pinch of salt
3 drops almond extract
   Red and green vegetable coloring
¼ pound blanched almonds, ground

Soak gelatin in cold water. Set over hot water to liquefy and then cool, stirring occasionally until it reaches the consistency of syrup (if too hot, gelatin will thin egg whites too much). Whip egg whites until stiff. Add sugar, salt, gelatin and flavoring, folding into the egg whites. Divide into three bowls. Color one part red or pink, one green, and to the remaining white mixture add ground

almonds. Pour in alternately colored layers into a loaf-shaped dish, making the center layer white. Chill in refrigerator, and when firmly set, slice like brick ice cream and top with almond-flavored Custard Sauce. Makes 18 servings.

**Custard Sauce for Almendrado:**

6 egg yolks
¼ cup sugar
⅛ teaspoon salt
2 cups scalded milk
¼ teaspoon almond flavoring

Beat egg yolks slightly with a silver fork; add sugar and salt. Add milk gradually, stirring constantly. Cook and stir in double boiler over hot, but not boiling, water until mixture coats the spoon, about 7 minutes. Add the flavoring and chill.

## DEL MONTE LODGE LEMON SOUFFLÉ

2 lemons, rind and juice
½ pound white bread crumbs
1 pint milk
5 ounces sugar
2 ounces butter
4 eggs, separated

Grate lemon rinds on bread crumbs. Bring milk and sugar to a boil, add bread crumbs and butter. Let cool. Add

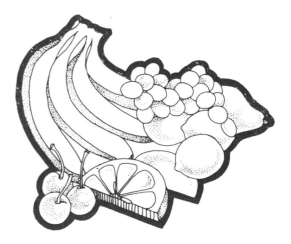

juice of lemons and egg yolks. Beat egg whites until firm and fold into mixture. Fill buttered 1½-quart mold ¾ full. Dust with powdered sugar. Bake in moderate 350° oven for about 1 hour and serve at once. Serves 8.

## BLAZING BANANA
  2 teaspoons butter
  3 teaspoons dark brown sugar
  1 ounce banana liqueur
  1 large banana, sliced
    Dash of nutmeg
  3 dips vanilla ice cream
  1 teaspoon flaming brandy

Place butter, sugar and liqueur in a chafing dish over low heat, mix until a paste. Add banana and nutmeg. Cook for about 5 minutes or until banana is soft. Pour over ice cream and top with flaming brandy. Makes 1 serving.

## PINEAPPLE AND BANANA FLAMBÉ

Cut stalks and ends from whole pineapple. Turn upside down and trim sides. Quarter and remove center core. Split pieces in half again.

Place 6 ounces butter in a flambé pan and melt. Add 2 teaspoons sugar and brown lightly. Peel 4 bananas and split in half. Add banana and pineapple to pan. Glaze lightly. Add juice from 1 lemon and 1 orange and 4 ounces banana liqueur. Flame with 2 ounces cherry brandy. Place fruits around 4 scoops of coffee ice cream and pour 1 ounce Kahlua over them. Makes 4 portions.

## CURRIED FRUIT
  14- ounce can sliced pineapple
  14- ounce can peaches
  14- ounce can pears
  1½ cups combined pineapple and
      pear juice
  ¾ stick butter
  ½ cup brown sugar

  2 tablespoons cornstarch
  4 teaspoons curry powder
  ½ lemon, juice

Arrange drained fruit in casserole. Add cornstarch to fruit juice. Cook until clear and somewhat thickened. Add butter.

Mix curry powder and brown sugar, pour hot sauce over mixture and stir until sugar melts. Add lemon juice. Pour over fruit. Bake 1 hour at 350°. Put in refrigerator overnight.

Heat about 45 minutes before serving. Delightful by itself, as a relish, and particularly good served over vanilla ice cream. Serves 8.

## PEARS BELLE HELENA
  1 cup hot chocolate sauce
  4 scoops vanilla ice cream
  8 Bartlett pear halves, canned
  1 cup whipped cream
  4 tablespoons green crème de menthe
  4 stemmed maraschino cherries
  4 sprigs fresh mint
    Sugar wafers

Place 2 teaspoons chocolate sauce in each of 4 hollow stemmed coupe glasses. Place scoop of ice cream in each. Arrange 2 pear halves cut side down on opposite sides of ice cream. Pour remaining chocolate sauce over pears and ice cream. Place 2 whipped cream rosettes between each pear half and a large swirl of whipped cream on top of ice cream. Garnish with crème de menthe, mint sprig and cherry. Serve with sugar wafer. Serves 4.

## FROZEN JOHNELLS

Soak 7 or 8 crumbled macaroon cookies in 1 cup of brandy combined with 1 cup of sugar. Whip 1 quart of whipping cream until stiff. Fold whipped cream into the macaroon mixture. Spoon into champagne glasses and freeze for 1 hour. Serves 8.

# MAIN COURSE DISHES

## SHEPHERD'S PIE
- 2 cups cooked, chopped lamb, beef, or veal
- 2 cups mashed potatoes
- 2 cups gravy, seasoned with salt, ¼ teaspoon pepper, and 1 teaspoon onion juice
- ¼ teaspoon paprika
- 2 tablespoons butter

Line bottom of a buttered baking dish or individual casseroles with hot mashed potatoes. Add thick layer of meat and seasoned gravy, then another layer of potato until dish is filled. Make top crust of potatoes. Dot with butter and sprinkle with paprika. Bake in hot oven until a golden brown.

## QUICHE LORRAINE
Line a regulation-size pie tin with a flaky-type crust. Do not bake. Cover with a layer of diced ham or diced half-cooked bacon. Put on a layer of Swiss cheese shavings. In a separate bowl prepare a custard mix of:
- 4 whole eggs and 2 yolks
- 1 quart homogenized milk or light cream
- Dash of salt, pepper, and nutmeg

Beat eggs until light and creamy. Add milk and spices, then stir thoroughly. Pour mixture over ham and cheese in the half-filled pie tin, bringing liquid level to edge of pastry. Bake 25 minutes in a slow oven (250°), or until custard is firm and golden brown. Will serve 4 to 6 as a main dish, or up to 12 as an extra. Plan it for a party menu over the holiday.

## TOURTIÈRE
- 1½ pounds fresh pork shoulder, medium ground
- 2 medium onions, chopped Melted butter
- 1 bud garlic, chopped Salt and pepper, to taste
- ½ bay leaf
- ½ teaspoon nutmeg
- 1½ tablespoons cinnamon
- 4 9-inch pie crusts

Toss onions lightly in melted butter, then add the meat. Cook slowly on top of stove 20-30 minutes. The meat should not be brown; the pink shade will turn light gray. Add seasonings and mix well. Line pie plates with pastry and fill with meat filling and cover with top crusts. Bake in a medium oven 45 minutes or until pastry is a golden brown. This makes two 9-inch pies.

## FRESH MUSHROOMS AND CHICKEN LIVERS ON WILD RICE
- 1 cup wild rice
- 4 cups water
- 1 pound mushrooms
- 1 pound chicken livers

¼ cup butter
4 tablespoons flour
2 cups chicken broth
½ teaspoon salt
¼ teaspoon pepper
¼ cup sherry wine

Boil rice briskly in water 30 or 40 minutes. Do not stir. Drain off water and steam until dry and fluffy. Sauté mushrooms and chicken livers in butter. Sprinkle with flour and mix well. Add chicken broth and cook until thickened. Season with salt and pepper. Add sherry. Serve over wild rice.

## CHINESE GREEN PEA CHOW YOKE

2 cups roast pork or beef, diced
2 medium-sized onions, chopped
2 tablespoons peanut oil
1 cup mushrooms
1 cup celery, chopped
1 cup water chestnuts
2½ cups bamboo shoots
2 cups green peas, rinsed with boiling water
Salt and pepper
1 tablespoon soy sauce

Sauté onions in peanut oil until they are golden brown. Mix diced meat and other ingredients together (except soy). Add to onions; simmer covered 15 minutes. Remove cover and cook 10 minutes, over medium fire. Add soy sauce. Stir occasionally. Serves 6.

## HAM SNAILS

For this recipe you will need 1½ cups sifted bread flour, 1 tablespoon baking powder, ½ teaspoon salt, 1 tablespoon sesame seed, 3 tablespoons shortening, ½ cup milk, melted butter, 1½ cups ground ham.

Mix flour, baking powder and salt. Add sesame seed. Then cut in shortening; moisten with milk. Roll dough into ½-inch-thick rectangle. Brush with butter and spread ham evenly over the surface.

Roll like a jelly roll. Cut into 1 inch slices. Bake on a cookie sheet 25 to 30 minutes at 400°. Serve with hot basil tomato sauce.

**Sauce:**

Sauté 1 ground onion in 2 tablespoons butter. Combine 2 tablespoons flour, 1 teaspoon sugar, 1 teaspoon salt and ¼ teaspoon finely ground basil and blend into onion mixture. To this add 1 cup canned tomatoes; cook till smooth.

## GUMBO

4-5 pound stewing hen
3 boxes frozen cut okra
4 cups onion, chopped fine
Bacon grease
3 tablespoons flour
1 No. 2 can tomatoes
1 12-ounce box frozen corn (fresh may be used)
2 12-ounce boxes frozen shrimp
Worcestershire sauce, to taste
Tabasco, to taste
5 cups cooked rice

Boil hen in 4 quarts of water, seasoned with celery and salt. Grind okra very fine and fry in bacon grease. Sift flour onto okra after it starts cooking. Fry onion separately, until soft, then combine with okra. Run tomatoes through sieve, then add to okra and onion mixture, allow to simmer for about 8 minutes. Remove chicken from water and add okra and onion mixture. Cut meat from hen, dice and return to pot. Grind corn and add. Boil shrimp 5 minutes and add, peeled and cleaned, to the mixture. Season liberally with Worcestershire sauce and Tabasco. Simmer for 1 hour. Serve with rice. Makes 10-12 servings.

## NEVER-FAIL CHEESE SOUFFLÉ

3 tablespoons minute tapioca
1 cup milk
3 eggs, separated
1 teaspoon salt
1 cup cheese, grated

Cook milk and tapioca together in double boiler until mixture is clear. Stir constantly. Add cheese, stirring until melted. Beat egg yolks and add to mixture while still over heat. Remove from heat, add salt and fold in beaten egg whites. Pour into buttered dish, 8 inches in diameter and 4 inches deep, and place dish in a shallow pan of water. Bake in a 350° oven for 50 minutes. Serve immediately. Six portions.

## CHICKEN ENCHILADAS WITH SOUR CREAM

 1 clove garlic, chopped
 2 pounds fresh green chili, toasted and peeled or 1½ cups prepared green chili
 5 ripe tomatoes, chopped
 2 onions, chopped fine
   Pinch of oregano
   Salt
 4 chicken breasts, cooked
 ½ pound Cheddar cheese
 1 pint sour cream
12 white corn tortillas
   Deep fat

Fry garlic in olive oil, lightly. Add green chili, tomatoes, onions, oregano and salt. Cover with water and cook until mixture thickens. In a bowl shred chicken meat, add grated cheese and sour cream. Fry tortillas in deep fat, one at a time, until soft. Then dip into chili mixture. Fill tortillas with chicken and sour cream mixture and roll up. Place rolls close together in a flat casserole. Pour on remaining green chili. Bake in 350° oven 10-15 minutes. Serve with chopped lettuce.

## MR. SEKO'S SUKIYAKI

2½ pounds sukiyaki beef strips (tender beef sliced ⅛-inch thick)
   Suet, as required
 1 small can bamboo shoots, sliced
 4 bunches green onion in 1½-inch lengths
 4 large dry onions, sliced
 1 small can yam noodles

**Sauce:**

Combine 1 cup soy sauce, 1 cup water, ¼ cup sugar and ¼ cup sake (optional). Render out suet and sear meat in fat until brown. Put meat to one side of pan, add vegetables, and pour sauce over all. Allow to simmer uncovered for 10 minutes or until vegetables are tender but crisp. Add noodles, heat through and serve with rice. All meat may be seared at one time, but it is advisable to cook only as much of the vegetables as needed for the first serving, adding more later for seconds. Serves 8.

## OYSTER SOUFFLÉ

 1 pint oysters
 1 teaspoon onion, finely minced
 ½ cup coarse cracker crumbs
1½ pints milk
 5 eggs, beaten
 1 teaspoon salt
 ½ teaspoon Ac´cent

Cut each oyster into three pieces. Combine oysters and onions and let stand, and add cracker crumbs, then liquid from oysters. Add beaten eggs to milk. Combine with oysters and add salt, Ac´cent and onion. Bake in a greased casserole in a 325° oven for 90 minutes. Serves 6-8.

## HAM AND YAM SURPRISE

Preboil 6-8 medium sweet potatoes or yams in salt water until tender. Peel and slice into greased casserole. Meanwhile, sauté 1 minced onion in 2 tablespoons butter or margarine until lightly brown. Blend 2 tablespoons flour into butter, then add 1 teaspoon salt, 2 teaspoons prepared mustard, ½ teaspoon Worcestershire, 2 teaspoons vinegar and 1 cup water. Mix well, remove from heat, and stir in ½ cup apricot syrup. Cook over low heat until slightly thickened. Mash ⅔ of a No. 3 can of apricot halves to a pulp and add to cooked mixture. Pour over potatoes. Take three 1-inch-thick ham steaks (1½ pounds each) and cut each slice in quarters, not quite to center bone; place on top of casserole. Stick cloves in side of ham around the edge. Bake in 325-350° oven for 50 minutes. Remove from oven and chill. Before serving, turn out from casserole on flat plate. Take balance of apricots and place around ham. Return to 350° oven for about 10 minutes. Garnish with parsley. Serves 9.

## SOUR CREAM NOODLE BAKE

Cook an 8-ounce package medium noodles in boiling salted water. Rinse and drain. Brown 1 pound ground beef in 1 tablespoon butter, then add 1 teaspoon salt, ⅛ teaspoon black pepper, ¼ teaspoon garlic salt and 1 cup tomato sauce or purée. Simmer 5 minutes. Combine 1 cup chopped green onions, 1 cup sour cream, 1 cup creamed cottage cheese and noodles. Alternate layers of noodle mixture and meat mixture in two-quart casserole, beginning with noodles and ending with meat. Top with 1 cup shredded sharp Cheddar cheese. Bake at 350° in preheated oven 20-25 minutes, until cheese is brown. Serves 8.

## MOTHER KAN'S STEAMED EGGS WITH MINCED CLAMS

8-10 ounce can minced clams
2½ cups cold water
4 large eggs
¼ teaspoon salt
½ Ac´cent
1 tablespoon soy sauce
Finely chopped green onions
Steamed or fried rice

Drain clam juice from can (which will yield about ½ cup) and mix with water in a saucepan. Heat until hot, then cool. Beat eggs well with fork; add clams, salt and Ac´cent. Mix well and add clam juice and water mixture. Pour into oiled shallow baking dish or casserole. Place casserole elevated on a trivet in large cooking utensil, such as Dutch oven or chicken fryer, that has a tight-fitting lid. Add enough water so that 2 inches of water surrounds casserole. Add boiling water to pan as needed. This is the Chinese method of steaming food. Cover and cook over moderate heat, removing cover of utensil frequently to drain moisture which will collect on inside of cover. This will prevent excess water from going into eggs. Cook 15-20 minutes or until knife blade comes out clean when inserted. Remove casserole from Dutch oven and sprinkle with soy sauce. Garnish with chopped green onions. Serve immediately over steamed rice. Makes 4 portions.

## SPINACH AND CHEESE PIE
1 large bunch fresh dill (about
    6 tablespoons chopped)
1 large bunch Italian parsley
6 scallions
2 pounds fresh spinach
1 cup olive oil
6 eggs
1 pound feta cheese, crumbled
1 pound phyllo pastry (obtainable
    in Greek specialty shops)

Marinate in olive oil, chopped dill, parsley and scallions (include scallion tops). Cook spinach very briefly, pour cold water over to stop the cooking and drain well. Add thoroughly drained spinach to olive oil. Beat eggs, add crumbled cheese. Add egg and cheese mixture to spinach, oil and herbs. Line a large (11 by 14 inches) baking pan with half the phyllo pastry, brushing it well with melted butter or oil. Place spinach filling on pastry and cover with remaining pastry, again brushing well with melted butter. Seal edges of pastry. Bake in 300° oven for 45 minutes or until well browned. Cut into squares. Makes 16 generous servings.

## "LOUIS" CHEESE FONDUE
Melt 1 teaspoon of butter in a casserole. Pour in 10 ounces of white wine. Let it warm. Crumble 1 pound of Swiss cheese (or use ½ Swiss and ½ Parmesan) and add a handful at a time. Mix until creamy. Add salt and pepper, and a few drops of kirsch. Have French bread previously cut in large cubes. Serve fondue on a heater. Everyone will dip bread in the cheese. (In case one drops the bread, the penalty is a bottle of wine!) Serves 4-6.

## MACARONI AND CHEESE CASSEROLE
Cook 4 ounces elbow macaroni in boiling salted water until tender. Mix with 3 well-beaten eggs, 1 tablespoon salt and pepper, to taste, 1 cup milk and ½ pound grated cheese. (Save some of the cheese to sprinkle on top.) Put in greased casserole and bake at 300° for about 30 minutes, then turn to 400° for a few minutes to brown top slightly. Serves 8.

## SWISS FONDUE
1 pound sharp Cheddar cheese,
    grated
1 pound aged Swiss cheese,
    grated
1 cup white wine
1 teaspoon dry mustard
½ teaspoon garlic, chopped
    Dash of Tabasco sauce
    Dash of Worcestershire sauce
    Toast squares

Combine ingredients in a saucepan and cook over low fire until smooth. Add 1 ounce kirsch and serve immediately on hot toast. Or serve Swiss style—dip pieces of French bread into bubbling fondue in a chafing dish. Serves 12.

## SWISS CHEESE FONDUE
Rub an earthenware casserole with a clove of garlic. Add 2 cups Neuchâtel wine and heat slowly over chafing dish burner. Lightly mix 1 pound shredded Gruyère cheese with ½ teaspoon flour. When the bubbles in the wine rise to the surface (do not boil) add cheese mixture, a handful at a time, stirring until each handful melts. Add freshly ground pepper, salt, nutmeg and 2 tablespoons kirschwasser; stir well. Turn heat low but keep fondue slowly bubbling.

Cut 1 loaf French bread into cubes, leaving one side of crust on each. Provide long-handled forks. Each guest impales a bread cube through the crust and dunks it into the fondue, stirring it around as he does. If fondue becomes too thick, add a little hot wine (never cold). Serves 4.

## TEPPAN YAKI (Mixed Grill)

On a lightly oiled hot griddle quickly grill 12 large raw shrimp, 12 stalks asparagus, 6 slices white onion and 2 cups bean sprouts. Then place on plates; keep warm. Grill six 8-ounce strip steaks to taste.

Cut steaks, shrimp and vegetables into bite-sized pieces so all can be eaten with chopsticks. Make a hot sauce by combining chili sauce, Worcestershire sauce, crushed sesame seeds and ground hot peppers or grated white radish, in proportions to your taste. Mix this sauce with equal parts of lemon juice and soy sauce. Serve with teppan yaki. Serves 6.

# MEATS

## SAUERBRATEN

2½ pound round roast
⅔ cup water
⅓ cup cider vinegar
1 tablespoon pickling spices
2 onions
2 carrots
2 celery stalks
   Gingersnaps

Pickle beef for three days in water and vinegar mixture with spices, chopped onions, carrots and celery. Roast as regular pot roast. When meat is done make gravy from juice and vegetable mixture, thickening it with gingersnaps. Served with noodles, potato dumplings and red cabbage, this makes a real Pennsylvania Dutch dinner. Serves 5.

## CORNED BEEF AND CABBAGE

3½ pounds brisket of corned beef
2 onions
2 carrots
   Celery leaves
1 head cabbage
   Bacon rind or ham bone
2 teaspoons salt
   Dash of pepper
4 tablespoons butter

Simmer beef slowly for 3 hours in water to which spices, 1 onion, carrots and celery leaves have been added. Boil cabbage in fresh water with bacon rind or ham bone. Flavor with an onion, salt and pepper. Cook until soft, about 20 minutes, and drain. Brown butter and pour over cabbage. Serve with corned beef. Makes 4 or 5 portions.

## HARTWELL FARM BAKED HAM

Bone and tie one 15- or 16-pound smoked ham. Place in roasting pan with 2 cups cold water. Make a "blanket" for the ham by adding cold water to 8 cups flour until mixture has consistency of biscuit dough. Turn onto a well-floured board and knead as much flour as possible into the dough. Roll out to a thickness of ½ inch. (The dough will be tough and will not roll easily.) Place blanket of dough over the ham. Put a tight-fitting cover on the roasting pan. Bake in a 375° to 400° oven 3 hours. Then test ham with fork to make sure it's cooked. If done, remove from oven. Take off dough and skin and cover with brown sugar. Poke cloves into fat. Return to oven, uncovered, till brown. Put on platter; cover with syrupy mixture from pan.

## DUTCH OVEN ROAST
    3- to 4-pound top round beef
    3 tablespoons beef fat
    1 onion, sliced
    2 small carrots, coarsely chopped
    ¼ stalk celery, coarsely chopped
    1 stalk leek, coarsely chopped
    3 tablespoons flour
    ½ cup tomato puree
    ½ glass red wine
    1½ quarts hot water or soup stock
    3 cloves
    1 bay leaf
       Black pepper and salt

Heat beef fat in Dutch oven until hot. Add meat. Turn meat until browned all over; remove from pan. Brown onion in beef fat before adding other vegetables to be browned. Blend flour and tomato puree into mixture. Pour wine and water (or stock) into Dutch oven. Boil a few minutes; then return meat to pan. Add seasonings. Cook slowly 2 to 2½ hours.

## HUNGARIAN BEEF GOULASH
    3 pounds beef, chuck or round
    ½ pound onions, diced
       Salt and pepper
    ½ pound fresh tomatoes
    2 ounces "rosen" paprika
    1 small clove garlic
    1 pinch chopped caraway seeds
       Bouquet of vegetables

    1½ pints water
    ¾ cup sour cream

Brown onions in saucepan with lard. Add beef cut in squares; season with salt and pepper. Cover pan and simmer 25 minutes in a moderate oven. Then stir in tomatoes, paprika, garlic, caraway seed, bouquet of vegetables and water. Continue cooking 1½ hours. Remove meat, strain sauce, then mix meat and sauce together again. Add sour cream and serve. Makes 6 good portions.

## BEEFSTEAK AND KIDNEY PIE
    1 pound veal kidney, diced
    1 pound round steak, diced
    ½ pound fresh mushrooms
    2 jiggers Burgundy wine
    ½ teaspoon salt
    1 bay leaf
    1 teaspoon Worcestershire sauce
    3 tablespoons flour
    1 pie crust, uncooked

Parboil the veal kidney in salt water for about 15 minutes; then wash it off in cold water. Parboil the round steak in salt water for 15 minutes and wash it off in cold water. Sauté steak till brown; add mushrooms and wine. Sauté mixture for 5 minutes. Add about 3 cups water to the round steak and add kidneys. Simmer for about an hour, with salt, bay leaf and Worcestershire sauce added for flavor. Make a paste of flour and ½ cup water to thicken gravy. Put filling into a casserole, cover with a flaky pie crust and bake for ½ hour at 375°.

## COLLOPS
    2¾ pounds round steak (beef)
    2 tablespoons butter or fat
    ¾ tablespoon salt
    ¾ tablespoon pepper
    ½ teaspoon allspice
    2 bay leaves
    1 large onion, sliced
       Water or weak stock
    2 tablespoons flour
    1½ cups cream

Cut beef in 1-inch cubes. Sear on all sides in fat; add seasonings, onion, and enough stock to cover these ingredients. Simmer about 2 hours. Strain and skim the juice in the pan, returning a little of the fat. Add flour mixed with 7 tablespoons water. Stir until browned. Add meat juice gradually. Pour in cream and cook gravy 8 to 10 minutes. Season and pour over meat.

## GREEK DALMADES
- 2 cups rice, uncooked
- 1 onion
- 1 celery heart
- 3 sprigs parsley
- 2 pounds choice ground beef
- 2 eggs
  Grape leaves or cooked cabbage leaves
- ¼ pound butter
- 1 quart water
- 1 pinch nutmeg
  Salt and pepper to taste

Boil rice. Chop onion, celery and parsley, and mix with beef. Season and add cooked rice and eggs. Make 1½-inch meat balls of mixture and wrap in grape leaves or cooked cabbage leaves. Place in pot with butter and water, and boil over slow fire for ½ hour.

**Sauce:**
- 3 egg yolks

- 1 tablespoon cornstarch
- 2 tablespoons water
  Juice of 3 lemons

Combine these ingredients with juice from dalmades and pour over wrapped meat balls before serving. Serves 8.

## ROAST STUFFED OPOSSUM
- 1 opossum
  Salt and pepper
- 1 chopped onion
- 1 tablespoon fat
- 1 cup bread crumbs
- ¼ teaspoon Worcestershire sauce
- 1 hard-boiled egg
- 1 teaspoon salt water
  Bacon

Rub the cleaned opossum with salt and pepper. Brown the onion in fat, add opossum liver, and cook until tender. To this add the bread crumbs, Worcestershire sauce, egg, and salt water. Mix these ingredients thoroughly and stuff the opossum with it. Then truss the opossum like a fowl and put it in the roasting pan with bacon across the back. Pour 1 quart water into the pan before placing the opossum in a moderate oven. Roast uncovered, basting every 15 minutes until the opossum is tender (about 2½ hours).

## STUFFED PEPPERS — CREOLE STYLE
- 8 medium-size peppers
- 2 onions, chopped
- 1 small can tomatoes
- 2 cups bread crumbs
- 2 tablespoons butter
- ½ cup cooked chopped ham
  Salt and pepper to taste

Chop 2 peppers before combining with onion, tomatoes, bread crumbs, butter, ham and seasonings. Cut tops off remaining 6 peppers, clean, and scald. Then stuff with filling. Sprinkle with cracker crumbs and bake for 40 minutes in a moderate oven.

## VEAL PAPRIKÁS

Dice 3 medium onions and sauté in 5 tablespoons of oil for 5 minutes over low heat in a heavy 5-quart casserole with a tight fitting lid. Stir frequently until the onions are golden. Take casserole off heat, add 3 tablespoons Hungarian paprika and mix well. Place 3 pounds of leg of veal (cut into one-inch cubes) on top of paprika mixture. Turn pieces to coat them well. Cook over low heat for a few minutes, stirring continuously so the paprika does not burn. Add 2 teaspoons salt, ½ teaspoon white pepper, 1½ cups of water and 1 large green pepper. Cook, uncovered, over low heat for 35 minutes. Taste for seasoning, remove green pepper and discard. Test veal for tenderness — do not overcook as meat will fall apart. Mix ½ cup sour cream with 1 rounded tablespoon flour and 1 tablespoon cold water in a separate bowl. Add 1 tablespoon paprika sauce from the cooked meat to the sour cream. Mix well. Add this to the sauce in the pot. Serve immediately with galuska (egg dumplings). Makes 6 portions.

## MINING CAMP PASTIES

- 2 **pounds roast of beef**
- ½ **cup red wine**
- ½ **cup brandy**
- **Salt and pepper**

- 6 **pounds boiled potatoes**
- 1 **No. 2 can carrots, diced**
- 1 **No. 2 can garden peas**
- **Worcestershire sauce**
- **Celery seed**
- **Garlic powder**
- 15 **circles pie crust — 6 inches in diameter**

Pressure-cook the meat until overdone, using red wine, brandy and salt and pepper to season. Chop or grind meat and potatoes, and mix with vegetables. Slightly over-season with Worcestershire sauce, salt, pepper, celery seed and garlic powder. Put about ¾ pound of the mixture, molded oval-shaped, on each pie-crust circle and fold over the sides. Pinch the ends together and brush with an egg-and-milk mixture. Bake at 375° for 20 minutes or until brown. Brown gravy made with the meat liquid is served hot over pasties.

## SWEETBREADS

- 2 **fresh sweetbreads**
- 1½ **cups water**
- 2 **beef bouillon cubes**
- 1 **cup small whole mushroom caps**
- 2 **tablespoons butter**
- 2 **tablespoons flour**
- ½ **cup thick cream**
- **Thyme and salt to taste**

Soak the sweetbreads in cold water 30 minutes, after removing fat and membrane. Cut in small pieces. Drop these in boiling beef stock (made with bouillon cubes and water) and cook 5 minutes. Drain (saving the stock). Sauté mushrooms quickly in 2 tablespoons butter; remove. Leaving the remaining butter in pan, combine this with 2 tablespoons flour, thyme and salt. Add beef stock slowly; boil 2 minutes. Add cream, sweetbreads and mushrooms. Bring to boil and serve on toast.

## BARBECUED BRISKET OF FRESH BEEF

8-10 pounds fresh brisket beef
  8 ounces Milani's barbecue sauce
  1 quart catsup
  6 ounces wine vinegar
  3 ounces Lea and Perrins sauce
  2 tablespoons liquid smoke
  2 tablespoons prepared mustard
  3 tablespoons fresh lime juice
  6 bay leaves
  1 clove garlic, crushed
 12 whole peppercorns
  1 cup consommé, if necessary

Wipe beef dry, trim, and rub with salt. Prepare sauce by combining remaining ingredients.

Place beef in heavy pan, pour the sauce over it, and cook for 3½ hours in a preheated oven at 350°. Turn and baste every half hour. If sauce becomes too thick, add a cupful of consommé. Serve with puree of split peas.

## BEACHCOMBER CANTONESE SPARERIBS

  2 sides pork spareribs
  2 cups Chinese soya sauce
  1 cup sugar
  2 teaspoons salt
  2 tablespoons catsup

Trim ribs and marinate for an hour in mixture of soya sauce, sugar, salt and catsup. Roast in 400° oven for approximately 30 minutes. Baste at least 3 times. Roasting time will vary with thickness of ribs. Serve with barbecue sauce.

This is a recipe ideal for an outdoor barbecue.

## HAMBURGER DE LUXE

  2 pounds ground sirloin
  1 raw egg
  2 cups chicken broth
 ½ teaspoon English mustard
  1 tablespoon salt
  1 teaspoon black pepper

  2 tablespoons Worcestershire sauce
  2 teaspoons chicken fat

Mix meat, egg and broth, then add the other ingredients. Use one full coffee cup of the mixture for each portion. Serve with braised onions or De Luxe Sauce. (To make this sauce combine: 2 cups brown sauce, either canned or from a beef roast; 1 tablespoon English mustard, 2 teaspoons Sauce Diable or A-1 sauce, 1 tablespoon Worcestershire sauce, ½ cup catsup, 2 pats butter. Boil together, adding a little parsley.) Pour over hamburgers.

## VERMLANDS FLÄSK KÖRV (SWEDISH PORK SAUSAGE)

  2 pounds pork shoulder
 ½ pound veal shoulder
 1½ pounds cold boiled potatoes
  2 tablespoons salt
 ¾ tablespoon sugar
 ¼ tablespoon each of white, pepper, ginger and ground cloves
   Pinch of saltpeter
 1¾ quarts milk
   Hog casing

Grind meat in fine grinder twice. Grind potatoes; mix with meat. Add condiments. Add milk slowly, mixing till smooth. Stuff loosely in casing. For brine: combine 2½ cups water, 1 pound sugar, 1 pound salt, 1 teaspoon saltpeter. Bring to a boil; chill. Coil sausage in a crock, cover with brine, and leave in refrigerator 2 weeks. To cook sausage: Place in cold water with bay leaf and allspice. Cook 20 to 30 minutes.

## VENISON STEW

Place 1½ pounds of shoulder or saddle of venison in an earthen jar and cover with vinegar, combined with 3 or 4 sliced onions and 6 bay leaves. Marinate in vinegar mixture for 2 days; then wash meat in cold water. Add to boiling water and stew slowly until meat is tender. When venison is cooked remove from water and bone. Dice 4 carrots, 5 celery stalks and cook in meat broth until tender. Cut meat in medium-size pieces and add to vegetable-broth mixture; thicken broth, salt and pepper to taste. Serves 6 to 8.

## ROAST HAM WITH CUMBERLAND SAUCE

Boil a whole ham until tender. Remove from kettle and crisscross fat into diamond pattern with knife. Sprinkle with sugar and ground cloves and bake in 400° oven until glazed brown.

### Cumberland Sauce:

Mince ½ dozen shallots and put in stewing pan with grated rind of 2 lemons and 2 oranges. Add 1 cup water; cook for 15 minutes. Add juice from the oranges and lemons and 2 quarts of stock, 2 teaspoons mustard, 1 cup port wine, ½ teaspoon ground ginger, 1 cup red currant jelly, 2 tablespoons vinegar, salt, pepper and cayenne to taste. Thicken with flour and strain. Serve on ham slices.

## BEEF STEW PRINTANIER

- 2 pounds shoulder beef
  Butter, for browning
- 1 soupspoon flour
- 6 ounces white wine
- 4 tomatoes, cut and diced
- 10 pieces turnip, cut into olive shapes
- 4 carrots, cut into olive shapes
- 10 small new onions
- 5 small new potatoes
- 2 tablespoons peas

Cut beef into pieces weighing about 2 ounces. Sauté in butter until golden brown. Add flour, wine and tomatoes. Add remaining vegetables in order listed. Add enough water to cover and season to taste. Cook over low flame for 2½ to 3 hours. Serves 6 in individual casseroles.

## VEAL BIRDS

- 1¼ pounds veal steak
- 3 tablespoons butter
- 1 small onion, chopped
- 1½ cups bread crumbs
- ¾ teaspoon salt
- ⅛ teaspoon pepper
- ⅛ teaspoon sage
  Bacon

Cut veal in strips about 2 inches wide and 5 to 6 inches long. Sauté onion in butter until light brown. Then stir in crumbs and seasonings. Spread this dressing on each strip of veal and roll as tightly as possible. Wrap a strip of bacon around each and secure with a toothpick. Arrange in a pan with a little water and bake in slow oven for about an hour. Garnish with parsley. Serves 4 to 6.

## ENGLISH STEAK AND KIDNEY PIE

- 2 pounds beef chuck, cubed
- 1 pound lamb kidneys, quartered and cut crosswise
- 1 piece beef suet, egg size
- 1 large onion, coarsely cut
- 1 cup rich beef stock

Salt and pepper, to taste
Pinch of cayenne pepper
1 teaspoon Worcestershire sauce
1 flaky pie crust, uncooked

Heat the suet in a stew kettle and brown onion in the fat. Brown beef and kidney, stirring constantly. Add beef stock and seasoning; stir well. Cover and simmer over low flame for 1¾ hours. If the liquid gets too thin, thicken with a little flour and water. When meat is tender, place in a casserole and let cool. Top with crust and bake for 10 minutes in hot oven. Lower heat to moderate and bake until crust is a delicate brown.

## SAUERBRATEN
4 pounds bottom round beef
2 large onions
2 large carrots
2 stalks celery
1 pint vinegar
1 pint water
3 tablespoons salt
Small handful pickling spice
1 cup tomato puree
12 gingersnaps

Cut vegetables in small pieces. Combine vinegar, water, seasoning and vegetables. Pour over meat and let stand in refrigerator 3 or 4 days. Remove meat and roast in moderate oven until tender, about 2½ hours. Baste occasionally with vinegar mixture. When meat is done, remove from pan, add remainder of vinegar mixture, tomato puree and gingersnaps. Allow mixture to boil. Strain, add flour to thicken.

## LINGNAN SPECIAL STEAK
12 ounces prime sirloin steak, cubed
½ ounce oyster juice
1 tablespoon soy sauce
1 ounce Chinese black mushrooms
½ ounce water chestnuts
1 ounce bamboo shoots
1 ounce snow peas
2 ounces Chinese vegetables
3 ounces celery

1 tablespoon flour
Salt and sugar, to taste

Sauté cubed steak with oyster juice and soy sauce. Add flour (to thicken), salt and sugar. Cook vegetables separately. Put steak on top of vegetables when served.

## SCHNITZ UN KNEPP
3 pounds smoked ham, 8-ounce slices
4 cups dried apples
2 tablespoons brown sugar
2 cups flour
4 teaspoons baking powder
¼ teaspoon pepper
1 teaspoon salt
1 egg, well beaten
⅓ cup milk
3 tablespoons butter, melted

Cover dried apples with water and soak overnight. In the morning, cover ham with cold water and boil for 3 hours. Add the apples and water in which they have soaked and continue to boil for another hour. Add brown sugar. Make dumplings by sifting dry ingredients together 3 times. Stir in beaten egg, milk and melted butter. Drop the batter by spoonfuls into the hot liquid with the ham and apples. Cover kettle tightly and cook dumplings 15 minutes. Serve piping hot. Serves 6.

## HAMBURGERS WITH MUSHROOM SAUCE

¼ pound mushrooms
½ teaspoon salt
½ teaspoon soy sauce
½ teaspoon Ac'cent
2 heaping tablespoons shortening
¼ cup flour
2½ pounds ground beef
   Hamburger buns, toasted

Slice mushrooms thin. Cook in 1½ pints of water, adding salt, soy sauce and Ac'cent. Let boil 15 minutes. Make a roux of shortening and flour and add liquid from mushrooms. Form hamburger patties and broil to taste. Serve on open toasted bun with mushroom gravy and garnish of coleslaw and sliced tomatoes. Serves 4 to 6.

## INTOXICATED LOIN OF PORK

1 loin of pork for roasting
   Seasonings: 2 tablespoons salt,
     1 teaspoon pepper, 1 teaspoon
     nutmeg, ½ teaspoon sage,
     ½ tablespoon marjoram
¼ cup bacon fat
3 cloves of garlic, cut
½ cup parsley, chopped
   Bouquet garni (1 large bay leaf,
     1 sprig thyme, 2 sprigs green
     celery leaves, 1-inch horse-
     radish root)
   Claret wine to cover
2 cups beef stock

Rub pork well on all sides with the seasonings noted. Sear it in hot bacon fat containing cut cloves of garlic and chopped parsley. Put pork in baking pan. Add bouquet garni tied up with heavy white thread. Cover with claret and bake at 375°, allowing 30 to 35 minutes per pound. Turn the meat once in a while as it roasts. When the pork is done the wine will have evaporated. Remove meat; pour in beef stock. Brown some flour and mix with a little stock. Pour this roux into remaining stock and, stirring, heat to boiling. Season.

## WEST VIRGINIA RABBIT STEW

2 rabbits, young
1 tablespoon butter
1 tablespoon flour
1 cup dry red wine
1 quart hot water or stock
3 cloves
2 cloves garlic, finely chopped
1 bay leaf
   Pinch of thyme
1 No. 2 can small white onions,
   drained
1 cup mushrooms

Disjoint rabbits and season with salt and pepper. Melt butter in pan, add rabbit and brown slowly. When nearly brown add flour and simmer for two minutes. Add wine and enough hot water or stock to cover, stir, and bring to a boil. Add cloves, garlic, bay leaf and thyme. Cover and place in 350° oven. After 45 minutes, add onions which have been lightly sautéed in butter. Add mushrooms and place stew back in oven for 15 minutes. Serves 4.

## BARBECUED SPARERIBS

- 2 sheets lean spareribs
- 1 teaspoon each: salt, black pepper and sugar
- ½ teaspoon cayenne
- 1 tablespoon chili powder
- 1 cup catsup
- ½ cup tomato puree
- 1 cup water
- 1 large onion, chopped fine
- 2 cloves garlic
- ½ green pepper
- 3 pieces celery
  Juice of 1 lemon

Cut ribs into serving portions and place in baking dish. Blend other ingredients and pour over ribs. Bake in a moderate oven for an hour, turning and basting often.

## JAWAHARLAL PANDIT'S LAMB CURRY

- 1 pound lamb
  2 to 3 small onions
- 2 cloves garlic
- 3 tablespoons oil
- 1 tablespoon curry powder
- ¼ teaspoon cayenne pepper
- 1 teaspoon sugar
- 2 teaspoons grated coconut
- 2 cups stock

Slice onions, chop garlic and fry to light brown in oil. Add curry powder, pepper, sugar and coconut. Season to taste with salt. When well mixed, add the stock and simmer for 20 minutes, stirring occasionally. Add meat (after cutting in 1-inch cubes) and simmer for 1 hour, or until meat is tender. Serve very hot with rice and chutney.

## KOUZOU KZARTMA

- 4 lamb shanks
- 2 cups water
- 2 tomatoes, quartered
- 2 teaspoons salt
- 1 teaspoon paprika
- 4 large pieces potato

Wash lamb and soak in water for 15 minutes. Cook for ½ hour at 375° in open roasting pan with tomatoes, salt, paprika and water. Turn meat over and cook another ½ hour. Add potatoes and roast 30 minutes more, then turn the meat and potatoes and roast another ½ hour. Serve with its own juice. This makes a complete meal for 4.

## BAKED PORK CHOP, ARABIAN STYLE

- 4 thick loin pork chops
  Salt and pepper, to taste
- 1 medium size tomato, sliced
- 1 cup wild rice, cooked
- 1 medium onion, sliced
- 1 medium green pepper, sliced
- 4 slices Cheddar cheese
- 2 tablespoons fat

Season chops, then put a slice of tomato on each one, followed by a layer of wild rice (ordinary rice may be substituted), slice of onion and green pepper. Bake in 300° to 325° oven for 2 hours. Then top each chop with a slice of cheese and fat; leave in oven until cheese melts and runs over the sides. Serves 4.

## CORNISH PASTY

  Pie dough to cover sides of 10x18-inch pan, 3 inches deep, and for top crust
- 2 pounds diced beef
- 1 large onion, sliced very thin
- 2 large potatoes, diced
  Salt and white pepper, to taste
- ½ cup beef stock or finely ground suet

Line pan with pie dough. Add a layer of diced beef, a layer of onion, and then potatoes and seasonings. Repeat this process until pan is reasonably full. Add beef stock or suet. Cover top with crust. Bake about 1½ hours in a 350° oven. This recipe will serve 12.

## BAKED PORK CHAMPVALLON

8 ½-inch thick pork chops
2 pounds potatoes, sliced
½ pound onions, sliced thin
   Salt and white pepper
   Chicken or beef broth

Dip pork chops in flour and sauté until brown. Mix potatoes and onion slices together. Place half on the bottom of a baking pan, lay pork chops over them and then another layer of potatoes and onions. Season with salt and white pepper. Add broth to level with the ingredients. Cover pan and bake 45 minutes at 350°.

## ROUND-UP STEW

2½ pounds stew meat, diced
½ cup suet, diced
½ teaspoon pepper
4 teaspoons salt
1 teaspoon paprika
8 carrots, chopped
3 medium onions
6 potatoes, cut small
4 stalks celery, chopped
¼ small cabbage

Braise meat and suet in Dutch oven, add seasonings and water to cover. Cook 2 hours, add carrots, cook 15 minutes. Then add remaining vegetables except cabbage, which is added when other vegetables are cooked. Leave 10 minutes and serve. Water will evaporate so check while cooking.

## SOUR BEEF POT ROAST

4 pounds beef (chuck, rump or round)
1 onion, sliced
3 bay leaves
1 teaspoon whole peppercorns
   Vinegar and water (half and half)
2 teaspoons salt
¼ cup white sugar
¼ cup brown sugar
4-6 ginger snaps

Sprinkle meat with salt and pepper and rub in. Put meat with onion, bay leaves and peppercorns into a deep earthenware dish. Heat water and vinegar, add salt and white sugar. Pour over meat to cover. Cover the dish and keep in a cool place 3-4 days. Turn daily. Put meat in pot, add onion and a little of the spiced vinegar, place it in a 400° oven and brown. Cover and simmer on top of stove for 3 hours or until tender. Add more vinegar during cooking if you want. Remove meat and slice. Strain liquid and skim off fat. Let ¼ cup brown sugar melt in an iron skillet and add gradually to the strained liquid, then add the ginger snaps. Cook until thick and smooth and pour over meat. Serves 6-8.

## HUNGARIAN GOULASH

2 pounds of steak and trimmings, cubed
1 pound onions, sliced
2 tablespoons butter
2 tablespoons paprika
1 clove garlic
   Pinch of caraway seed
   Slice of lemon peel
   Salt and pepper, to taste
1 cup stewed tomatoes (not too much juice)
   Beef stock, to cover

Melt butter in heavy pot. Put in meat, paprika and onions. Simmer until onions have disintegrated. Chop garlic and lemon peel fine and add to meat mixture with caraway. Season. Add tomatoes and beef stock to cover and simmer until meat is tender. Thicken gravy with a roux of flour and half-butter, half-lard. Serves 4.

## ROULADE OF STEER FILET MIGNON

1 4-pound steer filet, trimmed
½ pound prosciutto (Italian ham), sliced paper thin
16 slices bacon

Filling:
2 hard-boiled eggs, chopped
2 cups dry bread crumbs
½ teaspoon Italian oregano
1 clove garlic, chopped fine
2 teaspoons parsley, chopped
½ onion, chopped
Salt and pepper to taste

Cut trimmed filet in ½-pound pieces and flatten out to ¼-inch thickness. Place layer of prosciutto over filet steaks. Combine filling ingredients and place over filets. Roll up making sure stuffing cannot ooze out. Wrap each with 2 slices of bacon and hold together with toothpicks. Broil 7-10 minutes, turn once or twice. Serves 6-8. Top with mushroom sauce.

## GYPSY BEEF GOULASH

2½ pounds lean round of beef
3 tablespoons shortening
3 medium size onions, sliced thin
Salt and pepper, to taste
1 tablespoon paprika
1 blade marjoram
1 clove garlic, crushed
Beef stock or water, to cover
4 green peppers, cut in large pieces
1 tablespoon butter
1 tablespoon flour
1 cup sour cream
1 tablespoon caraway seeds

Cut meat into 1-inch cubes. Melt shortening in a skillet and brown the sliced onions. Skim out onions and place them in a stew pan. Brown the meat in the drippings, add paprika, salt, pepper, marjoram and garlic. Stir mixture in

skillet, then remove to stew pan. Add enough water or beef stock to cover meat. Simmer gently for 30 minutes. Add green peppers and cook until meat is tender. Cream flour and butter together and stir into sauce, cooking until smooth and thickened. Add sour cream and caraway seeds and cook a little longer. Serve over noodles. Makes 6 to 8 portions.

## ROAST SADDLE OF VENISON

4-pound saddle of venison
1 onion
1 carrot
Small piece of celery
1 sprig of thyme
2 bay leaves
2 cloves
1 teaspoon peppercorns
½ glass sherry wine
1 cup beef or chicken stock
1 tablespoon meat extract
2 ounces butter
Salt and pepper to taste

Spread butter (or lard) on venison and season. Put onion, carrot, celery, thyme, bay leaves, cloves and peppercorns in roasting pan. Roast in 325° oven and baste often. When the saddle is done (20-25 minutes a pound — medium rare) take out of the pan and drain off the fat. Put sherry in with cooking juices and reduce by boiling until nearly dry. Then add stock and meat extract with salt and pepper. Boil until reduced. Pour over venison or serve separately. Serves 6.

## FLÄSKKARRE

5-pound loin of pork
12 prunes, whole
12 dried apricots, whole
12 fresh apple slices, dipped in salt
1 teaspoon salt and ¼ teaspoon pepper
24 cloves (whole)
1 tablespoon brown sugar
1 tablespoon cinnamon

Have a butcher prepare roast for

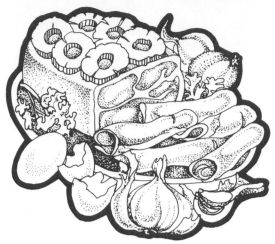

stuffing. Stuff with a mixture of dried prunes, apricots and fresh apple slices. Rub outside of loin with salt and pepper and roast in 300° oven uncovered for about 1½ hours or until lightly browned. Then remove from oven and stud with cloves and sprinkle with a mixture of brown sugar and cinnamon. Add 2 cups of water in bottom of roasting pan. Cover and return to oven for about 1 hour. Serve meat in 1-inch-thick slices topped with slightly thickened gravy made from juice in pan. Serves 8 generously.

## CHUTNEY MEAT LOAF
    2  cups soft bread crumbs
    1  tall can evaporated milk
    1  egg, beaten
    1  medium size onion
       Handful of parsley
    1½ pounds ground beef
    1½ teaspoons salt
    ¼  teaspoon pepper
       Apricot or peach chutney
    2  slices of bacon

With a fork mix bread crumbs, evaporated milk and beaten egg. Grind or chop onion and parsley; add to bread mixture with ground beef, salt and pepper. Mix well. Pack in a greased 8½x4½x3-inch loaf pan; spread with chutney; top with 2 slices of bacon. Bake at 350° for 1¼ hours. Serve hot or cold to 6.

## BAKED HAM LOAF
    1  pound ground smoked ham
    1  pound ground beef
    1  pound ground pork
    1  cup bread crumbs
    1  egg
    1  8-ounce can tomato puree or
       juice
       Tomato sauce or grilled pine-
       apple slices, for garnish

Combine ham, beef, pork, bread crumbs, egg and tomato puree. Place in a greased loaf pan. Steam for 1 hour and bake in 350° oven for ½ hour. Serve with tomato sauce or grilled pineapple slices. Makes 16 portions.

## HAM LOAF
    1  cup milk
    1  cup dry bread crumbs
    2  eggs, slightly beaten
    2  pounds ground smoked ham
    1½ pounds ground lean pork

Thoroughly combine all ingredients. To shape loaf, pack mixture in a 10x5-inch loaf pan, then invert on a shallow baking pan. Score top of loaf with handle of wooden spoon or knife. Bake in 350° for 1½ hours. Baste occasionally with brown sugar glaze. Makes 12 servings. Serve with horseradish sauce.
**Brown Sugar Glaze:**
Combine ¾ cup brown sugar, ¼ cup water, ¼ cup vinegar, and 2 teaspoons dry mustard.
**Horseradish Sauce:**
Combine ¼ cup horseradish, 1½ tablespoons vinegar, 1 tablespoon mustard, ½ teaspoon salt, 4 drops Worcestershire sauce, dash of cayenne pepper and paprika. Fold mixture into ½ cup heavy cream, whipped. Chill.

## SAVORY BAKED VEAL
    8  pounds rump of veal, boned
       and rolled
    1  clove garlic
       Salt and pepper, to taste

1 **pound butter**
1 **large onion, grated**
¾ **cup parsley, minced**
1 **can beef consommé**

Place veal on a breadboard, cut off and discard string. Rub unrolled meat thoroughly with cut clove of garlic and sprinkle with salt and pepper. Cream butter with a wooden spoon, then work in grated onion and minced parsley. Spread unrolled meat generously with seasoned butter. Roll meat up carefully tying with soft white twine in several places. Rub outside of roast with garlic and season with salt and pepper. Cover with a good coating of butter. Place on a rack in an uncovered roasting pan with the veal bones set around the sides. Brown in preheated oven of 450° for 15 minutes, then add consommé and equal amount of water to pan. Cook for 10 minutes, then turn heat down to 325° and continue cooking for about 2 hours, or until tender. A gravy may be made with pan drippings; add a small amount of red wine for flavoring. Makes 8-10 portions. Serve with potatoes roasted in with meat.

## BAKED PORK CHOPS
## À LA BORDEAUX

4 **heavy-cut loin pork chops**
  **Salt and pepper, to taste**
⅛ **teaspoon nutmeg**
⅛ **teaspoon ground cloves**
1 **tablespoon brown sugar**
1 **cup Bordeaux wine**
  **Spiced apples, for garnish**

Wipe chops dry and sprinkle with salt and pepper. Broil chops golden brown on both sides. Remove from broiler and drain excess fat. Sprinkle chops with nutmeg and cloves. Add brown sugar and wine to pan and bake covered in a 350° oven for 10 minutes. Remove cover and bake an additional 10 minutes. Serve on hot platter garnished with spiced apples and topped with a glass dome. Makes 4 portions.

## KIBBIE
**Meat Mixture:**
Grind together ¾ pound of beef, ¾ pound lamb, ½ small onion and ½ small bell pepper. Season with 1½ teaspoons salt, 1 teaspoon each cinnamon and allspice, and pepper to taste. Soak 1 cup crushed wheat germ in water until soft, then squeeze dry and blend with meat mixture.

**Filling:**
Sauté 1½ large chopped onions in lamb fat. Add ½ cup pine nuts or pecans. Season with salt, pepper and allspice as in meat mixture.

Spread meat mixture ½-inch thick on bottom of greased baking pan. Spread generous portion of filling over it. Put another ½ inch of meat mixture on top of filling and press down and smooth. Cut squares through meat, checkerboard style. Top with 2 ounces of flaked butter. Bake at 400° for 45 minutes. Makes 12 portions of this Oriental dish.

## BANCROFT
## CORNED BEEF HASH

1 **pound corned beef brisket,**
    **uncooked**
3 **cups cold boiled potatoes**
½ **cup cream**
  **Salt and pepper, to taste**
¼ **cup butter**

Boil corned beef until well done, about 3-4 hours. The meat should be coarsely ground or chopped. Dice or coarsely grind potatoes and add to corned beef.

Mix cream in well with a large spoon until all ingredients are thoroughly blended. Season to taste. Brown hash in butter over a slow fire. Turn hash over and brown on other side. Serve hot. Serves 4.

## HASENPFEFFER
1 medium-sized rabbit (about 5 pounds)
  White distilled vinegar, to cover
2 medium-sized carrots
2 medium-sized onions
1 small stalk celery
1 ounce whole mixed pickling spices
2 tablespoons salt
1 tablespoon pepper
3 cloves garlic
½ pound old-fashioned gingersnaps
2 ounces imported port wine

Cut rabbit into six equal portions and place in a crock. Cover with vinegar, vegetables, spices and garlic. Marinate for 3 days. Remove rabbit and sauté to a golden brown. Place in a roasting pan, strain the vegetables from the marinade and place over rabbit. Add gingersnaps and wine. Cover and roast at 425° for 1½ hours. For a real German feast, serve with potato pancakes.

## BUFFALO SWISS STEAK
Take 8 rounds of buffalo round steak cut in ¾-inch slices and cut into pieces for individual servings. Dredge in flour and brown in cooking oil which has been lightly flavored with garlic. Slice 4 green peppers, 6 large white onions and 12 ounces of mushrooms. Place a layer of meat in the bottom of a flat oven pan and cover with a separate layer each of onion, green pepper and mushrooms. Over the top pour 1 No. 10 can of tomatoes. Add salt and pepper to taste and bake in 250° oven until tender. Serves about 40. (If you are going to the trouble of finding buffalo steak, you might as well invite a large group.)

## JAGER HOUSE BEEF GOULASH
6 pounds shin or stewing beef, cut in 1-inch cubes
6 pounds onions, chopped fine (or better, grated)
½ cup vegetable shortening
1 pint unsalted beef stock or water
3 cloves garlic, crushed
  Pinch of freshly ground pepper
½ cup sweet Hungarian paprika
⅓ cup tomato puree
  Salt to taste
  Boiled potatoes or noodles

Brown meat very carefully in 350° oven, keeping watch so that meat does not dry out. Sauté onions in vegetable shortening until golden. Place browned meat in heavy pot with beef stock, garlic, onions, pepper, paprika, tomato puree and salt, to taste. Cook covered on top of stove over low fire for 2½ to 3 hours, or until tender. Add stock or water during the cooking if more liquid is needed. Serve over hot noodles or boiled potatoes. Serves 10-12.

## VEAL SCALOPPINE Á LA SAN REMO
Pound 1½ pounds thinly sliced veal cutlets until very thin. Cut veal into pieces about 6 inches square. Sprinkle with salt and pepper and flour lightly. Melt 4 tablespoons butter in large skillet and, when hot, put in veal and brown thoroughly on both sides, over high heat. When well browned add ½ cup Marsala

and let meat cook 1 minute. Turn heat down to simmer. Add ½ cup sliced mushrooms; over each piece of veal place a thin slice of prosciutto topped with a piece of thinly sliced mozzarella cheese. Add 4 tablespoons chicken stock and simmer for a minute or so. Place skillet under broiler until the cheese is melted. Serves 6.

## JAMAICAN GINGER BEEF

- 2 onions
- 3 cloves garlic
- 1½ teaspoons turmeric
- ¼ teaspoon dried chili peppers (optional)
- 5 teaspoons ginger (or 2-inch piece fresh ginger, chopped)
- 1½ teaspoons salt
- 1¼ pounds flank steak
- 3 tablespoons peanut or salad oil
- 1 No. 2 can tomatoes
  10½-ounce can condensed onion soup
- 4 to 6 cups hot cooked rice
  Pickled watermelon, for garnish

In chopping bowl, combine onions, garlic, turmeric, chili peppers, ginger and salt; chop fine. Add flank steak cut diagonally into thin slices or 2-inch by ½-inch strips and toss together. Stand to season in refrigerator from 15 minutes to 3 hours. Heat oil in Dutch oven, add steak and onion mixture and brown lightly. Add tomatoes, then cook uncovered over high heat for 10 minutes. Add soup, cover and simmer 1 hour if steak is sliced; or 1½ to 2 hours if in the thicker strips. To serve, form hot rice in a mound in center of serving platter, spoon a few pieces of steak over rice then spoon rest of mixture around it. Garnish at both ends with pickle. Serves 4 generously.

## DANISH ROAST LEG OF LAMB

Make about 6 slits in a 6- to 8-pound leg of lamb. Stuff slits with ½ pound of salt

pork cut into small pieces, and whole parsley sprigs. Roast meat in 325° oven for 3-4 hours for medium. Cook 2 small heads of cauliflower and 16 asparagus spears to desired tenderness. Boil and peel 1 pound small red potatoes. Brown 2 tablespoons sugar in a heavy skillet, then add ¼ pound butter and blend. Add potatoes, turning carefully until each is glazed. Place roast on large platter, surround with cauliflower and asparagus topped with 1 cup of hollandaise sauce and glazed potatoes. Serves 4-6.

## SAUERBRATEN

Cover a lean, 4-pound piece of beef round with the following mixture: 1 cup of vinegar; 3 cups of water; 2 cloves garlic; 2 sliced onions; 1 cut carrot; salt and pepper to taste; 1 bay leaf and a generous tablespoon pickling spices. Marinate 5 days in refrigerator. Remove meat from the marinade, dust with flour and brown in 3 tablespoons corn oil in oven. When meat is brown, add 1½-2 cups of the marinade (depending on the pan size), the vegetables, 1 teaspoon sugar and 1 diced tomato. Braise until meat is tender. Strain the sauce left in the pan, thicken with 4 or 5 gingersnaps and correct seasoning. Meat should be sliced thin, 5 or 6 slices per person, topped with the gravy, garnished with potato pancakes.

**Potato Pancakes:**

Grate or grind — never use blender — 4 medium-sized peeled potatoes and 1 small onion into a sieve. Remove as much water as possible. Then transfer to bowl, add three eggs, 1 tablespoon flour, 1 teaspoon baking powder, and ½ teaspoon salt. Gently mix. Fry in ¼-inch hot corn oil. For thick, fluffy pancakes, slide a spoonful of batter gently into the hot oil, heaped high. Turn once. When pancakes are a golden brown, remove and blot. Makes 8 pancakes, serves 4.

## CHARCOAL-BROILED PORK CHOPS MARINADE

Mix and bring to a boil: 2 cups soy sauce, 1 cup water, ½ cup brown sugar, 1 tablespoon dark molasses and 1 teaspoon salt. Place 6 center-cut pork chops, bone side up, in pan and pour cooled marinade over chops and let stand overnight in refrigerator. Next day place chops in baking pan and cover tight with foil. Place in 375° oven and bake until tender, about 2 hours.

**Red Sauce:**

While chops are baking, combine 1 tablespoon dry mustard, ¼ cup of water, 1 cup brown sugar, leaving no lumps. Combine with 1 regular size bottle catsup and 1 bottle chili sauce, place in heavy pan or double boiler and bring to a slight boil. When chops are tender, remove from oven, dip in red sauce and bake for 30 minutes in uncovered pan at 350° until slightly glazed. Keep chops at room temperature until ready to put on charcoal pit. Over small bed of coals raised as high as possible, grill chops up to 15 minutes. Serves 6.

## BRAISED LAMB SHANK GEMÜSE

4 lamb shanks, ¾ to 1 pound each
   Bouquet garni (2 bay leaves, 2 mashed garlic cloves, 1 dozen peppercorns, ¼ teaspoon summer savory, ¼ teaspoon thyme and ¼ teaspoon marjoram, in cheesecloth bag)
1 cup each: diced onion, celery and carrots
   Red wine and beef stock, equal parts
1 cup each: peas and green beans
   Flour, to thicken
   Kitchen Bouquet and salt, to taste

Sauté lamb shanks till well browned, place in Dutch oven with bouquet garni, onions, carrots, celery and enough wine and stock to cover. Braise in oven at 375° covered, until lamb shanks are tender, about 2½ hours. In the last half-hour of cooking add peas and beans, and remove bouquet garni. Blend in flour-and-water mixture (1 tablespoon flour with ¼ cup water for each cup of liquid, to thicken). Add Kitchen Bouquet to desired brownness, and salt to taste. Serves 4.

## BEEF SUKIYAKI

1½ pound rib steak or top sirloin steak
1 cake tofu (soybean curd), cut in small pieces
1 No. 2 can bamboo shoots, sliced thin
½ pound mushrooms, sliced thin
1 pound fresh bean sprouts
1 pound white onions, sliced thin
1½ pounds spinach, cut 2 inches long
2 bunches green onions, 2-inch pieces
   (Celery and other leaf vegetables may be added if some vegetable items are not available)
½ teaspoon monosodium glutamate

Heat a thick 10-inch skillet and melt a piece of beef fat in it. Spread extra-thin beef slices over bottom of pan and sear. After meat is browned add vegetables and other ingredients on top of it. Lower heat. Then add about half of the Sukiyaki Sauce and cook. Let mixture simmer uncovered until the vegetables are cooked. Serve while the vegetables are still crisp. Add remaining Sukiyaki Sauce, a little sugar, sake (rice wine) or sherry to suit your taste. Do not overcook! In Japanese cooking this is important. Serve directly from the pan to the plate. Serves 4.

**Sukiyaki Sauce:**

½ cup Japanese soy sauce
½ cup consommé or beef stock
2 teaspoons sugar, or to taste
2 ounces sake (Japanese rice wine), or sherry or sauterne

Blend and stir over medium flame until sugar dissolves. Cooking time 6-10 minutes.

## LAMB CHOPS STROGANOFF

- 8 **thick loin lamb chops, fat removed**
  **Salt and pepper to taste**
  **Flour**
- ½ **teaspoon mace**
- 2 **ounces butter**
- 1 **ounce brandy**
- 2 **small onions, sliced thin**
  **Bacon drippings**
- 1 **tomato, sliced thin**
- 1 **slice dill pickle, chopped fine**
- 1 **teaspoon lemon rind, grated**
- 1 **cup sour cream**
- 2 **to 3 ounces Madeira**
- 4 **cups steamed rice**

Salt and pepper the lamb chops and dip in flour seasoned with mace. Brown on both sides in butter, add brandy and light. Sauté onions in bacon drippings and add to lamb chops, together with tomato, dill pickle and lemon rind. Over all of this pour sour cream mixed with the Madeira. Cover skillet and simmer over low fire until done: medium rare, 10 minutes; or well done, 15 minutes. Serve on steamed rice. Serves 8.

## BRAISED OXTAILS

- 3 **pounds oxtails**
- 2 **cups stewed tomatoes**
- 5 **cups beef stock**
- 1 **bay leaf**
  **Dash of Worcestershire sauce**
- 3 **cups diced carrots**
- 3 **cups diced celery**
- 1 **green pepper, diced and seeded**
- 1 **large onion, chopped**
- 1 **clove garlic, finely minced**
- 1 **cup cooked new peas**
- 3 **tablespoons cornstarch**
  **Salt and pepper**

Disjoint oxtails with a knife to prevent bone fragments from splintering. Bake them in a 400° oven for 1 hour to

render fat. Turn every 15 to 20 minutes until oxtails are browned on all sides. Put in a large pot with tomatoes, beef stock, bay leaf, Worcestershire sauce, carrots, celery, green pepper, onion, garlic and salt and pepper to taste. Braise until tender, about 2 hours. When almost done, thicken with cornstarch moistened with a little water. Garnish with new peas. Serves 6 to 8.

## SYRON'S IRISH STEW

- 2 **pound lean lamb, 1½-inch cubes**
- 1½ **cups flour**
- 3 **teaspoons salt**
- 1 **teaspoon pepper**
  **Lamb, veal or beef drippings**
- 4 **medium onions, quartered**
- 1 **bay leaf**
- ½ **teaspoon thyme**
- 4 **carrots, sliced thick**
- 3 **stalks celery, 1-inch diagonal cut**
- 4 **potatoes, quartered**

Coat lamb with flour, salt and pepper. Using a heavy Dutch oven, sauté the onions in meat drippings until golden; remove from pan. Sauté coated lamb cubes until brown; add sufficient hot water or stock to cover meat, cover tightly and simmer for 1 hour, skimming occasionally. Add bay leaf, thyme, celery and carrots. Cook gently 20 minutes. Then add potatoes and continue cooking until potatoes are done and meat is tender. Adjust seasonings and thicken if desired. Add chopped parsley to your own dumpling recipe; cook dumplings on top of simmering stew. Garnish with chopped parsley. Serves 4 to 6.

## ROAST PORK WITH SWEET-AND-SOUR SAUCE

Place four 1 pound center-cut rib (not loin) pork roasts in pan, bone side down, and brown at 450° for 30 minutes. Transfer to deep baking dish. Pour Sweet-and-Sour Sauce over pork and roast at 300° for 2½ hours, or until tender. Baste occasionally. Serve with some sauce ladled over meat and garnished with baked apples. Serves 4.
**Sauce:**
Combine 2 cups sugar, 1 cup white distilled vinegar, 2 tablespoons chopped green pepper, 1 cup water, 1 teaspoon salt; simmer 5 minutes. Thicken sauce

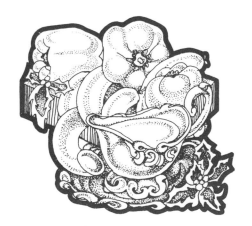

with 4 teaspoons cornstarch dissolved in 2 tablespoons water. Add 2 teaspoons paprika and a bit of finely chopped parsley. Makes 2 cups.

## CHRISTMAS SUCKLING PIG

Select a suckling pig — the average weight is about 30 pounds. Clean and dry very well. Season interior with 2 tablespoons salt, 2 teaspoons pepper and 1 teaspoon nutmeg.
**Stuffing:**
Chop pig liver very fine and sauté in butter for 5 minutes. Chop 2 medium-size onions and sauté in butter. Soak 1 loaf of dry bread in warm water for 15 minutes, then press out water and add the following:

  3 **eggs**
  1 **tablespoon salt**
  2 **teaspoons pepper**
  1 **tablespoon sage**
  ½ **teaspoon nutmeg**
  ½ **pound sausage**
  1 **tablespoon chopped fresh parsley**

Combine sautéed liver and onion with bread mixture and stuff pig. Sew opening very tightly and place on barbecue skewer. Turn slowly over hot coals for about 3 hours, baste frequently with drippings. Serve with gravy made from drippings. Serves 40 to 50.
**Alternate Method:**
Place pig on large flat pan and roast in 350° oven for 6½ hours. Tuck legs under body and baste often.

# PANCAKES, CREPES & FRITTERS

## MAINE BLUEBERRY GRIDDLE CAKES

2 eggs
2 cups buttermilk
1 teaspoon soda
2 cups all-purpose flour
2 teaspoons baking powder
1 teaspoon salt
2 teaspoons sugar
4 tablespoons melted butter
1 cup fresh blueberries or frozen blueberries, thawed and drained

Beat eggs and add buttermilk mixed with soda. Sift flour, baking powder, salt and sugar into this mixture; then pour in melted butter. Fold blueberries into batter, and fry on a hot griddle. Serve with maple syrup and sausage and you have the perfect breakfast for cold winter mornings.

## ADIRONDACK FLAPJACKS

4 eggs, separated
2 tablespoons sugar
½ teaspoon salt
2 cups milk
4 tablespoons butter, melted
2 cups flour
2 teaspoons baking powder

Beat egg whites and yolks separately. Then beat together egg yolks, sugar, salt, milk, butter, flour and baking powder. Add whites last. Pour out individual flapjacks on a hot griddle. Serve with melted butter and hot maple syrup which has been boiled until thick. Top with whipped cream.

## BANANA FRITTERS

8 bananas, sliced
1 cup flour
1 teaspoon baking powder
1 teaspoon sugar
Pinch of salt
1 egg
½ cup milk

Mix a batter with the flour, baking powder, sugar, salt, egg, and milk. Beat well and dip thick slices of banana into the batter. Drop a teaspoon of banana and batter into deep fat and fry until golden brown and fluffy. This recipe will make 8 hearty servings. Try these fritters as something different in a fruit or vegetable course!

## FRENCH PANCAKES À LA GELÉE

½ cup sifted all-purpose flour
1 egg
1 egg yolk
⅛ teaspoon salt
5 tablespoons milk (approximately)
3 tablespoons currant or red raspberry jelly
Powdered sugar

Combine flour, egg, egg yolk, salt, and milk. Beat with rotary beater until smooth. If necessary, add more milk to make batter the consistency of light cream. Cover; chill for ½ hour in refrigerator. Heat heavy iron skillet; wipe out with waxed paper which has been dipped in butter. Pour in enough batter to barely cover bottom of skillet, tipping while adding batter. Brown pancake on both sides. Remove from skillet; spread with jelly; roll up jelly-roll fashion. Sprinkle with a little powdered sugar. Place under broiler to glaze. Serve immediately. Yields 12 to 15 5-inch pancakes.

## RHODE ISLAND JOHNNY CAKES
1 cup white corn meal
¼ teaspoon salt
½ teaspoon sugar
1¼ cups boiling water
¼ cup milk

Warm all utensils. Mix corn meal with salt and sugar. Pour boiling water over dry ingredients and stir well. When thoroughly mixed, add milk. Drop by tablespoonfuls on hot, heavy iron skillet. Turn and cook other side as you do pancakes. Serve cakes hot with butter and maple syrup. Serves 4.

## CLAM FRITTERS
1 cup sifted flour
¼ teaspoon salt
½ teaspoon sugar
1 teaspoon baking powder
1 beaten egg
¼ cup milk
1 tablespoon melted butter
1 cup drained and chopped clams

Combine the sifted flour, salt, sugar and baking powder, and set aside. Mix together the egg, milk, melted butter and clams. Stir lightly into the dry ingredients. Drop from spoon into hot deep fat or oil, fry until brown, turning once, drain on absorbent paper.

## WAFFLES
1 level teaspoon baking soda
1 teaspoon baking powder
1 level teaspoon salt
2 cups flour
½ cup Wesson oil
3 eggs
1½ cups buttermilk

Sift dry ingredients together. Add oil and eggs and beat well. Stir in buttermilk. (It may be necessary to use more buttermilk if batter is very thick.) When waffles are baked, place on a rack in a warm oven to crisp before serving. Serve with butter and maple syrup.

## CORN FRITTERS
2 cups cream-style corn
6 cups flour
1 teaspoon salt
2 tablespoons sugar
1 quart milk
4 eggs, separated
2 tablespoons baking powder
Hot lard, for frying

Blend all ingredients together except egg whites and lard. Beat egg whites and fold into dough mixture. Heat inch-deep lard in heavy iron skillet over a moderate flame. Drop 1 tablespoon dough mixture into lard for each fritter. Brown on one side, turn. Then place skillet with fritters in 450° oven for about 2 minutes before serving. Makes 50.

## POTATO PANCAKES
5 uncooked potatoes
1 medium onion
½ teaspoon salt
Dash of pepper
2 eggs
1 tablespoon parsley, chopped
2 tablespoons flour

Grate potatoes and onion. Add salt, pepper, eggs, parsley and flour. Mix well and drop by tablespoonfuls into very hot fat in a heavy frying pan. Fry until

golden brown, turning once. Serves 6.
Try these pancakes with sauerbraten.

## CHEESE BLINTZES

- 2 eggs
- 2 cups water
- ⅛ teaspoon vanilla
- 2 cups flour
- ⅛ teaspoon nutmeg
- 4 tablespoons sugar
- ¾ teaspoon baking powder
- ⅛ teaspoon salt

Beat eggs and add water and vanilla.
Blend dry ingredients and combine with
egg mixture with a few strokes. Heat a
5-inch skillet and grease with a few
drops of oil. Add small amount of batter
and tip skillet to spread batter over
bottom. Brown on one side only and
turn out on a plate brown-side up. Fry
all the blintzes.

### Filling:

Combine 6 ounces dry cottage cheese
and 6 ounces cream cheese and place a
spoonful of this mixture on each blintz.
Fold blintz edges toward middle so they
lap over filling. Return blintzes to skillet
and sauté in butter on both sides until
lightly browned. Serve with powdered
sugar and sour cream. Makes about 15
blintzes.

## EGG ROLL

- 3 eggs
- 1 quart cooking oil
- 1 cup fresh bean sprouts
- ½ cup celery, finely diced
- ½ cup pork strips, finely sliced
- ½ teaspoon salt
- ¼ teaspoon pepper

Beat 2 eggs until well blended. Pour half
of eggs into a heavy 8-inch frying pan
that has been lightly greased and heated.
Cook quickly on one side. Turn over
with a wide spatula so the egg remains
as a large thin pancake. Cook until done.
Prepare remaining egg the same way.
Combine other ingredients (except oil

and third egg); divide them between the
2 egg rolls. Fold lower third of egg roll
over filling. Turn the ends in about ½
inch to seal. Brush the top third of egg
roll with slightly beaten egg to seal and
fold this over the rolled mixture. Place
rolls in a basket and steam 20 minutes.
Then brown in 2 inches of 350° oil.
Brown rolls about 3 to 5 minutes on
each side. Serve hot with mustard and
soy sauce. Serves 4.

## FRIED CORN MEAL MUSH

- 4 cups boiling water
- 1½ teaspoons salt
- 1½ cups corn meal
- 1 cup chopped ham or bacon
  Parsley, to taste
- 1 egg
  Cracker crumbs and flour
  Bacon slices, cooked
  Molasses or maple syrup

Add salt and corn meal to boiling water
and cook well. Then add ham and
parsley. Pour into a well-greased loaf
pan and cool. Cut into slices ½ inch thick
and roll in mixture of egg, cracker
crumbs and flour. Fry to a golden
brown. Strip with bacon slices and top
with molasses or maple syrup. Makes 6
servings.

## APPLE PANCAKES

Whip 4 eggs; then add 1 pint coffee cream, ½ grated lemon rind, ¼ grated orange rind, dash of vanilla, 4 tablespoons sugar, ¼ tablespoon salt and pinch of nutmeg. Mix and add 1¾ cups flour. Peel and slice 3 medium apples; sprinkle with cinnamon and sugar and fry lightly. Add 2 ounces whipped cream to batter just before frying. Heat an 8- or 10-inch skillet. Put in 6-ounce ladle of batter per pancake and cook slowly on one side; add apples, and then turn over and put in 325° oven for 5 minutes. Take out of oven and turn, sprinkle with cinnamon, sugar and return to oven for 1 to 2 minutes. Put on plate and serve with lemon wedge. Serves 8. (Do not use syrup as pancakes are very sweet.)

## CORN FRITTERS

- 2 cups whole kernel corn
- 1 heaping teaspoon salt
- 1 teaspoon sugar
- 2 tablespoons melted shortening
- 1 egg, beaten
- 1 cup flour
- 1 teaspoon baking powder
  Milk

Combine corn, salt and sugar. Stir in shortening and egg. Mix flour and baking powder together and add to corn mixture. Add enough milk so that mixture will be correct consistency (quite thick) to drop off tablespoon into deep hot fat (350° to 375°). Makes 12 large fritters.

## CRÊPES MAISON

To 9 tablespoons of flour add 1 tablespoon sugar and a pinch of salt. Beat in 3 eggs one at a time, then add 1 teaspoon melted butter and 2 cups milk. When batter is smooth, butter a 5-inch skillet or a crêpe pan and pour a small amount of batter on the heated pan. Turn with spatula so it is cooked on both sides. Keep warm. Makes 18.

### Crabmeat Filling:

Sauté 3 chopped shallots and 1 tablespoon chopped onion in 2 tablespoons of butter. Then add 1 cup dry white wine, 1 cup tomato puree, 2 tablespoons béchamel (cream) sauce, ¾ pound crabmeat, 1 pint whipped cream, and salt and pepper to taste. Bring to a boil and simmer. Then drop a spoonful of mixture on each crêpe and roll up around the filling.

To 1 cup béchamel sauce add ½ pint of whipping cream, whipped. Mix and pour over crêpes. Place under broiler for a minute or so until sauce is browned. Serves 6.

## STRAWBERRY CRÊPES

### Basic Crêpe:

Beat 3 eggs well with a fork, add 1 cup unsifted flour and ⅛ teaspoon salt. Beat until batter is smooth. Gradually add 1 cup milk and ¼ cup water, beating until smooth. Melt 2 tablespoons butter and set aside.

Before preparing each crêpe, brush an 8-inch crêpe pan or skillet with butter. Add batter to cover entire bottom of pan. Cook 1 minute or until lightly brown. Flip, brown lightly for about 30 seconds. Makes 12 crêpes.

### Strawberry Filling:

Mix 1 cup fresh sliced strawberries with 2 tablespoons brown sugar. Place 4 tablespoons sliced berries in the center of the crêpe. Spoon 3 tablespoons sour or whipped cream over mixture. Fold edges of crêpe over to make a roll.

Garnish crêpe wth 2 tablespoons sour or whipped cream and whole strawberries.

## CRÊPES AUX FRAISES FLAMBÉES

Sift together ⅔ cup flour, 1 tablespoon sugar and a pinch of salt. Beat 2 whole eggs and 2 egg yolks; add to flour mixture. Add 1¾ cups milk, blend smooth. Add 2 tablespoons melted butter and 1 tablespoon rum or cognac. Let batter stand for 2 hours, then make 12 crêpes in the usual way.

Mash about 36 strawberries and add 2 tablespoons Cointreau. Melt 6 pats of butter in a large skillet over low heat, cover bottom with Melba Sauce, adding a few drops of Cointreau. In the pan, roll each crêpe around 1 tablespoon strawberries. When all are rolled, add Cointreau to pan and ignite. Place 2 crêpes on each plate; spoon sauce over them; place 1 tablespoon ice cream on 1 side of crêpe and 1 tablespoon whipped cream on the other, topped with a whole berry. Serves 6.

**Melba Sauce:**

Blend: 4 tablespoons strawberry preserves; 2 tablespoons currant jelly; 2 tablespoons red food coloring, and 1 tablespoon strawberry extract.

# PICKLES, RELISHES & PRESERVES

## WALPOLE WOODCHUCK RELISH

1 medium cabbage, shredded
2 green peppers, cut julienne
2 sour pickles
2 ounce can pimentos
  Celery seed
  Garlic powder
  Olive oil
  Vinegar
  Pepper
  Salt
⅛ teaspoon sugar

Combine vegetables. Add celery seed, garlic powder, olive oil, vinegar, pepper, and salt to taste. Sprinkle sugar over relish. Delicious with meat.

## SUNSET FARM PLUM RUM JAM

3½ cups plums, chopped fine
½ cup lemon juice
7½ cups sugar
½ bottle pectin
¼ cup good dark rum

Combine plums, lemon juice and sugar in a kettle; boil hard for 3 minutes, stirring constantly. Then add pectin and rum; stir at intervals for 5 minutes. Pour into jam jars and seal.

## SWEET-SOUR CUCUMBERS

1 dozen medium-size cucumbers
2 tablespoons salt
1 medium-size onion

2 cups sugar
½ teaspoon pepper
1 pint sweet whipping cream
1 pint vinegar

Wash, peel and slice cucumbers and place in earthen jar. Add salt and sliced onion, then cover jar with cheesecloth, plate, and weight. Let stand 6 hours and drain off water. Add sugar and mix until dissolved; then add pepper and vinegar. Stir in cream. Put in refrigerator till cold and crisp.

## WATERMELON RIND PICKLE
    2 quarts watermelon rind
    2 quarts lime water (1 teaspoon dehydrated lime to 1 quart water)
    2 quarts water
    1 quart vinegar
    4 to 6 cups sugar
    1 tablespoon whole allspice
    1 tablespoon whole cloves
    1 stick cinnamon
    1 tablespoon ginger root

Trim green skin and pink flesh from rind. Cut in small pieces, ½ inch or smaller. Soak in lime water for 4 hours. Drain and rinse. Boil in 1 quart water for 1 hour. Boil vinegar, sugar, second quart of water and spices together. Add rind. Cook until tender and translucent. Add a jar of maraschino cherries, if desired. Pack pickles in hot jars and seal at once. Makes about 3 pints.

## SPICED CARROTS
    2 quarts carrots
    1 quart white vinegar
    ½ cup mixed pickling spices
    1 cup sugar
    1 teaspoon Maggi

Cook carrots whole or in chunks and let cool. Bring vinegar, spices, sugar and Maggi to a boil. Pour over carrots while vinegar mixture is still hot. Let stand overnight. Try this with lamb or veal.

## WINTER JELLY
Mix 2 cups apple juice, 2 cups orange juice, 2 cups crushed pineapple and 8 cloves (or 4 pieces dried ginger). Stir in 1 package Sure Jell and bring to boil. Add 7 cups sugar and stir constantly. Season to taste with 2-5 teaspoons concentrated lemon juice. Boil to jelly stage, about 5 minutes. Skim and pour into 10 jelly glasses. Seal with hot wax.

## PEPPER RELISH
    6 green peppers
    6 sweet red peppers
    6 onions
    1 cup sugar
    2 tablespoons salt
    1 pint cider vinegar

Grind peppers and onions in a meat grinder, then cover with hot water and let stand five minutes. Drain and add sugar, salt and vinegar. Boil 20 minutes. Put into small jars and seal while hot. Serve with meats. Makes about 1 quart.

## KIDNEY BEAN RELISH
Chop together 1 small onion, 3 stalks celery and 1 or 2 hard-boiled eggs. Add 2 cups drained kidney beans. Mix in 1 tablespoon mayonnaise, 2 teaspoons mustard relish, 1 teaspoon curry powder, ¼ teaspoon white pepper and ½ teaspoon salt. Serve cool and keep under refrigeration. Makes 6 portions.

## WAYBURY HOT FRUIT COMPOTE
Combine ½ cup each: prunes, pears, peaches and pineapple with 1½ cups applesauce and arrange in casserole. Then add 1 teaspoon cinnamon and ½ teaspoon each ginger and nutmeg. Add the juice of ½ lemon and its rind, chopped. Mix the fruits and place covered in a 250° oven for at least 1 hour before serving. The longer it bakes the better it is. Other fruits can be substituted and either fresh or canned

container. Mix other ingredients with 1 quart water, separately from carrots, bring to a boil and pour over carrot sticks while mix is hot. Cool before covering. Not necessary to seal. Keep under refrigeration. As carrots cool they will absorb mix. Let stand 3 to 5 days for best flavor. Carrot sticks will keep for several months under refrigeration. Delicious as an appetizer or as a relish.

## CORN RELISH
- 2 **dozen ears sweet corn**
- 1½ **quarts sugar**
- 4 **cups ground onions**
- ¼ **cup salt**
- 6 **green peppers, ground**
- 1½ **teaspoons turmeric**
- 4 **cucumbers, ground**
- 4 **cups vinegar**
- 4 **cups ground peeled tomatoes**
- 1½ **teaspoons dry mustard**
- 6 **red sweet peppers, ground**

Remove corn from ears and combine with remaining ingredients in a large kettle. Boil for 1 hour. Turn into sterile jars, fill to overflowing and seal. Makes about 12 quarts.

## PICKLED BEETS FARM STYLE

Trim 6 bunches of small beets of uniform size (6 or 7 beets to a bunch) leaving 2 inches of stem and the entire root. Cook until tender. Drain, saving 2 cups of the water in which beets were cooked. Plunge the beets into cold water and slip off skins. Remove roots and stems. If only large beets are available, slice them.

Make a syrup by cooking 2 cups vinegar, 2 cups sugar and 2 cups beet water and the following spices tied loosely in cheesecloth: ½ teaspoon whole cloves, 1½ teaspoons allspice, and 1 teaspoon whole black peppers. Stir until the sugar is dissolved. Pour over the beets and simmer 15 minutes. Remove the spices. Pack the beets into sterile jars and fill to overflowing with syrup. Seal and store.

may be used. Serve hot with meat or fowl.

## RHUBARB CONSERVE

Combine: 1 cup crushed pineapple, 1 cup raisins, 4 cups fresh rhubarb cut in 1-inch pieces, 4 cups sugar and the juice and grated rind of 1 orange. Cook these ingredients over low heat, stirring frequently until thick, about 1 hour. Add ½ cup chopped nuts. Refrigerate. Use as a cold relish.

## CINNAMON CARROT STICKS
- 8 **pounds large carrots**
- 1 **quart water**
- 2¼ **cups cider vinegar**
- 2¼ **pounds granulated sugar**
- 6 **drops cassia oil (oil of cinnamon— use eyedropper)**

Slice carrots vertically into thick sticks. Cook in water until tender, not soft. Drain and place carrots in 1-gallon glass

# PIES

## COCONUT CREAM CHIFFON PIE

1 tablespoon gelatin
¼ cup cold water
3 eggs, separated
½ cup sugar
¼ teaspoon salt
1 teaspoon vanilla
1 cup scalded milk
2 cups heavy cream, whipped
1 baked pie crust
¾ cups shredded coconut

Sprinkle gelatin in cold water. Combine egg yolks, sugar, salt and vanilla. Add to hot milk. Cook in double boiler until mixture coats spoon. Add gelatin to hot mixture; stir until dissolved. Chill until syrupy. Fold in stiffly beaten egg whites and 1 cup whipped cream. Pour into crust-lined pan and chill. Top pie with remainder of whipped cream and sprinkle with coconut.

## MEMORY INN MINCEMEAT

4 pounds cooking apples
2 pounds lean boiled beef
½ pound suet, chilled
1 pound seeded raisins
1 pound seedless raisins
1½ pounds currants
⅓ pound ground citron
1 teaspoon salt
½ teaspoon pepper
1 teaspoon allspice
1 teaspoon mace
1 teaspoon ground cloves
1 teaspoon nutmeg
2 tablespoons cinnamon
1 pound brown sugar
1½ quarts cider
1 cup brandy
1 cup Madeira wine

Peel and chop apples and combine with chilled beef and suet, also chopped. Mix in other ingredients except 1 pint cider and the brandy and Madeira. Boil this cider down to a cup of liquid; then add to mixture. Heat mixture through over low flame, stirring constantly. Remove, cool, and add brandy and Madeira.

## FROZEN LEMON PIE

3 egg yolks
⅛ teaspoon salt
½ cup sugar
¼ cup fresh lemon juice
½ teaspoon grated lemon rind
3 egg whites
1 cup cream, whipped
¾ cup crushed vanilla wafers

Beat yolks, salt and sugar in top of double boiler. Stir in lemon juice and grated rind; cook over hot, not boiling, water until mixture thickens and coats spoon. Remove from fire and chill. Beat egg whites until stiff, and fold in whipped cream and cooked mixture.

Sprinkle half of the wafer crumbs in freezing tray, then pour in mixture. Top with remaining crumbs and freeze until firm. Serve in finger-length slices.

## DELUXE PEANUT PIE
 1 cup parched peanuts
 2 eggs, beaten
 1 cup Karo syrup (Blue Label)
 ⅛ teaspoon salt
 1 teaspoon vanilla
 1 cup sugar
 2 tablespoons melted butter
    or margarine
 1 pie shell, unbaked

Mix ingredients together, adding peanuts last. Pour into 9-inch pie pan lined with unbaked crust. Bake in hot oven, 400°, for 40 minutes or until filling fails to adhere to a silver knife inserted in the center of the pie. If you prefer, tarts may be made from this recipe. It will serve 6 to 8.

## KENTUCKY LEMON PIE
 5 eggs
 1½ cups Karo syrup (white)
 1 cup sugar
    Juice of 2 lemons
    Rind of 1 lemon, grated
 ¼ cup butter

Beat eggs well; add syrup. Add sugar, lemon juice and grated rind. Add butter and beat together until well mixed. Pour into unbaked pie shell and bake on the lower shelf of a moderate (375°) oven for 10 minutes; move to a middle shelf and reduce the heat to 350° for 30 to 40 minutes.

## COCONUT PIE
 1½ cups fresh shredded coconut
 1 tablespoon granulated gelatin
 4 eggs, separated
 1 cup sugar
    Pinch of salt

 ½ cup cream
 ½ cup cream, whipped
 1 teaspoon vanilla or sherry
    flavoring

Soak gelatin in ½ cup cold water 5 minutes. Beat egg yolks, adding ½ cup sugar, salt, and ½ cup cream. Cook in double boiler until thick and add the soaked gelatin. Beat whites stiff, gradually adding the other ½ cup sugar. When the custard mixture has cooled, fold in the whites, coconut and flavoring. Pour in pie shell and chill thoroughly in refrigerator. Just before serving, spread ½ cup cream that has been whipped and sweetened over top of pie and sprinkle with coconut.

**Pie Crust:**

Crush 20 chocolate cookies until very fine and add ¼ cup melted margarine. Pat into 9-inch pie pan and chill in refrigerator.

## CHOCOLATE RUM PIE
 2 cups milk, scalded
 4 eggs, separated
 ½ cup sugar
 1¼ tablespoons cornstarch
 1½ squares chocolate
 1 teaspoon vanilla
 1 cooked pie crust
 1 tablespoon gelatin
 3 tablespoons rum
 ¼ teaspoon cream of tartar
 1 cup whipped cream
    Chocolate slivers

Combine milk, egg yolks, sugar and cornstarch. Cook 20 minutes, stirring, till mixture forms thin custard. To 1 cup of this, add chocolate squares and vanilla; pour mixture into crust. To remaining custard, add gelatin softened in 4 tablespoons water. Let mixture cool but not get too thick. Beat egg whites into meringue; add rum and tartar. When custard in crust sets, add this mixture. Chill till firm. Top with whipped cream and chocolate slivers.

## SOUR CREAM RAISIN PIE

- 1 cup brown sugar
- 2 tablespoons flour
- ½ teaspoon nutmeg
- ½ teaspoon cinnamon
- ¼ teaspoon salt
- 1 cup sour cream
- 3 egg yolks
- 1 cup raisins
- 3 egg whites
- 6 tablespoons sugar
- 1 baked pie shell

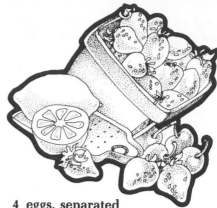

Combine brown sugar, flour, spices, salt and sour cream in top of a double boiler and cook until thick. Beat egg yolks in separate dish and blend a little of the hot paste with them before stirring into mixture in double boiler. Cook for 5 minutes and add raisins. Cool. Place in baked pie shell and cover with meringue made with egg whites and sugar. Brown in oven.

## SOUR CREAM RAISIN PIE

- 1 cup raisins
- 1 cup sugar
- 1 cup water
  Pinch of salt
- 2 tablespoons flour
- 2 egg yolks, well beaten
- 1 cup sour cream
- 1 teaspoon vanilla
- 1 9-inch pie shell, unbaked
  English walnuts
  Meringue

Cook raisins, sugar, water and salt over slow heat till quite thick. Cool; then stir in flour, egg yolks, cream and vanilla. Pour mixture into pie shell and sprinkle top with walnuts. Bake at 400° for 20 minutes; then at 350° till filling is firm (about 40 to 45 minutes). Cool pie; then top with meringue and brown in slow oven.

## NESSELRODE PIE

- 1 tablespoon plain gelatin
- 2 cups light cream
- ¼ cup sugar plus 6 tablespoons

- 4 eggs, separated
- ½ teaspoon salt
- ¼ cup each, rum and cherries
  soaked in rum (optional)
- 2 teaspoons lemon juice
- 1 9-inch pie shell, baked
  Bitter chocolate

Soak gelatin in ¼ cup cold water 5 minutes. Scald cream in double boiler, add ¼ cup sugar and egg yolks, slightly beaten. Cook until somewhat thickened. Remove from fire. Add gelatin and salt and chill until slightly thickened. Beat egg whites until stiff, add 6 tablespoons of sugar, and fold into chilled custard. Add rum and lemon juice, and cherries. Pour into pie shell, chill until set. Shave 1 or 2 squares bitter chocolate over the top.

## STRAWBERRY ANGEL PIE
### Crust:

Beat 4 egg whites until frothy. Add ¼ teaspoon cream of tartar, beat until stiff. Add 1 cup sugar and beat until glossy. Spread evenly over a 9-inch pie plate and bake in a 280° oven for 20 minutes; then increase heat to 300° for 40 minutes more.

### Filling:

- 4 egg yolks
- ½ cup sugar
- 1 teaspoon lemon juice
- 1 teaspoon gelatin
- ¼ cup cold water
- 1 cup heavy cream, whipped
- 1½ cups crushed strawberries,
  drain juice

Cook egg yolks, sugar, lemon juice and strawberry juice until thick. Mix gelatin with cold water and add to mixture. When cool add crushed strawberries. Spread thin layer of whipped cream on shell. Cover with filling and top with thin layer of whipped cream.

## PINEAPPLE WHIPPED CREAM PIE
1 No. 2½ can crushed pineapple
1 cup sugar
  Pinch of salt
  Juice of ½ lemon
2 tablespoons cornstarch
1 unbaked pie shell
  Whipped cream

Cook pineapple with sugar, salt and lemon juice. Thicken with cornstarch. Pour into unbaked shell and bake for 30 minutes. Let cool; then serve topped with whipped cream.

## GLAZED APPLE PIE
Crust:
2 cups flour
1 teaspoon salt
⅔ cup vegetable shortening
⅓ cup margarine
5½ tablespoons cold water

Blend flour, salt, and shortenings and enough cold water to hold mixture together. Roll out pastry and line a 9-inch pie plate. Roll out top crust.

Filling:
  6 to 7 cups sliced tart apples
1 cup granulated sugar
1 teaspoon cinnamon
⅓ cup orange juice
¼ cup confectioners' sugar
2 teaspoons water

Heap apples into crust shell. Blend granulated sugar, cinnamon and orange juice and pour over apples. Cover with top crust, sealing the edges. Bake in 425° oven for 15 minutes; then lower heat to 325° until apples are tender. When pie is cool, brush mixture of confectioners' sugar and water on top.

## COFFEE CHIFFON PIE
1 tablespoon unflavored gelatin
¼ cup cold water
4 large eggs, separated
1 cup sugar
1 cup coffee, cold and strong
1 10-inch pie shell, baked
¼ cup nuts

Combine gelatin and water. Let stand 5 minutes. Combine egg yolks with ½ cup sugar, then add coffee and stir well. Cook in double boiler until mixture coats a spoon. Add gelatin. While mixture is still warm fold into meringue made with stiffly beaten egg whites and the remaining ½ cup sugar. Fill baked pie shell and top with nuts. Chill in refrigerator before serving.

## LEMON SPONGE PIE
2 tablespoons butter
1 cup sugar
3 eggs, separated
2 tablespoons flour
2 cups milk
  Juice of 3 lemons
  Grated rind of 1 lemon
1 pie shell, uncooked

Cream butter and blend with sugar, egg yolks, flour, milk, lemon juice and rind. Beat egg whites separately and fold into mixture. Roll out a single pie crust and line a regular-sized pie tin. Then pour lemon mixture into shell and bake in slow (350°) oven for approximately 45 minutes.

## DAMSON PLUM PIE

2 eggs
⅓ cup butter
⅓ cup sugar
⅓ cup milk
⅓ cup Damson plum preserves
1 teaspoon cornstarch
1 pastry shell, uncooked

Separate eggs and beat. Cream butter and sugar together and stir into beaten egg yolks. Add milk, preserves and cornstarch. Fold beaten egg whites into mixture and pour into pie tin lined with pie crust. Bake in 350° oven for 40 minutes.

## ALMOND PIE

¼ pound butter
1 cup sugar
6 eggs
1½ cups Blue Label Karo syrup
1½ cups chopped almonds
2 teaspoons vanilla
2 pie shells, uncooked

Cream the butter and sugar, add eggs, syrup, almonds and flavoring. Bake in uncooked pie shells for 30 minutes, at 350°. (This recipe makes enough filling for 2 pies.)

## CHRISTMAS PIE

**Crust:**

Combine 1½ cups finely ground Brazil nutmeats with ½ teaspoon sugar. Press this mixture to sides and bottom of 9-inch pie tin. Bake in 400° oven for 8 minutes or until lightly browned.

**Filling:**

Soak 1 envelope of gelatin in ¼ cup of water. Beat 3 egg yolks with fork and add ¼ cup sugar and ⅛ teaspoon salt. Gradually stir in 1½ cups scalded milk. Cook in double boiler over hot, not boiling, water till mixture coats spoon. Remove from fire and stir in gelatin. Chill custard till thickened. Beat till smooth. Add 1½ cups thinly sliced maraschino cherries, 3 tablespoons rum or

flavoring. Beat 3 egg whites. Then add ¼ cup sugar, continuing to beat till whites are stiff. Fold into custard; pour into crust. Top with whipped cream.

## CHOCOLATE FUDGE PIE

1 cup sugar
½ cup butter, melted
2 eggs
⅔ cup flour, sifted
1 square bitter chocolate, melted
1 teaspoon vanilla

Beat sugar and butter together, then add eggs. Beat until thoroughly mixed, add flour and blend well. Add chocolate and vanilla. Pour into a greased Pyrex pie plate (no crust) and bake in preheated 325° oven for 25 minutes. Serve with vanilla ice cream. This recipe yields 8 servings.

## SIMSBURY HOUSE WINTER PIE

1½ cups mincemeat
¼ cup peach brandy
¾ cup strained pumpkin
1 egg, lightly beaten
½ teaspoon cinnamon
½ teaspoon ginger
　Piece of mace (less than ⅛ teaspoon)
¼ teaspoon salt
½ cup heavy cream
½ cup milk
　9-inch pie shell, unbaked

Cover bottom of pie shell with mincemeat which has been moistened with brandy. Combine remaining ingredients and pour over mincemeat. Bake at 425° for 10 minutes and lower to 350° until the pumpkin custard is set and nicely browned.

## BITTERSWEET MINT PIE

Sift 1 tablespoon gelatin over ½ cup cold milk. Scald 1½ cups milk and add ¾ cup sugar, 1 tablespoon cornstarch and 3 egg yolks that have been mixed together with a little of the hot milk to liquefy them. Cook (over double boiler) until mixture coats the spoon. Add softened gelatin and chill until fairly firm. In meantime, melt 2 squares unsweetened chocolate over hot water and cool. Beat 3 egg whites until stiff. When custard is chilled, beat until smooth and fluffy and then combine egg whites and beaten custard. When thoroughly blended, fold in ½ cup cream, whipped. Divide custard in half. Add chocolate to one half and ¼ cup creme de menthe and a few drops green color to other half. Place chocolate mixture in bottom of a 9-inch baked pie shell and top with mint half. Then chill. Serve topped wth whipped cream and grated chocolate.

## RASPBERRY CHIFFON PIE

1 large egg white
1 cup sugar
1 teaspoon cream of tartar
½ cup boiling water
1⅓ tablespoons plain gelatin
1 cup raspberry juice
1 baked pie shell

In bowl place egg white, sugar, cream of tartar and boiling water. Beat at medium

speed for 20 minutes. While mixture is beating, dissolve gelatin in ¼ cup of juice over low heat. Add rest of juice and set in coldest part of refrigerator until ropey but not firm. Add to egg white mixture beating until blended. Pour into pie shell and keep in refrigerator until ready to serve. May be served plain or with whipped cream.

## FRESH COCONUT CREAM PIE

2 cups milk
2 egg yolks, beaten
7 tablespoons sugar
2 tablespoons cornstarch
3 tablespoons butter
⅛ teaspoon salt
   Vanilla, to taste
1 9-inch baked pie shell
1 cup freshly grated coconut

Bring ½ cup of milk to boil. Add sugar and cornstarch to egg yolks and remaining milk. Add this mixture to hot milk and cook until thickened in double boiler. Stir constantly. Add butter and salt and when cool, add vanilla. Fill baked pie shell with cream mixture. Cover with whipped cream, then sprinkle with coconut.

## PEANUT PIE

3 eggs
½ cup sugar
1 cup white Karo syrup
1 teaspoon vanilla
1 teaspoon butter
   Pinch of salt
2 tablespoons peanut butter
1 9-inch unbaked pie shell
¾ cup of toasted peanuts, chopped
   and lightly buttered

Beat eggs, then add sugar and beat well together. To this add syrup, salt, butter and peanut butter. Mix at medium mixer speed for 5 minutes or until thoroughly blended. Pour into pie shell and sprinkle peanuts over top. Bake in 300° oven for 45 minutes. Cool before slicing.

## CRANBERRY CHIFFON PIE

1 envelope unflavored gelatin
¼ cup cold water
1 pound can cranberry jelly
⅛ teaspoon salt
1 teaspoon grated lemon rind
2 teaspoons lemon juice
2 egg whites
2 tablespoons sugar
   8-inch pastry shell, baked
   Whipped cream (optional)

Place gelatin in a custard cup. Add cold water and let stand 2 minutes. Place custard cup in pan of boiling water until gelatin dissolves. Add to jellied cranberry sauce (crushed with a fork) or whole sauce. Add salt, lemon rind and lemon juice; chill until mixture begins to set. Beat egg whites until stiff and beat in sugar. Fold into cranberry mixture. Pour filling into baked pastry shell and chill until firm. Top with whipped cream, if desired.

## APPLE BUTTER PIE

6 egg yolks
3 cups apple butter
3 tablespoons butter, melted
2 tablespoons flour, sifted
2 tablespoons light corn syrup
1 pint cream
½ cup sugar
1 teaspoon cinnamon
½ teaspoon nutmeg
½ pint whipping cream
2 9-inch pie shells

Beat egg yolks until thick. Add apple butter and stir in butter, sifted flour and syrup. Blend in cream and add sugar and spices. Pour into pie shells and bake 40 minutes at 375°. When pies cool, top with whipped cream. Halve recipe for one pie.

## BLACK BOTTOM PIE
### Filling:

2 cups milk, scalded
4 egg yolks, beaten
½ cup sugar
1½ tablespoons cornstarch
1½ squares bitter chocolate, melted
1 teaspoon vanilla
1 tablespoon gelatin
4 tablespoons water

Add yolks slowly to hot milk. Mix sugar and cornstarch, stir into milk. Cook mixture in double boiler for 20 minutes, stirring occasionally until it coats spoon. Remove from fire. Take 1 cup hot custard and add chocolate to it. Beat well as it cools. Add vanilla to mixture and pour into 9-inch gingersnap crust. Chill. Dissolve gelatin in cold water and add to remaining warm custard. Cool.

### Meringue:

Beat 4 egg whites, ½ cup sugar and ¼ teaspoon cream of tartar until stiff. Then add 2 tablespoons whiskey. Fold meringue into plain custard mixture and pour into pie shell. Top with 1 cup whipped cream and ½-square shaved bitter chocolate. Chill.

## PEACH COBBLER

3 cups sliced fresh peaches
1 cup sugar
6-8 tablespoons butter
   Pie crust, approximately enough
     for a 2-crust pie

Make a layer of half the peaches in a 6x9x3-inch deep pan, sprinkle with sugar and liberal dabs of butter. If peaches are a naturally sweet variety, less sugar can be used, and if they are of firm, not

juicy variety, more butter is needed. Place thin strips of pie crust dough over this layer. Place another layer of peaches on top of crust, and sugar and dot with butter. Lay on top crust, either laced or perforated. Bake in 400° oven until brown. Serve with cream or ice cream. Makes 6 portions.

## THE INN'S OWN APPLE PIE
- 4-6 tart apples
- 1½ cups sugar
- 1 tablespoon flour
- ¼ teaspoon salt
- ¼ teaspoon cinnamon
- ¼ teaspoon nutmeg
- ⅛ teaspoon ground cloves
- ⅛ teaspoon allspice
- 2 tablespoons melted butter
  Juice of half a lemon and lime
  Grated rind of half lemon
- ⅔ cup of water from simmered apple peels
  Pastry for 9-inch crust and strips

Peel and core apples. Cover peels and cores with water and simmer. Dice apples in small cubes. Mix flour and sugar and add salt and spices. Line pie tin with bottom crust and sprinkle half of sugar mixture on it. Add apples and cover with remaining sugar. Sprinkle with butter, fruit juice, rind and water from peels. Cover pie with latticed strips of crust. Bake at 425° for 15 minutes; then at 375° until fruit is tender.

## FUDGE PIE
- ¼ pound butter
- 3 squares unsweetened chocolate
- 4 eggs
- 3 tablespoons white Karo syrup
- 1½ cups sugar
- ¼ teaspoon salt
- 1 teaspoon vanilla
  9-inch unbaked pie shell

In top of double boiler melt butter and chocolate together. Cool slightly. Beat eggs until light, then beat in syrup, sugar, salt and vanilla. Add cooled chocolate

mixture and mix thoroughly. Pour into pie shell. Bake at 350° for 25-30 minutes, or until top is crusty and filling is set but still somewhat soft inside. Do not overbake. Pie should shake like custard so it will not be too stiff when cool. May be served plain or with a thin topping of vanilla ice cream.

## RICH LEMON PIE
- 6 ounces sweet butter
- 1 cup sugar
- 2 lemons, juice and grated rind
- 3 egg yolks (save whites)
- 1 whole egg
- 1-2 slices white bread
- 6 tablespoons sugar
  8-inch pie shell, baked

Melt butter over very low heat; stir in sugar and lemon rind and juice. Beat yolks and whole egg together and add to mixture when sugar is dissolved. When thickened, remove from heat. Don't allow to boil! Remove crusts from bread and cut or tear gently into large crumbs and scatter over bottom of pie shell. Make a stiff meringue of the egg whites sweetened with 6 tablespoons sugar. While lemon mixture is still hot, spoon it over bread crumbs and cover with meringue. Seal meringue to edges of pie shell. Brown in 350° oven. Cool and serve at room temperature.

## BUTTERSCOTCH PEANUT CHIFFON PIE
- ¼ cup cold water
- 1 tablespoon gelatin
- ¾ cup brown sugar
- 1 cup milk
- 2 tablespoons butter
- ¼ teaspoon salt
- 1 teaspoon vanilla
- 4 eggs, separated
- ¼ cup roasted peanuts, chopped
- ¼ cup white sugar
- 1 cup whipping cream, whipped
  8-inch pie shell, baked

Combine cold water and gelatin and let stand. Stir together in a double boiler: brown sugar, milk, butter, salt, vanilla and beaten egg yolks. Cook until mixture is consistency of custard. Remove from fire, stir in gelatin and chill. Add roasted peanuts to chilled mixture. Whip room temperature egg whites until stiff, beating in white sugar. Fold in chilled ingredients and pour into baked pie shell. Decorate with whipped cream squeezed from a pastry bag.

## PUMPKIN-MINCE PIE

    1 cup canned pumpkin
    ½ cup brown sugar
    1 teaspoon pumpkin pie spice
    ½ teaspoon salt
    2 eggs, slightly beaten
 14½ ounces evaporated milk
    2½ cups mincemeat
        9-inch unbaked pie shell

Combine pumpkin, sugar, spice, salt, eggs and milk and beat until smooth. Spread mincemeat evenly over pie shell. Ladle pumpkin mixture carefully over mincemeat. Bake at 450° for 10 minutes, then at 350° about 45 minutes, until filling is firm in center.

## JEFFERSON DAVIS PIE

    ½ cup butter
    2 cups light brown sugar
    4 eggs, separated
    2 tablespoons flour
    1 teaspoon cinnamon
    1 teaspoon freshly grated nutmeg
    ½ teaspoon allspice
    1 cup cream
    ½ cup pecans, chopped
    ½ cup raisins
    ½ cup dates, chopped
        10-inch pie shell

Cream butter and sugar together, then beat in egg yolks. Sift flour, cinnamon, nutmeg and allspice into mixture. Add cream, pecans, raisins and dates. Brown empty crust in 450° oven for 5 minutes; add filling. Bake in 300° oven until set,

about 40 minutes. When cool, top with meringue made of egg whites. Brown meringue in 300° oven 15-20 minutes.

## GINGER PIE

    ¼ pound butter
    ¾ cup confectioners' sugar
    2 tablespoons coffee cream
    ¼ cup preserved ginger, grated
    2 tablespoons syrup of ginger
    2 cups whipping cream
    1 10-inch layer of cake,
        ¼-inch thick
    1 tablespoon semi-sweet chocolate,
        melted

Cream butter and sugar together. Thin slightly with coffee cream and mix thoroughly. Add ginger and syrup in which ginger is preserved. Whip cream and fold into mixture. Place cake layer in 9-inch pan so that it forms side "crust" for pie. Pile filling onto cake and smooth top surface. Drizzle melted chocolate over top in lacelike pattern. Refrigerate for at least 3 hours. Serves 8-10.

## CONCORD GRAPE PIE

    2 quarts Concord grapes
    ½ cup sugar
    ½ tablespoon cornstarch
    1 tablespoon butter, melted
        Pastry for two 9-inch crusts

Wash grapes thoroughly (as skins are to be used). Remove skins from grapes. Heat pulp and strain through colander to remove seeds. Mix sugar and cornstarch with a little cold water, then add to pulp along with skins. Add butter and stir mixture well. Pour into lower crust and then top with crust, making slits for steam. (Be sure pie pan is perforated to permit proper baking of lower crust.) Bake in 450° oven for 10 minutes, then in 350° oven for another 35 to 45 minutes. Cool. Delicious served à la mode.

## PEANUT BUTTER ICE CREAM PIE
Line a 9-inch pie pan with graham cracker crust. Thaw 1 quart of vanilla ice cream, put in mixing bowl with 1 cup of peanut butter and mix thoroughly. Fill crust with mixture and freeze. Serve frozen. Serves 8.

## SCHULER'S GRASSHOPPER PIE
**Crust:**

Combine 1¼ cups crushed chocolate cookie wafers with ⅓ cup melted butter. Pat into deep 9-inch pie pan and chill.

**Filling:**
- ⅔ **cup milk, scalded**
- 24 **marshmallows**
- 2 **ounces green crème de menthe**
- 1 **ounce white crème de cacao**
- ½ **pint whipping cream, whipped**

Add marshmallows to scalded milk in double boiler, stirring often until they blend into smooth mixture. Cool to room temperature. Then add crème de menthe and crème de cacao. Fold whipped cream into mixture and pour into chilled chocolate crust. Freeze a minimum of 2 hours. If frozen overnight, it should be partially thawed before serving. Serves 8.

## BULGUR PECAN PIE
- 3 **eggs**
- ¼ **cup vegetable oil**
- ½ **cup brown sugar**
- 1 **cup maple syrup**
- ¾ **cup milk**
- 1 **teaspoon vanilla**
- ½ **teaspoon salt**
- ¼ **cup bulgur**
- 1 **cup pecans**
  **9-inch pie shell, unbaked**

Beat eggs, then mix in all remaining ingredients in order given. Pour into an unbaked pie shell, and bake at 350° for 35 to 40 minutes. (Bulgur is an ancient food, resembling cracked wheat, developed for modern taste by the Kansas Wheat Commission.)

## DEEP DISH CHEHALEM BLACKBERRY PIE
- 3 **cups Chehalem blackberries**
- 2 **cups sugar**
- ¼ **teaspoon salt**
- 4 **tablespoons cornstarch**
- 1 **cup water**
- 1 **9-inch baked pastry crust**
  **Vanilla ice cream**

Pour ¾ cup water over 3 cups Chehalem blackberries and let stand at room temperature for 2 hours. Drain juice through colander into saucepan. Add sugar and salt and bring to boil. Immediately add cornstarch that has been dissolved in ¼ cup water. Stir until dark and clear. Fold in uncooked blackberries gently. The secret is *not to cook berries.* Serve in individual deep dishes topped with pie crust and vanilla ice cream. May be warmed before serving, but *do not cook.* Serves 6-8.

## LEMON CHESS PIE
- 2 **cups sugar**
- 1 **good pinch salt**
- 1 **tablespoon water-ground white or yellow cornmeal**
- 1 **tablespoon flour**
- ¼ **cup melted butter**
- ¼ **cup milk**
- 2 **lemons (juice and grated rind)**
- 4 **eggs**
  **9-inch unbaked pie shell**

Combine sugar, salt, cornmeal and flour. Add melted butter (slightly cooled), milk, lemon rind and juice; add eggs; beat well. Slip the unbaked pie shell under the hot broiler for 60 seconds to improve the crust, then pour pie mixture into it. Bake at 350° for 40 minutes, center should be barely firm. Serves 6.

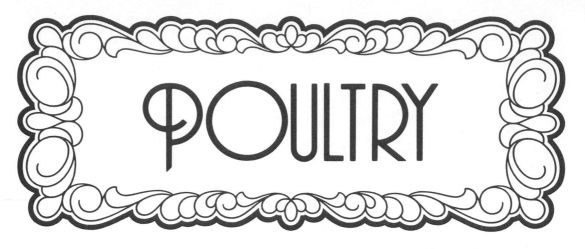

# POULTRY

## BONELESS BAKED CHICKEN

- 3 3-pound broilers, split and boned
- 7 ounces bread crumbs
- 11 ounces lukewarm water
- 1 medium Spanish onion, sliced
- 4 ounces rendered chicken fat
- 4 ounces fresh chicken livers
- 1 teaspoon chopped parsley
- ¼ ounce salt
  - Pinch of black pepper
  - Dash of thyme
  - Dash of basil
  - Dash of oregano

Combine bread crumbs and water in mixing bowl and allow to stand for 10 minutes. Brown onion in fat, then sauté chicken livers in it. Put onion and liver through meat grinder and mix with bread crumbs and seasonings. Place in refrigerator overnight. Use as stuffing for boned broilers. Form each chicken around dressing to get a chicken-like shape. Lightly broil, then bake 20 minutes. Serves 6.

## BAKED CHICKEN BIRD AND BOTTLE

- 3 broiler chickens, split in half
- 2 tablespoons onion, chopped
- 3 tablespoons green bell peppers, chopped
- 2 tablespoons celery, chopped
  Garlic clove, chopped fine, mashed
- 3 tablespoons parsley, chopped

- 1 cup chopped oysters, drained
- 1 teaspoon salt
- ½ teaspoon ground black pepper
- ¼ teaspoon cayenne pepper
- 5 tablespoons butter
- 1 cup bread crumbs
- ½ cup oyster juice

Sauté vegetables, oysters, and seasonings in butter. When tender, remove from pan. Add crumbs, oyster juice. Place chickens in pan, skin side up, ½ teaspoon butter on each half. Add ½ cup water. Bake (375°) 20 minutes. Remove, turn over, and fill cavity with heaping spoonful dressing. Sprinkle with crumbs, melted butter. Bake 15 minutes. Garnish with cranberry or lingonberry preserve.

## CHOW MEIN

- Meat of one large boiled fowl cut julienne
- 1 stalk celery
- 1 pound white onions
- ½ pound fresh mushrooms
- ¼ pound ground beef
- 1 pint water chestnuts
- 1 pint bamboo hearts
- 1½ cups stock from the fowl
- ½ quart bean sprouts
  Soy sauce

Slice celery, onions, and mushrooms in a pot with a small amount of stock. Cover tightly and allow to simmer slowly so they will make their own liquor. When these are half cooked, add ground beef and stock of fowl. Boil slowly for 1 hour. Add chestnuts, bamboo hearts, dark meat of fowl, and bean sprouts. Bring to a boil, season, add soy sauce to taste, and serve with fried noodles and boiled rice. Garnish with white meat of the fowl. Serves 8.

## CHICKEN COUNTRY CAPTAIN

3 fryers cut in pieces
1 teaspoon salt
½ teaspoon pepper
  Paprika
2 cloves garlic, chopped
4 medium onions, chopped
3 green peppers, chopped fine
3 No. 2 cans tomatoes
1 dash cayenne
½ teaspoon thyme
1 teaspoon curry powder
½ cup chopped parsley
1 cup currants
½ pound blanched toasted almonds

Roll chickens in mixture of flour, salt, pepper and paprika. Fry in deep fat until golden brown. Place in a roaster, add ½ cup hot water, and steam slowly. To small amount of fat add garlic, onions, and green peppers, and brown slightly. Add ½ cup water and cook 10 to 15 minutes. Blend in tomatoes and remaining seasonings. Cook until smooth. Pour over chicken and cook until tender, about 1 hour. Add currants and almonds and serve with wild rice.

## DOMESTICATED RING-NECK PHEASANT WITH WILD RICE

Clean pheasant; split it down both sides of backbone. (Use backbone and neck in stock pot.) Split down breastbone, making two halves. Wipe thoroughly with clean dry cloth. Season well with salt and pepper; dust with flour. Fry in hot fat until golden brown. Make a thin, well-seasoned sauce of stock and cream (one part of each). Put pheasant in a pot, cover with cream sauce, put on slow fire

and simmer. When almost done, add about 1 ounce of sherry. Serve with wild rice.

Steam ½ cup rice until tender and fluffy. Put in colander to drain and cool. Chop ½ onion and about 3 strips bacon; sauté in a frying pan until brown; now add rice. Season with salt and pepper. Thoroughly heat on a quick hot fire.

## EAST-WEST CURRIED TURKEY

Melt ¼ pound butter in a flat saucepan and add 1 pound breast of turkey, cooked and cubed, and 2 pineapples, cut in chunks. Sprinkle mixture with 1 teaspoon curry powder, 1 tablespoon flour, and 3 to 4 cups light cream. Boil 5 minutes. Add salt and lemon juice to taste. Peel 2 ripe avocados, halve, and dip in lemon juice to keep from discoloring. Fill avocado halves with turkey and fruit mixture and sprinkle with grated cheese or Hollandaise sauce mixed with cheese. Bake for about 30 minutes at 350° to 375°. Garnish with sliced mango, peach, or apricot. Arrange with rice. Serves 4.

## CHICKEN CACCIATORE

2 3-pound chickens
  Salt and pepper, to taste
½ cup olive oil
1 onion, chopped fine
½ cup dry white wine
1 bay leaf
  Pinch of rosemary
4 fresh tomatoes, cut in small pieces
  Garlic, to taste

Cut each chicken into 6 pieces and season with salt and pepper. Cook chicken in olive oil for about 20 minutes or until brown. Then add onion and cook until transparent. Stir in wine and add remaining ingredients and cook for about 15 minutes.

## BRUNSWICK STEW

1 6-pound chicken
2 cups lima beans
4 cups tomatoes
2 large onions, sliced
4 medium potatoes, diced
2 cups okra
4 cups corn
2 teaspoons salt
½ teaspoon pepper
1 tablespoon sugar

Cut chicken in 8 pieces and simmer 2¼ hours in 1 gallon water. Remove chicken. Add beans, tomatoes, onions, potatoes and okra to broth. Simmer until limas are tender, about an hour. Add hot water if necessary and stir to prevent scorching. Add corn and chicken, boned and diced, seasonings, and sugar. Cook till corn is done. Serves 8 to 10.

## CHICKEN SHORTCAKE

Heat ½ pint of cream and 1 cup milk in a double boiler. Add to this ¾ cup chicken fat. To ⅛ pound melted butter slowly add and blend ½ cup flour, 1½ teaspoons salt and a dash of pepper. Add cream mixture. Stir in 2 ounces chopped pimento, 4 ounces diced mushrooms and 4 cups cooked, diced chicken. Serve over hot egg bread slices, biscuits or pastry shells. Six servings.

## CHICKEN CACCIATORE

2 fryers, disjointed
  Olive oil
2 large onions, chopped
1 pound mushrooms, sliced
1 No. 2½ can tomatoes
1 clove garlic
1 tablespoon oregano
1 tablespoon salt
  Black pepper, to taste
1 cup Rhine wine
1 cup chicken stock
½ cup pitted, sliced green olives
  Mostaccioli noodles

Sauté chicken in olive oil till brown. Add onions, mushrooms, tomatoes, garlic,

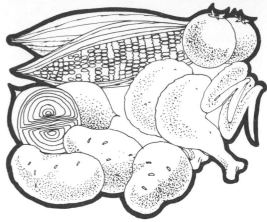

oregano, salt, pepper. Brown slightly. Add wine and simmer for 20 minutes. Add chicken stock, reduce heat and add sliced olives. Serve with noodles. Serves 6.

## CHICKEN PAPRIKASH

  4-pound spring chicken
3 medium onions, sliced
2 tablespoons paprika
1 tablespoon shortening
2 cups broth or cold water
3 tablespoons flour
⅛ teaspoon red pepper
1 tablespoon salt
½ cup sour cream

Sauté onions and paprika in shortening slowly for 10 minutes. Add disjointed chicken. Cover pan; simmer slowly until golden brown. Add broth; cook till tender — 1 to 1½ hours. Add water if needed. Blend flour, seasonings and sour cream about 5 minutes before chicken is done. Stir into chicken mixture slowly. Serve with dumplings or noodles.

## CHICKEN AND DUMPLINGS

Take 1 fat hen and cook whole or disjointed in 1½ quarts of water seasoned with salt. Cook for about 3 hours. When tender, lift out of broth and cool. Pick meat from bones and cut in small pieces. Thicken broth with 7 tablespoons flour and ¾ cup water. Mix smooth with egg beater. Season to taste with salt and pepper. Add a few drops of yellow food coloring. Strain over chicken. Reserve 4 cups of gravy in a flat stew pan for dumplings.

## Dumplings

1 egg
⅔ cup milk
1 tablespoon oil or melted shortening
1½ cups flour
⅔ teaspoon salt
4 level teaspoons baking powder

Sift dry ingredients into liquid and stir briskly until blended. Drop dumpling batter by teaspoonfuls into boiling gravy. Cover and cook gently for 8 to 10 minutes or until done.

## ROCK CORNISH GAME HEN BON VIVEUR

1 Rock Cornish game hen
1 thin slice salt pork
3 tablespoons butter
1 small onion, quartered
1 carrot, quartered
1 stalk of celery, quartered
Pinch of thyme
Salt and pepper
½ cup chicken broth
5 ounces of good red wine
1 tablespoon brandy

Clean and dry bird. Place pork over breast. Sauté in butter. When meat is well browned add vegetables and seasonings. Roast in moderate oven for 25-30 minutes. Remove bird from pan when cooked. Add to cooking pan: broth, wine and brandy. Cook over a high fire for 5 minutes. Place bird in a serving dish and strain sauce over it. Garnish with a rondelle of foie gras. Cover dish and leave on fire for a few minutes and let it get very hot. Serve with wild rice and currant jelly.

## ROAST WATERTOWN GOOSE WITH STEWED APPLES

Have a 12-pound fat young goose cleaned and drawn. Chop off wings, neck, head and feet. Wash goose inside and out, drain. Cover with cold water and let soak 15 minutes. Drain; pat dry. Rub with salt inside and out. Place in baking pan. Add 4 cups water, ½ onion, sliced, and 6 peppercorns. Roast in 325° oven. When water has boiled down, baste frequently with ¼ pound melted and browned butter. A young goose should be cooked 15-20 minutes a pound. Remove goose to warm platter. Place pan on top of range and sift 2 tablespoons flour into juice. Stir, then add 2 cups water. Let boil 2-3 minutes, stirring constantly. Serve gravy with goose. Makes 6 portions.

### Stewed Apples:

Wash, peel and core 2 pounds of apples. Cut in thick slices. Sauté in 2 tablespoons butter for 2-3 minutes. Sprinkle with ½ cup sugar. Add ½ cup water, ½ cup white wine, small piece of lemon peel and 1 tablespoon lemon juice. Cover, cook slowly until apples are tender. Serves 6.

## ROCK CORNISH GAME HEN FLAMBÉ AU COGNAC

6 1-pound Rock Cornish game hens
Melted butter
Salt, pepper and paprika
½ ounce brandy

Fill game hens with dressing and brush with melted butter. Sprinkle each lightly with salt, pepper and paprika. Roast in 300° oven for about 1½ hours. Serve in chafing dish — pour Cherry Sauce over hens just before serving. Pour brandy over sauce; light with match. Makes 6 servings.

### Dressing:

Cook ¼ pound sausage, chopped, in a large skillet. Add 4 tablespoons water, 1 medium onion, chopped fine, and 3 mushrooms, sliced thin. Sauté until meat is well done. Add 1 cup cooked rice and season to taste with salt, pepper, poultry seasoning and 1 tablespoon brandy. Add ¼ cup bread crumbs and mix ingredients thoroughly.

**Cherry Sauce:**
Combine 1 cup water, ¼ cup Burgundy wine, ¼ cup sugar; add ¼ teaspoon salt. Bring to a boil and thicken slightly with cornstarch. Add 1 No. 2½ can black Bing cherries.

## ARROZ CON POLLO

- 1 frying chicken
- 2 buttons garlic
- 1 onion, chopped
- 2 ounces tomatoes or 3 fresh tomatoes
- 1 pinch saffron
- 4 ounces lard or 2 ounces olive oil
- 2 tablespoons salt
- 1 bay leaf
- ½ pound rice
- 2 green peppers
- 1 quart water
- 2 ounce can small peas
- 2 pimentos

Cut chicken in quarters and fry until slightly browned in lard or oil with onion and garlic. When done, add tomatoes and water. Boil 5 minutes. Add bay leaf, salt, rice, saffron and green pepper. Stir thoroughly and place in moderately hot oven for 20 minutes. Garnish with peas and pimentos. Serves four.

## CHICKEN PIE (two layer)

- 3½ pound hen, boiled
- 3 cups chicken broth
- 2½ cups milk
- ¼ pound butter or margarine
- 6-8 tablespoons flour
  Salt and pepper, to taste
- 4 hard-boiled eggs, sliced
  Pastry for crusts

Remove bones and skin from chicken. Cut into chunks. Heat broth, milk, butter and seasonings to boiling point. Thicken with flour mixed to a smooth paste with water. Cook a couple of minutes. Arrange half of chicken and eggs in a greased casserole 13x9x2½ inches. Add half the liquid and top with pastry strips.

Brown in 450° oven. Top with remaining chicken, eggs and liquid, and cover with pastry crust. Bake in 350° oven from 30 to 45 minutes. Serves 10 to 12.

## BROILED SQUAB WITH WILD RICE DRESSING

Prepare 4 whole young squabs, 13-ounce size is best. Rub inside and out with butter and salt. Stuff with dressing.

### Wild Rice Dressing

Steam 8 ounces wild rice in 2 cups chicken stock until fluffy. Finely mince 1 stalk celery, 1 bunch parsley, 1 green pepper, 1 Bermuda onion and 4 hard-boiled eggs. Sauté vegetables slowly in 2 tablespoons butter. Mix with cooked rice, moistening entire dressing with chicken stock and stuff into squabs tightly.

Place whole birds, breast side down, 6 inches below broiler flame. After 15 minutes brush generously with butter and turn. Baste and broil breast side for 15-20 minutes, or until brown. Sauté 8 ounces mushrooms and 1 cup toasted almonds in 2 tablespoons butter; spread over birds. Garnish with peeled orange slices and serve with cream sherry on the side. Makes 4 portions.

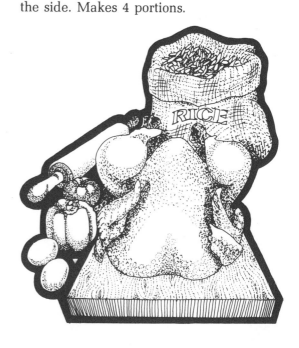

## CHICKEN À LA COPENHAGEN WITH HORSERADISH SAUCE

Simmer a 3½-pound spring chicken with a small onion, salt and pepper, until chicken is tender. Disjoint cooked chicken with poultry shears; place in warm casserole and cover with piping hot horseradish sauce. Makes 6 portions.

### Horseradish Sauce
    3 tablespoons butter
    3 tablespoons flour
    1½ cups half-and-half cream and milk,
        enough to make a smooth sauce
    4 tablespoons horseradish
    2 tablespoons sugar
    1 tablespoon vinegar

Melt butter and blend in flour. Slowly stir in milk and cream mixture. Add remaining ingredients, mix well and bring to a boil. Pour over chicken.

## ROAST LONG ISLAND DUCKLING WITH WILD RICE AND BURGUNDY WINE JELLY

### Duckling:
To serve four, select a 4½ pound bird. Place duck in 350° oven. Baste frequently until done. Roast about 20 minutes per pound weight after it has been cleaned. Split and cut into four pieces. Serve with wild rice and jelly.

### Wild Rice:
Wash a cup of wild rice thoroughly, place in a pot and cover with salt water. Boil until tender, remove from heat and drain well. Sauté chopped green onions in pure butter. Add to wild rice and mix well.

### Burgundy Wine Jelly:
Add 6½ cups sugar to 3 cups of Burgundy wine. Simmer over low heat and stir constantly. Add 1 bottle fruit pectin, then bring to a boil for one minute. Pour into individual molds and chill.

## SUPRÊME OF PHEASANT GRAND VENEUR

Remove the breast of a pheasant (one makes 2 servings), leave skin on. Marinate for 24 hours in a mixture of: 2 ounces olive oil; 2 ounces brandy; 2 ounces sherry wine; 1 bay leaf; 2 whole cloves; a few parsley sprigs; ¼ stalk celery, diced; salt and pepper, to taste; ½ cup onion, diced; 4 shallots, diced, and a pinch of 4 spices (select your own favorites).

After 24 hours remove pheasant from marinade and dry in clean towel. Lightly brown in a hot thick skillet with clarified butter. Place in 350° oven for 25-30 minutes, until done and golden brown. Remove fat from pan, then add 6 ounces fresh mushrooms, diced; 2 ounces shallots, chopped; and 3 ounces sherry. Let simmer covered in oven for five minutes.

Set pheasant breasts on toast squares covered with ham slice; arrange on serving dish. Keep covered and hot while finishing sauce. Add 3 ounces coffee cream to simmering sauce and boil together until it thickens. Put in 1 ounce game meat glacé, 2 ounces sweet butter, juice of ½ lemon and 1 tablespoon freshly chopped parsley. Pour a little sauce over pheasant and serve rest from a separate dish. Garnish platter with gondolas of sweet potatoes filled with candied fruit and topped with marshmallow glaze, and glazed pineapple rings with kumquats. Serve hot wild rice separately.

## MADRAS CHICKEN CURRY

Cut meat from two 2-pound frying chickens; slice into 1-inch squares, not more than ½-inch thick. Dust with flour and sauté in 3 tablespoons hot butter until lightly browned on both sides; remove to platter and keep warm.

To butter remaining in pan add 3 onions

and 1 clove garlic, minced; sauté until golden.

Melt 3 tablespoons butter in another saucepan and stir in 1½ tablespoons curry powder until smooth. Gradually add 2 cups hot chicken stock; 2 tablespoons chutney, chopped; ½ cup seedless raisins; 2 tart apples, peeled and sliced; ½ teaspoon powdered ginger and ½ teaspoon salt. Cover and simmer 30 minutes.

Meanwhile, chop ¼ cup blanched almonds and sauté in 1 tablespoon butter until golden. Turn nuts into mortar or electric blender and convert to smooth paste. Stir nut paste gradually into ½ cup hot cream and cook over low flame for 5 minutes. Add almond cream to curry mixture, then add onion mixture and chicken; simmer uncovered for about 15 minutes or until sauce is thickened. Add juice of ½ lemon and serve over 3 cups cooked rice. If sauce is reduced too much, thin with a little hot chicken stock. Serve with condiments such as fresh grated coconut, toasted dry coconut, crisp bits of fried bacon, chopped peanuts, India relish, Major Grey's Chutney, French-fried onion rings and raisins. Makes 6 portions.

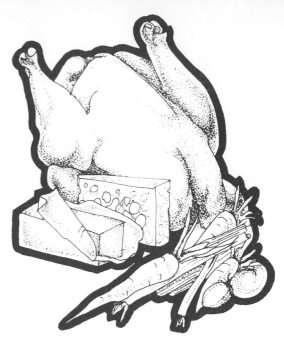

## BREAST OF CHICKEN CORDON BLEU

    Whole breast of a 4-pound chicken
2   thin slices cooked ham
2   slices Swiss cheese
    Salt, pepper and paprika
    Worcestershire sauce
1   egg, well beaten
1   cup fine bread crumbs
½   cup flour
½   cup salad oil
1   cup tomato sauce or
      basic white cream sauce

Split breast of chicken in half, bone completely, and flatten each half. On half of each chicken breast place slice of ham and Swiss cheese, sprinkle with paprika and season with salt, pepper and a few drops of Worcestershire sauce. Fold chicken pieces over, flour each side well and dip into beaten eggs and roll in fine bread crumbs. Preheat shortening in a heavy skillet over medium heat and sauté chicken until well browned on each side. Serve topped with hot tomato sauce or white sauce, which should be fairly thin. Makes 2 portions.

## TAK BOK KIM (KOREAN STYLE CHICKEN)

2   broiler chickens, disjointed
1   cup Japanese soya sauce
1   cup dry sherry
1   tablespoon garlic powder
1   teaspoon ginger powder
2   teaspoons monosodium glutamate
1   cup green onions, chopped
2   tablespoons sesame oil or
      crushed sesame seeds

Combine all ingredients and marinate chicken for at least 4 hours. Can be marinated for up to 48 hours. Broil skin side down, then turn. Cook until not quite done. Dip in sauce and return to broiler skin side up. Cook 5-6 inches below broiler until done. Chicken meat should be very moist with a nicely browned skin. Serves 4.

## CHICKEN MARENGO

**3½ pound chicken, cut in**
**serving pieces**
**Chicken fat or oil**
**Salt and garlic powder, to taste**
**¼ teaspoon each: thyme and pepper**
**6 medium green onions, sliced**
**¼ cup black olives, sliced**
**1½ cups chicken broth**
**¾ cup sauterne**
**3 tablespoons tomato paste**
**1 tablespoon flour**

Fry chicken pieces golden brown on both sides in fat or oil. Season with salt, pepper, thyme and garlic powder. Transfer to baking dish. Sprinkle with sliced onions and black olives. Add ½ cup of chicken broth. Bake, uncovered, at 325° for 30 minutes. Add ½ cup of wine combined with tomato paste, cover and bake for 20 minutes or longer. Uncover, bake 10 more minutes. Remove chicken pieces and add remaining wine and broth, with flour, to the sauce. Cook until thickened. Pour hot sauce over chicken and serve. Serves 4.


## CHICKEN PAPRIKASH

**4 2-pound oven-ready chickens**
**½ pound butter**
**¼ cup sliced carrots**
**¼ cup chopped celery**
**¼ cup chopped onions**
**1 cup flour**
**2 teaspoons paprika**
**1 quart chicken broth**
**½ pint sour cream**
**Salt, pepper and garlic to taste**
**Cooked noodles or steamed rice**

Cut the chickens in half and brown on both sides in skillet in a little butter. Drain. Place in baking pan and cover with following sauce:

**Sauce:**

In the same skillet, sauté carrots, celery and onions until tender. Melt the remaining butter and cook the flour and paprika until light brown; pour in chicken broth and vegetables and cook until smooth. Then mix in sour cream. Add salt, pepper and garlic. Pour the sauce over the chicken and bake in 325° oven for 45 minutes. The chicken is then served on cooked noodles or steamed rice. Serves 8.

## CHICKEN VERACRUZ

Bone ten 8-ounce chicken breasts. Pound with a wooden mallet until chicken is about ½ inch thick. Marinate for 24 hours in the following mixture: 1 quart oil; 1 cup sherry; 2 cloves garlic; 1 tablespoon black pepper; pinch of salt and a dash of paprika and oregano. Sauté marinated chicken in butter until brown on both sides. Bake uncovered in 350° oven for 10 minutes. Serve with broiled tomatoes, sliced avocado, rum-fried bananas, and Rice Ortega. Serves 10.

### Rice Ortega

Sauté ½ cup chopped onions until light brown in 3 tablespoons butter. Add 4 cups cooked rice; 1 small Jalapeño pepper, finely ground (or other small hot red or green pepper); 1¾ cups sour cream; ½ pound cottage cheese, ½ pound grated longhorn cheese; ½ bay leaf, crumbled; salt and pepper. Alternate layers of rice mixture and canned Ortega chili strips to form 4 layers in greased casserole. Bake at 375° for 25 minutes. Top with ½ cup additional grated cheese and bake for 10 minutes. Makes 10 portions.


## PHEASANT SOUVAROFF

**2 2-pound pheasants**
**Pork fat, sliced**
**Salt and pepper, to taste**
**8 ounces imported foie gras, diced**
**8 medium-size truffles**
**2 ounces Madeira**
**1 ounce cognac**
**1 cup brown chicken gravy**
**1 pound flour and 1½ cups water,**
**for dough**
**1 egg yolk**

Truss the birds and wrap them in slices of pork fat. Sprinkle with salt and pepper. Roast in 400° oven for 30 minutes. Unwrap birds and stuff them with foie gras. Remove birds to casserole adding truffles previously boiled in Madeira. Drain fat from the pan in which pheasants were roasted. Flambé the stock with cognac, add gravy and Madeira in which truffles were cooked. Pour the sauce over the birds in casserole. Place lid on casserole, seal edges with dough. Brush dough with egg yolk. Place in oven and heat for 15 minutes. Serves 4.

## CHICKEN CYNTHIA À LA CHAMPAGNE

- 2 2½-pound chickens
- 1 cup flour
- 1 teaspoon salt
- 1 tablespoon butter
- 1 tablespoon oil
- 1 ounce Curaçao (or other orange-flavored liqueur)
- 6 ounces dry champagne
- 1 cup consommé or bouillon
- 1 cup mushrooms, sliced and sautéed
- ½ cup whipping cream
  Orange wedges and seedless grapes, for garnish

Disjoint the chickens. Set wings and legs aside and bone remaining parts. Salt and flour chicken legs and wings and boned parts. Sauté in butter and oil, 10 minutes on each side. Remove from frying pan and continue browning in 350° oven for 20 minutes. Remove from oven and pour on Curaçao and champagne. Then cover with consommé and let chicken simmer on top of stove until tender, about 20 minutes. Add sautéed mushrooms and cream. Garnish with orange wedges and grapes. Serves 4.

## BEGGAR'S CHICKEN

Wash a 3-pound chicken. Mix: 2 teaspoons sesame oil, 1 teaspoon cornstarch, ¼ teaspoon anise seed, and ½

teaspoon salt. Rub this mixture over chicken, inside and out. Heat 1 tablespoon sesame oil in a skillet and sauté ⅓ cup dried mushrooms which have been soaked in water 2 hours, then sliced thin. Stir for 2 minutes before adding ½ cup boneless pork and ¼ cup bamboo shoots, both sliced thin. Blend in 1 tablespoon soy sauce and cook for 2 minutes. Stuff this mixture into chicken. Wrap bird in 2 layers of foil and 1 layer of butcher's paper. Encase wrapped chicken in wet clay about ¼ inch thick. (Ceramic clay may be found at most art supply shops.) Bake in preheated 400° oven for 50 minutes. Lower heat to 200° and bake another hour. To serve, crack clay with mallet and open paper. Serves 4.

## MOLE DE POLLO

Cook 2 stewing chickens and cut into pieces. Reserve broth. Blend in blender until smooth: ⅓ cup toasted almonds, 10-ounce can tomatillos (green tomatoes), 3 peeled tomatoes, ½ cup toasted pumpkin seeds, 2 ounces Mexican chocolate (or semi-sweet), and an 8½-ounce jar of Doña Maria Mole en Pasta Sauce. Add a little warm chicken broth.

Combine this mixture with about 2 quarts chicken broth and strain through a coarse sieve. Heat ½ cup of shortening, add strained sauce and simmer until it thickens.

Add salt to taste. Combine with chicken and heat thoroughly. Serves 10. (Check Mexican markets for special ingredients or write La Preferida, 11 Bronx Terminal Market, New York, New York 10451.)

## ROAST DUCKLING

Rub a 4½-lb. duckling inside and out with chef's salt — a mixture of 1 cup table salt, 1 tablespoon black pepper, 1 tablespoon Hungarian or Spanish paprika and 1 teaspoon garlic salt or ¼ teaspoon garlic powder. Put 3 generous tablespoons lard, duck fat or chicken fat in a roasting pan.

Place the duckling, breast side down, on the fat. Coarsely dice 1 carrot, 1 medium-sized onion and 2 stalks celery and add 1 or 2 cloves thinly sliced garlic. Sprinkle this mixture inside, on and around the duckling. Add 2 inches water to the pan, cover tightly and roast in preheated 300° to 325° oven for 2 hours. Cool completely, at room temperature.

Split the duckling lengthwise. Place the 2 halves, skin side up, on a slightly greased cookie sheet in a 425° to 450° oven for 18 to 22 minutes. Before serving remove first 2 joints of wing.

## BAKED CHICKEN OREGANATI

**4 chickens halved (2 to 2½ pounds each)**
**1 teaspoon oregano**
**⅓ pound melted butter**
  **Salt and pepper, to taste**
  **Juice of 2 lemons or ⅓ cup lemon juice concentrate**

Lay chicken halves on roasting pan and brush with melted butter. Bake at 400° for about 15 minutes or until brown. Blend the rest of the melted butter with lemon juice and oregano and heat slightly. Add salt and pepper to taste. Pour 1 cup water in the bottom of the baking pan to give proper steaming. Reduce heat to 300° and bake chicken for about 1 hour, basting with butter mixture at 20-minute intervals. Serves 8.

## CHICKEN BREASTS, EDEN ISLE

**6 chicken breasts, halved**
  **Pepper**
**12 bacon slices**
  **Package of dried beef**
**2 cans cream of chicken soup**
**1½ cups sour cream**
**3 ounces cream cheese**
**4 cups hot rice**

Pepper, but do *not* salt, chicken breasts. Wrap 1 slice of bacon around each half.

Place a layer of dried beef (not corned beef) in the bottom of baking dish. Arrange bacon-wrapped chicken on beef slices. Combine chicken soup, sour cream and cream cheese; pour over chicken. Cover pan tightly with foil.

Place in 325° oven for two hours. When meat is tender remove foil and let brown slightly. Serve on bed of hot rice. Serves 12.

## CHICKEN SAUTÉ

Use only the breasts and legs from two 3-pound chickens. Remove the bones. Dip chicken lightly in flour and place in frying pan with melted butter. Sauté chicken in covered pan until brown on all sides (about 20 minutes). Separately prepare ¼ pound wild rice according to directions on package.

In another frying pan place 2 tablespoons melted butter; 12 hearts of artichoke; 12 fresh mushrooms, sliced; 1 ounce sherry; 1 teaspoon lemon juice; 4 tablespoons Escoffier Sauce (or other good meat sauce) and salt and pepper to taste.

Cook mixture until artichoke hearts and mushrooms are done and ingredients well-blended (about 10 minutes). Place the hot wild rice in a serving dish, top with chicken pieces. Spoon artichoke-mushroom mixture over all. Serves 4.

## TURKEY MORNAY

- 7 tablespoons melted butter or margarine
- 7 tablespoons flour
- ½ pint scalded milk
- ½ pound mild Cheddar cheese, grated
- 12 thick, cooked turkey slices
- 6 pieces toast

Melt butter or margarine, blend in flour and cook for 2 minutes. Add scalded milk and grated cheese, beat until creamy and smooth. Place turkey on toast slices. Cover with cheese sauce and bake in 375° oven until golden brown. Serves 6.

## DOVE OR QUAIL WITH RICE DRESSING

Wash and dry 16 to 20 cleaned birds. Rub with salt and flour and sauté lightly in butter. Place in roasting pan. Then lightly sauté ¼ cup finely chopped onion, ½ cup finely chopped mushrooms and 1 tablespoonful chopped parsley. Combine with ½ cup of white wine and pour over birds. Cover pan and roast at 375° until tender. Serve with rice dressing. Serves 15.

Rice Dressing:

- 2 cups Uncle Ben's converted rice
- 3 large onions
- 4 stalks celery
- 1 green pepper
  Giblets of 4 birds
- ½ cup butter
- 1 tablespoon salt
- 1 tablespoon poultry seasoning
- 2 eggs
- 1 cup chopped pecans
- ½ cup chopped parsley
  Mushrooms (optional)

Cook rice as directed on package. Grind giblets. Chop onions, celery and pepper fine; then combine with ground giblets and sauté in butter until thoroughly cooked. Add seasonings.

Beat eggs until frothy. Combine onion mixture with rice, then fold in beaten eggs. Add chopped nuts and parsley, and mushrooms if desired. Bake in shallow greased casserole 25 minutes at 350°. (This is also good with chicken or turkey.)

## VERMONT CHRISTMAS GOOSE, COLONEL SCHIFFELER

- 1 oven-ready 8- to 12-pound goose
- 1 pound chopped onion
- 1 cup goose fat
- 6 apples, peeled and sliced
- 6 eggs
- 1 quart sauterne
- 1 tablespoon salt
- ⅛ teaspoon pepper
- ⅛ teaspoon thyme
- 2 pounds dry rolls, crumbled, or 1 loaf dry white bread

Soak the goose overnight in water with a little salt, drain. To prepare stuffing, sauté onions in goose fat; add apples. Remove from fire when apples are tender-crisp.

Beat eggs into sauterne, add salt, pepper and thyme, and pour over crumbled rolls. Let rolls absorb wine mixture, add cooked onions and apples, stuff goose and sew up cavity. Roast at 375° for 4½ to 5 hours, basting occasionally.

## ROAST DUCKLING DAVENPORT

Stuff a 5-pound duckling with fresh parsley and a slice of ginger root the size of a quarter. Truss it and season with salt and pepper. Place it on a rack, breast side up, in a roasting pan; add 1 cup water. Arrange aluminum foil loosely over the top and roast at 450° for 45 minutes.

Remove foil; pour off excess grease. Pour ½ cup sherry into the duck cavity and continue roasting at 325° for 30 minutes or until done. Remove from pan and remove parsley and ginger root from cavity. While duckling is still hot, cut into thin slices and serve with plum sauce (next page).

**Plum Sauce:**

Combine 1 cup granulated sugar, 1 cup white vinegar, 1 cup water and 4 tablespoons cornstarch; bring to a boil. Add 1 cup Chinese plum sauce and 1 piece ginger root the size of a quarter. Simmer 10 minutes.

# PUNCH

## MULLED CIDER

- 1 gallon apple juice or pasteurized cider
- 2 cups light brown sugar
- 5 sticks cinnamon
- 1 tablespoon whole cloves
- ½ tablespoon allspice

Heat combined ingredients. Do not let come to a boil. "Mull" for at least an hour. Serve hot with wedge of lemon. This drink with a small piece of butter and a jigger of rum makes a real New England hot buttered rum.

## EMERALD FROST

Heat ½ cup mint jelly and ½ cup water to make a syrup. Cool, then add 3 teaspoons lime juice. Fill 8 tall glasses with scoops of lemon sherbet; top each with 2 teaspoons of the mint syrup. Fill each glass with lemon-lime carbonated beverage and garnish with a slice of lime.

## SANGRIA WINE PUNCH

Make syrup by adding 1 cup sugar to 2 cups water. Heat, stirring until sugar is dissolved; bring to boiling point. While still hot, add 1 each of thinly sliced orange, lemon and lime. Marinate for at least 4 hours before using. Place about 12 ice cubes in a pitcher with 6 marinated fruit slices and ½ cup of syrup. Then add 1 bottle Chilean wine, red or white, and about 8 ounces of seltzer water. At serving time, place 2 slices of fruit in each glass and fill from pitcher.

## WASSAIL BOWL PUNCH

- 6 small apples, peeled and cored
- 1 tablespoon brown sugar
- 1 teaspoon nutmeg
- 1 gallon fresh apple cider (unpasteurized)
- 2 teaspoons cinnamon
- 1 cup white sugar
- 1 quart dry sherry
- 4 thin lemon slices

Slice apples, place in a shallow pan and sprinkle with brown sugar. Cover and bake about 20 minutes at 325°. Set aside. Bring cider to a boil and then add all remaining ingredients, stirring until sugar is dissolved.

# RICE & PASTA

## RICE MANGALAIS WITH CURRY SAUCE

1½ cups rice, uncooked
2 onions, chopped fine
1 clove garlic
2 teaspoons curry powder
¼ pound currants
¼ pound almonds, chopped
3½ cups chicken broth
   Salt and pepper to taste

Braise onions and add garlic and rice. Cook for 1 minute. Stir in curry powder, currants, almonds, and chicken broth. Add salt and pepper. Bake in moderate oven for 18 minutes. Serves 10.

Curry Sauce:

2½ tablespoons curry powder
3 onions, chopped
1 cup diced ham
2 apples, diced
2 tablespoons flour
1½ quarts chicken broth

Mix all ingredients together. Cook for ½ hour and serve with Rice Mangalais. Strain and season to taste.

## GREEN RICE

1½ cups rice, cooked
2 tablespoons finely chopped onion
¼ teaspoon minced garlic
3 tablespoons olive oil or butter
½ cup ground or finely chopped
   parsley

1 cup milk
1 teaspoon salt
1 teaspoon Worcestershire sauce
1 cup grated Cheddar cheese
2 eggs, slightly beaten

Sauté chopped onion and minced garlic in olive oil or butter. Measure cooked rice and ground parsley into a mixing bowl; then add milk, salt, Worcestershire sauce, Cheddar cheese, and slightly beaten eggs.

Add sautéed onion and garlic; mix thoroughly and pour mixture into buttered baking dish. Bake in a moderate oven (350°) for about 40 minutes. Serves 6.

## SPAGHETTI AND CRAB

½ cup chopped onions
1 teaspoon chopped celery
1 teaspoon chopped garlic
1 teaspoon chopped parsley
¼ cup olive oil
1 cup solid-pack tomatoes
1 cup tomato sauce
1½ cups water
1 teaspoon black pepper
2 teaspoons salt
½ teaspoon paprika
¼ cup sherry
   Grated cheese
1 pound fresh or canned crab meat
1 pound spaghetti

Braise onions, celery, garlic, and parsley in oil until golden brown. Add tomatoes, tomato sauce, water, and seasonings. Simmer for 1 hour. Add crab meat and wine and simmer a few minutes. Cook spaghetti. Drain but do not wash. Add to sauce. Mix well. Pour on platter and sprinkle with grated cheese.

## SPAGHETTI AND MEAT BALLS

**Sauce:**

Combine 1 No. 2-½ can tomatoes; 1 10-ounce can tomato puree; 1 can tomato paste; salt, to taste; 2 tablespoons parsley, dried; 2 tablespoons oregano; 1 tablespoon basil leaf; 3 bay leaves; 3-4 cloves garlic.

Bring to a boil. Simmer uncovered for 3-4 hours, adding water as sauce thickens. At least 2 hours before sauce is done, fry one small piece pork neck bone and add it with juice to sauce for flavor. Add meat balls and serve hot over spaghetti. Serves 4.

**Meat Balls:**

Combine 1 pound ground beef; 1 egg and ¾ cup of bread crumbs in a bowl. Moisten with water until meat will form balls easily. Add salt and pepper, to taste; 2 tablespoons parsley; 2 tablespoons oregano; 1 tablespoon basil leaf; 3-4 cloves garlic, minced, and 3-4 pieces orange peel, minced. Mix thoroughly. Fry in pork fat until browned and add to sauce ¾ of an hour before serving.

## SPAGHETTI WITH CLAM SAUCE

  2  **large cloves garlic, minced**
  ½  **cup olive oil**
  ¼  **cup parsley, chopped fine**
  ½  **teaspoon pepper**
  2  **cans minced clams and juice**
       **(7½-oz. size)**
  ½  **teaspoon salt**
  1  **pound fine spaghetti, cooked**

Brown garlic lightly in the olive oil over low heat. Add clam juice (but not clams)

and remaining ingredients except spaghetti, and cook over higher heat while stirring constantly. Add clams, bring to a boil. Serve over hot spaghetti. Serves 4.

## GNOCCHI

Boil 3 cups water with 1½ teaspoon salt and 2 tablespoons butter. Slowly add 1¾ cups French's instant potatoes until water is absorbed. Spread mixture on a large buttered baking sheet to cool. Beat 4 eggs lightly and stir into potatoes. Add 2¾ cups flour; knead until flour is absorbed.

Roll small chunks of dough quickly on well-floured board into finger-thick rolls and cut into 1-inch lengths. Drop a small quantity of gnocchi pieces into 1½ quarts salted boiling water for 10 minutes, stirring. When pieces come to the surface, remove them with a slotted spoon. Top with tomato sauce and Parmesan cheese. Serves 8.

# SALADS & DRESSINGS

## CORNED BEEF SUPPER SALAD

    3 cups ground corned beef
    1 package prepared aspic
    2 cups boiling water
    ½ teaspoon Worcestershire sauce
    4 hard-boiled eggs, chopped
      Shredded cabbage
      Marinated raw carrots
    6 tablespoons mayonnaise

Add boiling water to aspic; cool in refrigerator. Add corned beef, Worcestershire sauce and eggs; pour into ring mold and allow to set. Turn out on platter and fill center with shredded cabbage and raw carrots which have been marinated in French dressing. Garnish with unpeeled, scored cucumber slices. Serve with mayonnaise. Serves 6 to 8.

## FROZEN GINGER ALE SALAD

    1 tablespoon plain gelatin
    2 tablespoons cold water
    ¼ cup ginger ale, heated
    ¼ cup lemon juice
    1½ cups ginger ale, cold
    ¼ cup celery, chopped
    ½ cup seedless grapes
    ½ cup pineapple, crushed
    ½ cup preserved ginger, chopped
      Lettuce
      Cream mayonnaise (½ whipped
        cream and ½ mayonnaise)

Soak gelatin in cold water; add heated ginger ale and dissolve. Stir in lemon juice and cold ginger ale. Place mixture in refrigerator to set. When it begins to stiffen, add celery and fruit. Return to refrigerator to set. Serve on high beds of lettuce cut square. Garnish with cream mayonnaise.

## HOLIDAY SALAD

    1 cup sugar
    1 cup raw cranberries, ground
    1 package lemon gelatin
    ½ cup boiling water
    1 cup orange juice
    2 teaspoons grated orange rind
    9- ounce can crushed pineapple
    ½ cup pecan meats, broken
    1 cup chopped celery

Mix sugar and berries together, and let stand several hours. Add gelatin to boiling water, stirring until dissolved. Stir in orange juice and other ingredients. Pour into mold and set in refrigerator. Serve on crisp lettuce garnished with mayonnaise.

## TOSSED APPLE SALAD BOWL

    2 raw apples, unpeeled
    2 oranges
    ¼ cup peanuts, chopped
    2 teaspoons onion, minced
    2 cups raw green cabbage, finely
      shredded
    ¼ cup French dressing

Cut apples into small wedges and divide orange into sections. Place in salad bowl with peanuts, onion, and cabbage. Add dressing before serving and toss well. Serves 4.

## SPANISH SALAD DRESSING
  2 stalks celery
  ½ green pepper
  ½ medium onion
  2 cloves garlic
  ½ cup chili sauce
 2¼ cups catsup
  ¼ cup vinegar
    Juice of 1 lime
  ½ cup good oil
  ½ bay leaf
  2 cloves, ground
  2 celery leaves
  ½ teaspoon oregano
  2 level teaspoons salt
  2 tablespoons chopped parsley
    Sugar to taste

Put celery, green pepper, onion, and garlic through the fine knife of a food chopper. Add remaining ingredients. This recipe makes a quart and can be stored in the refrigerator. In fact the longer it stands, the more pungent and subtle the flavor.

## CORNHUSKER SALAD
Break crisp head lettuce into small pieces. Add sliced radishes, cucumber, a quartered tomato, julienne-cut green pepper, celery, carrots, green onions, and fresh watercress. Mix these ingredients with special olive oil dressing and top salad bowl with anchovy fillets, capers, and quartered hard-boiled egg. Serve with garlic bread.

**Special Olive Oil Dressing:**
  2 freshly peeled garlic cloves
  ½ teaspoon salt
  ¼ teaspoon dry English mustard
  ⅛ teaspoon white pepper
  ¼ cup wine vinegar
  ¼ cup tarragon vinegar

    Juice of 5 large lemons
  ¼ cup finely cut chives or onion tops
    Dash of sugar, Maggi seasoning and
      Worcestershire sauce
  1 quart pure olive oil

Crush garlic with salt. Mix with dry ingredients. Add vinegars, lemon juice, chives, sugar, Maggi seasoning, and Worcestershire sauce. Mix well. Add olive oil, stirring constantly. Makes a little over a quart of dressing.

## ROMAINE SALAD
3-4 heads romaine, cut and chilled
  2 handfuls crisp croutons
  6 tablespoons garlic oil
    Salt to taste
    Black pepper
  1 tablespoon Lea and Perrins sauce
  2 ounces olive oil
  6 ounces salad oil
  6 heaping tablespoons freshly grated
      Romanello cheese
  1 egg
    Juice of 3 lemons

Arrange the ingredients (all but egg and lemon juice) in salad bowl in order listed. Break egg over salad and pour lemon juice over egg. Toss salad from bottom. With salad serve garlic toast.

## WHITE SALAD
  4 egg yolks, beaten and slightly
      sweetened
  1 cup milk
  1 teaspoon gelatin
  1 pint cream, whipped
  1 No. 2½ can pineapple chunks
  1 No. 2½ can white cherries, seeded
      and halved
  ¾ pound marshmallows, cut
    Juice of 1 lemon
  ½ pound chopped blanched almonds

Mix beaten egg yolks with milk and scald in a double boiler. Soak gelatin in water to moisten and add to mixture. Fold in whipped cream and remaining ingredients. Let stand 24 hours in cool place. Garnish with lettuce. Serves 20.

## FRUIT SALAD DRESSING
2 cups pineapple juice
2 cups orange juice
1 cup lemon juice
2 cups sugar
6 egg yolks
2 heaping tablespoons cornstarch
1 tablespoon butter

Mix juices with sugar in top of double boiler. When hot, add egg yolks, slightly beaten and blended with cornstarch. Cook 15 to 20 minutes; stir in butter after removing from stove. Dressing may be served plain or folded into whipped cream for fruit salad topping.

## FROZEN FRUIT SALAD
4 ounces marshmallows, cut in pieces
1 cup fruit cocktail
12 apricot halves, cut in pieces
12 maraschino cherries, cut in pieces
3 slices pineapple, cut in pieces
½ cup boiled dressing
½ cup mayonnaise
½ cup whipping cream, whipped
  Dash of salt

Combine all ingredients and freeze. Cut in squares and serve on lettuce with salad dressing. Serves 12.

## OLD-FASHIONED COLESLAW
1 large cabbage
⅓ cup vinegar
½ teaspoon salt
½ teaspoon pepper
1 cup sour cream

Scoop out the center section of the cabbage, leaving only a shell. Shred the center section and soak in ice water for 30 minutes. Drain and dry thoroughly. Add vinegar and seasoning. Toss, and let marinate for an hour. Drain again, squeezing cabbage slightly to remove any excess liquid. Pour sour cream over cabbage and toss lightly. Place slaw in chilled shell of cabbage and serve salad. Makes 12 portions.

## FRENCH HERB SALAD DRESSING
⅛ teaspoon dry mustard
1 teaspoon sweet paprika
1 teaspoon dill
1 teaspoon tarragon
1 teaspoon fennel
1 teaspoon anise
2 tablespoons sugar
2 teaspoons salt
¼ teaspoon pepper
⅔ cup tarragon malt vinegar
1 pint olive oil
2 tablespoons Worcestershire sauce
  Dash of Tabasco sauce
  Juice of 1 lemon
1 clove garlic or 1 onion, whole

Mix herbs, sugar, salt and pepper well with vinegar. Then add olive oil and beat thoroughly. Add remaining ingredients. Keep cool but not too cold. Shake before serving.

## TROPICAL SALAD AND DRESSING
4 cups palm or lettuce hearts
1 cup pineapple, cubed
¼ cup dates, chopped
¼ cup candied or preserved ginger, chopped

**Dressing:**

- 4 tablespoons vanilla ice cream
- 2 tablespoons each, mayonnaise and crunchy peanut butter
  Pineapple juice or preserved ginger juice

Mix ice cream, mayonnaise and peanut butter thoroughly. Thin with either pineapple or ginger juice, pour over salad, toss and serve.

## SPECIAL SALAD CUP

- 1 cup orange sections
- 1 cup grapefruit sections
- ½ cup papaya or Honey Rock melon, diced
- 1 cup pineapple, diced
- 1 cup bananas, sliced
- ½ cup walnuts, broken
  Lettuce
- 1 small package cream cheese
- 1 tablespoon honey
- 1 tablespoon lemon juice
- 1 tablespoon orange juice
- ½ cup whipping cream
  Maraschino cherries

Fruits should be thoroughly chilled and drained. Combine them (all but the cherries) with nutmeats. Arrange lettuce cups in salad bowls and fill with fruit. Mash cream cheese, add honey, lemon juice and orange juice. Whip cream lightly and add to cheese mixture. Pour over fruit; top with cherries. Serves 6.

## COLESLAW

- 2 pounds cabbage
- 2 bell peppers
- 2 onions
- 2 carrots
- 1 tablespoon salt
- 3 tablespoons sugar
- 1 cup vinegar

Finely grate cabbage, peppers, onions, and carrots. Add salt, sugar, and vinegar. Mix several ice cubes in with slaw to chill it. Serves 6.

## CELERY SEED DRESSING

Mix together ½ cup sugar, 1 teaspoon dry mustard, 1 teaspoon salt, and ¼ grated onion. Then take ⅓ cup vinegar and 1 cup salad oil. Add a little bit of vinegar to mixture and blend thoroughly. Add vinegar and oil alternately and beat well. Add 1 tablespoon celery seed. Cover and store in refrigerator. Excellent on fruit salad.

## MOLDED CRANBERRY SALAD

- ½ cup strawberry gelatin
- 1 cup boiling water
- 1 cup cranberry sauce, strained
- ½ cup apples, chopped
- ½ cup celery, chopped
- ¼ cup nuts, chopped

Dissolve gelatin in boiling water. Add cranberry sauce and whip to dissolve. Cool, add apples, celery and nuts. Chill. Serve in squares on lettuce with sal d dressing.

## CHOP SUEY SALAD

- 2 cups cooked meat, cubed
- 2 cups cooked red kidney beans
- ¼ cup diced red pimento
- 1 cup diced celery
- ½ cup diced onions
- 2 cups bean sprouts (marinated in French dressing)
  Chop suey sauce, to taste
  Salt and pepper, to taste
- ½ cup mayonnaise

Add ingredients in order given and mix thoroughly in the salad bowl. Makes a tasty luncheon meal by itself or may be served as the dinner salad course. Try it when you have some left-over meat.

## HERRING SALAD

  3 cups pickled herring, diced
1½ cups boiled potatoes, diced
1½ cups pickled beets, diced
  ½ cup apples, diced
  ¼ cup onion, chopped
  ⅓ cup pickled gherkins, diced
  4 tablespoons vinegar
  2 tablespoons water
  2 tablespoons sugar
    White pepper, to taste
  1 pint sour cream, beaten stiff

Thoroughly mix herring, potatoes, beets, apples, onion and gherkins. Blend vinegar, water, sugar and pepper before adding to herring mixture; toss gently. When ready to serve, pour sour cream over top and garnish with hard-boiled eggs and parsley.

## FAMOUS GREEK SALAD

Decorate salad platter with lettuce leaves from a crisp head of lettuce. Place a cup of potato salad in the center and top with chopped lettuce and sprigs of roka (Florida watercress). Quarter 1 tomato and stand up around potato salad. Slice cucumber lengthwise and place on end between tomato sections. Fill spaces in between with 4 slices avocado. Lean 2 green onions upright against this circle. Place a slice of Greek feta cheese on top of salad and then 2 rings of green pepper and 2 beet slices. Place 4 Greek black olives and 6 Greek pickled peppers all around salad. A half pound of peeled and boiled shrimp and 2 anchovies top the completed salad. Sprinkle ⅓ cup vinegar over salad and follow wth ⅓ cup olive oil. Sprinkle with ½ teaspoon oregano. Serves 2.

## JADE MOLDED SALAD

  1 package lime gelatin
  1 cup cucumber, grated
  ¼ cup onion, grated
  1 cup cottage cheese
  1 cup mayonnaise
  1 cup whipping cream, whipped

Dissolve gelatin in 1 cup boiling water and cool it until it begins to set. Fold remaining ingredients into gelatin and pour into ring mold. Serves 6.

## HOT BEET SALAD

10 medium beets, cooked and diced
  1 medium onion, grated
  3 tablespoons sugar
  1 orange, juice and grated rind
  1 tablespoon vinegar
  1 tablespoon butter
    Salt, to taste

Mix ingredients in saucepan. Cover and place over low heat. Allow to simmer 15 minutes (may need additional vinegar). Serves 4-6.

## KOLB'S SPECIAL SALAD

  1 head lettuce
  2 heads chicory
  1 head escarole
  1 bunch watercress
  3 fresh tomatoes, quartered
  1 cup peas, cooked
  1 cup cooked carrots, diced
  2 cups white crabmeat
  2 cups shrimp, cooked and cleaned
  6 strips anchovy
  3 hard-boiled eggs

Wash and separate leafy vegetables. Put all ingredients except anchovy and egg into a mixing bowl and toss until well mixed. Distribute into 6 small salad

bowls, placing 2 quarters of egg and one strip of anchovy on each salad. Top with French dressing. Serves 6.

**French Dressing:**

Mix 2 cups oil; 1 cup vinegar; 1 teaspoon onion, grated; 1 teaspoon salt and 1 clove garlic minced in a mixing bowl. While mixing gradually add mustard and paprika. When thoroughly mixed, pour over salad.

## TOSSED GREEN GORGONZOLA SALAD

 1 **average head crisp lettuce, chopped**
 1 **green pepper, chopped**
 1 **tomato, peeled and chopped**
 2 **tablespoons celery, chopped**
 1 **small onion, chopped**
   **Freshly ground pepper, to taste**
 4 **tablespoons cider vinegar**
 4 **tablespoons salad oil**
   **Grated Gorgonzola cheese**

Rub wooden salad bowl with strong garlic. Add lettuce, green pepper, tomato, celery, onion and pepper. Mix vinegar and oil well, then sprinkle on salad. Completely cover top of salad with grated Gorgonzola. Toss gently with two forks and serve at table from bowl. Serves 4.

## THANKSGIVING SALAD MOLD

 2 **cups juice of any fruit except lemon or grapefruit**
 1 **package lemon gelatin**
 1 **cup whole cranberry sauce**
 1 **cup fresh apple, diced**
 1 **cup celery, diced**
 ½ **cup pecans, chopped**
 ½ **cup Tokay grapes, halved**
   **Tiny marshmallows (optional)**

Heat fruit juice over low fire and add gelatin, stir until it dissolves. Add remaining ingredients and pour into 12 individual molds. Refrigerate.

## FROZEN FRUIT SALAD

Dissolve 1 package lime gelatin in 2 cups

boiling water. Cut 2 packages cream cheese into small pieces and blend into gelatin. Let cool, then add 1 medium can or 1½ cups fruit cocktail or equal amount of fresh fruit. Cut 12 marshmallows and ½ cup pecans and fold into mixture. Whip ½ pint whipping cream and fold in. Pour in pan. Place in freezer 3-4 hours. Serves 12-15.

## LETTUCE AND BOILED EGG SALAD

Combine the following ingredients in a salad bowl: ½ head of firm lettuce, broken in pieces; 2 medium onions, sliced in rings; and 6 hard-boiled eggs, sliced. Mix together and pour over salad a dressing made of: ½ cup mayonnaise; 1 tablespoon prepared mustard; 2 tablespoons vinegar; ½ teaspoon pepper; and 1 teaspoon salt. Toss and serve to 6.

## HOSTESS SALAD DRESSING

Combine: 1 tablespoon green onions, chopped; 1 cup mayonnaise; ¼ teaspoon garlic, chopped; 1 teaspoon parsley, chopped; 1 pint yogurt or sour cream; ½ pound blue cheese, crumbled; 1 teaspoon anchovy paste; 3 drops Tabasco sauce; ⅛ teaspoon red pepper; 3 tablespoons lemon juice. Stir well. Store in refrigerator.

## FRANKENMUTH BEAN SALAD

 1 **pound small navy beans**
 1¼ **cups celery, diced**
 ½ **cup onions, chopped**
 ½ **cup green pepper, chopped**
 ½ **cup French dressing**
 ½ **cup vinegar**
 ½ **cup sugar**
 1 **teaspoon dry mustard**
 ½ **teaspoon garlic salt**
 ¼ **teaspoon paprika**
 ¾ **teaspoon monosodium glutamate**
 ½ **teaspoon salt**
   **Several pimentos, sliced**

Soak beans overnight. Cover beans with water and simmer on top of stove until tender. Drain well and cool. Then add remaining ingredients. Let stand about 4 hours in refrigerator before serving. Serves 10-12.

## CHICK-PEA SALAD

  1 quart chick peas, cooked
  1 cup vinegar
  ½ cup oil
  1 medium onion, chopped
  ½ cup celery, chopped
  ¼ cup pimento, chopped
  ¼ cup green pepper, chopped
  ½ teaspoon oregano
  ½ teaspoon salt
  ¼ teaspoon pepper
  ¼ teaspoon ground garlic

Drain chick peas and combine remaining ingredients into a well-mixed dressing. Add to chick peas and keep refrigerated until serving. May be served as a relish for buffet service. Serves 20.

## HOT GERMAN POTATO SALAD

  4 pounds potatoes
  3 medium onions, coarsely chopped
  ¾ cup sugar
    Salt and black pepper, to taste
  ½ pound bacon, diced
  ¾ cup very hot water
  ¾ cup cider vinegar
    Hard-boiled eggs and greens for garnish

Boil potatoes until tender; pare and slice while still warm. Heap chopped onion in center of potatoes. Top with sugar, salt and pepper. Fry diced bacon until crisp. Skim bacon from frying pan and set aside. Add water and vinegar to bacon grease and bring to a boil. Pour over potatoes and onions and toss lightly to mix well. Add bacon and garnish with hard-boiled eggs and greens. Serves 8-10.

## LETTUCE AND SPINACH WITH SWEET-SOUR BACON DRESSING

  6-8 slices bacon
  1 head lettuce
    Crisp spinach, to blend
  3 teaspoons sugar
  ½ teaspoon salt
    Dash of pepper
  ½ cup cider vinegar
  ½ cup sliced scallions (optional)

Cut bacon into small pieces, sauté until crisp, drain on paper towel, saving fat. In a large salad bowl break lettuce into bite-size pieces. Add enough spinach to blend, and scallions if desired. Add bacon bits. Toss.

Add sugar, salt, pepper and vinegar to 2 tablespoons of the bacon fat and bring to a boil. Pour over greens and toss until each leaf is coated. Serve at once. Serves 6 to 8.

## BACON BEAN SALAD

  ⅔ cup cider vinegar
  ¾ cup sugar
  1 teaspoon salt
  1- pound can cut green beans
  1- pound can cut wax beans
  1- pound can kidney beans, rinsed and drained
  1 pound can lima beans
  1 medium-sized onion, quartered and sliced fine
  1 medium-sized green pepper, chopped
  ½ teaspoon freshly ground pepper
  ⅓ cup salad oil
  1 pound unsliced bacon, cut in 1-inch cubes
    Lettuce

Blend vinegar, sugar and salt in a small saucepan. Heat until the sugar is dissolved and set aside. Drain all beans and toss with onion, green pepper, vinegar mixture and pepper. Pour oil over all and toss to coat evenly. Store in a large covered container in refrigerator for at least 8 hours. When ready to serve, fry bacon until crisp, and dry it on absorbent paper. Toss the bacon with the bean mixture. Place portions in lettuce cups. Serves 12.

## SALAD CURRIED RICE WINSTON

- 3 cups raw rice
- 1 tablespoon lemon juice
- 1 pound raw zucchini, sliced
- 1 teaspoon Ac'cent (MSG)
- 1 pound bean sprouts
- 1 teaspoon salt
- 1 dash yellow color
- 1 heaping tablespoon curry
- 1½ cups mayonnaise
- 4- ounce can water chestnuts, sliced

Stir rice into 6½ cups boiling water. Add salt, lemon juice and yellow color. Bring to a rolling boil, reduce fire as low as possible, cover and cook 25 minutes. Remove from fire and allow to reach room temperature. Combine with remaining ingredients.

## FRENCH DRESSED CANTALOUPE

This is a specialty of Engine Company No. 10, San Francisco. Cut 2 medium-sized cantaloupes in half crosswise and remove seeds. With a melon cutter, scoop melon balls into a bowl. Smooth inside of shells, chill.

Cut 2 medium-sized tomatoes into thin wedges; dice half a green pepper, cut 3 green onions, including part of green tops, into thin slices; then combine these 3 ingredients with melon balls and pour ½ cup oil and vinegar French dressing over them. Cover and chill for 4 hours. Heap marinated mixture into chilled cantaloupe shells. Serves 4 as a salad or appetizer.

# SANDWICHES

## COACH HOUSE HOT BROWN

For each portion remove crust from a well-toasted slice of white bread, cut bread diagonally, and place halves on oven-proof plate. Cover toast with either chicken or turkey sliced very thin. Cover this with your favorite medium cream sauce, sprinkle with sliced fresh mushrooms and Parmesan cheese and a dash of paprika. Edge the cream sauce with 4 cubes of fresh tomato. Place under broiler until cream sauce starts to bubble. Then remove and cross plate with partly cooked bacon. Return to the broiler until plate is very hot. Garnish with a sprig of parsley. This is a wonderful way to make a party dish of leftover holiday fowl.

## SOUFFLÉ SANDWICHES

Cut crusts from 12 bread slices and butter each on 1 side. Place 6 slices, buttered side down, in a greased flat pan. Put a slice of ham or cheese (or both) on each and cover with another slice, buttered side up.

Beat 4 eggs slightly, add 2 cups milk, 1 teaspoon salt and 1 teaspoon paprika. Blend well. Pour over sandwiches and refrigerate for several hours, or overnight. Bake at 350° for 45 minutes. Serve hot with asparagus or mushroom sauce.

**Sauce:**

Melt 2 tablespoons butter and blend with 2 tablespoons flour. Gradually stir in 1½ cups milk. Cook, stirring constantly until smooth and thick. Season with 1 teaspoon salt and ¼ teaspoon pepper. Add either ½ pound sliced mushrooms sautéed in 3 tablespoon butter, or a 9-ounce package of frozen asparagus, cooked and drained. Serve hot over sandwiches.

# SAUCES

## CUMBERLAND SAUCE
    3 tablespoons red currant jelly
    2 tablespoons strained
        orange juice
    1 tablespoon strained
        lemon juice
    1 teaspoon mustard
    1 teaspoon pepper
    ½ teaspoon ground ginger
        Peel of one orange

Stir jelly in saucepan over low flame until liquid. Cool, then add orange juice, lemon juice, mustard, pepper and ginger. Peel orange so that white pulp is removed from skin; shred and cover with cold water and bring to a boil. Drain off water and add shredded orange peel to the mixture. This delicious sauce is often served with hot or cold slices of Virginia Smithfield ham.

## RAW CRANBERRY SAUCE
    1 quart cranberries
    2 Delicious apples
    ½ orange peel
    2 large oranges
    2 cups sugar

Put cranberries, apples and orange peel through food chopper. Cut oranges in small sections with scissors and add sugar. Stir mixture well and set in refrigerator. It will keep for several days. Serve as a sauce or, congealed, as a salad with 2 cups of pecans added; or as a dessert in little parfait glasses. Halve this recipe for a small family.

## TARTAR SAUCE
    1 tablespoon sour pickles
    1 tablespoon dill pickles

1 tablespoon parsley
1 tablespoon green olives
1 tablespoon chives
½ cup mayonnaise

Chop pickles, parsley, olives and chives into fine pieces. Drain or even wring these ingredients in a clean cloth to prevent mixture from curdling due to excess vinegar. Combine with mayonnaise, preferably homemade with an olive-oil base. Serve with your favorite fish.

## PINK SAUCE FOR CRAB
1 cup mayonnaise
1 cup chili sauce
1 teaspoon Worcestershire sauce
2 teaspoons horseradish
4 sweet pickles, chopped fine
2 stalks celery
4 green onions
4 sprigs parsley
1 tablespoon sugar

Mix all ingredients together and serve over crab.

## HARD SAUCE
¼ pound butter
1 pound confectioners' sugar
2 eggs
Vanilla or liquor

Cream butter and sugar. Then blend in eggs. Add enough vanilla or liquor to bring to desired consistency and flavor.

## FOAMY SAUCE
¼ pound butter
½ pound confectioners' sugar
1 egg, well beaten
¼ cup hot water
1 teaspoon flavoring

Cream butter and sugar; then slowly add egg and hot water. Flavor. Heat over hot water until thick. Serve hot over plum pudding or fruit cake slices.

## REMOULADE SAUCE
2 eggs
4 tablespoons paprika

2 teaspoons salt
½ cup Creole mustard
1½ pints vegetable oil
½ cup vinegar
1 lemon
½ cup each, shallots and celery
3 cloves garlic, crushed
2 stalks parsley
¼ cup tomato catsup
3 bay leaves
2 tablespoons horseradish
Tabasco sauce, to taste

Put eggs, paprika, salt and Creole mustard into a mixing bowl. Add oil slowly; after mixture is thick, add vinegar. Grate lemon rind into mixture, then quarter lemon and squeeze in juice. Finely chop celery, garlic, parsley and shallots, add to mixture. Blend in catsup, bay leaves, horseradish and Tabasco. Chill for 6 hours. Serve with cold fish or meat. Makes 1½ quarts.

## ANCIENT BARBECUE SAUCE
1 pound tallow or suet
1 tablespoon sage
1 tablespoon thyme
1 tablespoon rosemary
1 pint olive oil
2 pints catsup
8 cloves garlic, crushed
1 pint steak sauce

Cook tallow for 20 minutes before adding spices and remaining ingredients. A really old recipe handed down for many generations, this sauce is excellent with spareribs, lamb, or beef.

# SEAFOOD

## SPAGHETTI SICILIENNE WITH CLAMS

    2  pounds spaghetti
   60  cherrystone clams and liquid
    2  large onions, sliced
   12  filets of anchovies
   10  fresh tomatoes, chopped
    4  green peppers, chopped
    1  clove garlic
    8  ounces tomato puree
       Salt and pepper to taste

Sauté onions in oil until slightly brown; then add clams and anchovies and cook together 5 minutes. Mix in tomatoes and green pepper, together with garlic and tomato puree; continue to cook for 20 minutes. Season to taste. Serve over spaghetti. Cook spaghetti separately (2 pounds for 10 servings).

## TERRAPIN À LA COLLIGAN

    1  quart terrapin meat
    1  tablespoon dry mustard
   ½  pound butter
    1  quart milk
       Salt and pepper to taste
       Pinch of cayenne pepper
    1  jigger sherry

Heat terrapin and mustard in pan with a little butter; add milk and let come to a boil. Stir in remaining butter with salt and pepper. Add sherry at the last; then remove mixture immediately from heat and serve.

## LOBSTER THERMIDOR

   1¼  pounds hot boiled lobster
    6  medium mushrooms, cooked
    1  teaspoon chopped parsley
   ½  teaspoon paprika
   ¼  teaspoon dry mustard
   ⅛  teaspoon salt
       Few grains pepper
   ½  teaspoon butter
       Juice of ⅛ lemon
    1  tablespoon sherry
   ½  cup cream sauce
    1  tablespoon Parmesan cheese

Remove lobster meat from claws and body of lobster. Save shell to refill. Leave small claws on—they will help shell to stand upright. Cube meat and combine with mushrooms, chopped parsley, paprika, dry mustard, salt, pepper, butter, and lemon juice, and sauté in melted butter. Remove from fire; add sherry and cream sauce (combine 1 cup cream, ¾ ounce flour, ¾ ounce butter). Refill lobster shell with mixture. Sprinkle with cheese and bake in moderate oven. Serves 1.

## BAKED INDIVIDUAL LOBSTER PIE

    1  cup buttered and seasoned
          bread crumbs
   1¼  pound lobster, boiled and shelled
   ¼  cup lobster stock
   ¼  cup milk
   ¼  cup drawn butter

Cover bottom of individual casserole with the bread crumbs. Dice lobster meat into large pieces and put in casserole on top of crumbs. Cover with lobster stock and milk. Make a topping of the bread crumbs and bake until heated through and crumbs are a golden brown (15 minutes in a hot oven). Moisten completely with drawn butter after baking. Garnish with small lobster claws; place wedge of lemon on lettuce leaf.

## BOUILLABAISSE À LA MARSEILLAISE

- ¼ **pound chopped onions**
- 2 **leeks (white part only), diced**
- 3 **ripe tomatoes, peeled**
- 1 **clove garlic, crushed**
- 1 **teaspoon chopped parsley**
- 1 **pinch saffron**
- ½ **cup olive oil**
- 1 **bay leaf**
- 1 **pound wall-eyed pike, boned and cut in squares**
- 1 **pound sole, boned and cut in squares**
- 1 **pound haddock, boned and cut in squares**
- 2 **dozen oysters**
- ½ **pound shrimps**
  **Salt and pepper**

Place this mixture in a frying pan and fry for about 5 minutes, then add: 1 live lobster, cut in chunks.

Cover ingredients with water. Cook 20 minutes. Serve hot in casserole surrounded with dried French toast. Serves 10.

## FROGS' LEGS SAUTÉ PROVENÇALE

Pare legs and soak in cold running water until the are rosy white. Dip in mixture of eggs and milk before rolling in seasoned flour. Fry in very hot clarified butter or good oil. Cook fast enough so they turn golden as they cook. Dry on a clean towel and arrange on a hot plate, and sprinkle with chopped parsley and lemon juice. Brown 2 tablespoons of butter, then add a little chopped garlic, shaking pan to brown garlic on all sides. When lightly colored, pour over legs and serve.

## SEA FOOD À LA LOFFLER

- 1 **pound filet of fish**
- 4 **lobster tails**
- ½ **pint scallops**
- ½ **pint shrimp**

Cut fish in strips 1½ inches wide. Split lobster tails. Steam scallops, shrimp, lobster tails (with shell), and fish until tender. Shell and de-vein shrimp. Remove meat from lobster tails. Combine ingredients, divide into four portions and place in individual casseroles. Pour sauce over them and broil in oven under medium heat until golden brown. Serve immediately.

**Sauce:**

Melt ¼ pound butter in pan and add ⅓ cup flour. Slowly stir in 2½ cups milk and season with salt, pepper, ¼ pound grated cheese, and 1 teaspoon sherry. This sauce also blends well with other dishes.

## FISH LOAF

- 2 **cups flaked cooked fish**
- 1½ **cups bread crumbs**
- ½ **teaspoon baking powder**
- ⅔ **cup chopped celery**
- ⅓ **cup chopped onion**
- 1 **tablespoon lemon juice**
- 1 **cup milk**
- 1 **tablespoon minced pimento**
- 1 **tablespoon chopped green pepper**
  **Salt and pepper**

Mix ingredients and form loaf in an oiled loaf pan. Bake in moderate oven (350°) until brown and firm. Serve with desired cream sauce. This is a recipe guaranteed to make your family fish eaters!

## SALMON STEAK, CALCUTTA STYLE

    Boneless salmon in slices about
        1½ inches thick
    Salt and pepper
½ cup sherry
½ cup fish stock
    Pepper oil

Put salmon slices in flat oiled pan. Season with salt and pepper. Add sherry and stock. Cover with pepper oil and cook in oven 20 minutes. Then put fish on platter and keep hot. Cover with sauce.

Sauce:
1 shallot, chopped
1 teaspoon flour
1 teaspoon curry powder
    Broth from fish cooked above
1 pint fish stock
2 egg yolks
½ cup cream

Sauté shallot with flour and curry powder. Heat through. Add broth and fish stock. Boil 2 minutes. Blend with beaten egg yolks and cream. Strain and pour over fish.

## ROLLED SMELTS

2 pounds smelts, boned and cleaned
3 cups water
1 cup vinegar
½ cup sugar
2 bay leaves
10 whole allspice

Roll smelts up lengthwise and secure with toothpicks. Mix other ingredients and bring to boil. Put in the smelts and boil 2 minutes. Cool smelts in brine before serving.

## NEW ENGLAND FISH BALLS

2 cups codfish, cooked and shredded
4 medium potatoes
3 eggs
    Deep fat, for frying

Rinse fish with hot water, then press water out. Boil potatoes and put them through a ricer. (Potatoes must be freshly boiled and still hot when combined with fish.) Then mix fish and potatoes and break eggs into mixture, stirring as little as possible. Drop mixture from a spoon and fry in deep fat at 350° until brown. Serve with New England baked beans. Makes enough fish balls to serve 4.

## BAKED OYSTERS ON HALF SHELL

32 fresh oysters on the half shell
¼ pound each, butter, lard
1 or 2 cloves garlic, finely chopped
2 tablespoons parsley, chopped
1 tablespoon Worcestershire sauce
½ teaspoon each, salt and paprika
1 ounce anisette
1 ounce gin
¼ pound cracker meal
    Dash of Tabasco (optional)

Cream butter and lard; add remaining ingredients (except oysters) and mix well. Drop teaspoon of dressing on each oyster. Bake at 400° until dressing turns golden brown (8 or 10 minutes). Garnish with lemon wedges. Serves 4.

## OYSTER STEW

1 quart oysters
1 quart hot milk
¼ pound butter
⅓ teaspoon salt
⅛ teaspoon celery salt
⅛ teaspoon pepper
⅛ teaspoon mace
1 tablespoon parsley, chopped
1 tablespoon onion juice (optional)

Place oysters in strainer and wash with 1 pint water. Keep liquid. Remove all shell pieces, heat liquid and strain through cheesecloth. Cook oysters in this strained liquid until they are plump and the edges curl. Scald milk and add butter and seasonings. Keep oysters and milk hot in separate containers. When serving, place about 7 oysters in each bowl and cover with the seasoned milk.

## SEAFOOD EN SOPÉE

½ pound filet of sole
½ pound lobster meat
½ pound shrimp
½ pound scallops
3 tablespoons butter
1 pint milk
½ cup flour
  Light cream
½ teaspoon salt
3 tablespoons white wine
  Toast points

Cut sole and lobster into 1-inch squares. Cut shrimp in half. If sea scallops are used cut into quarters; use bay scallops whole. Place seafood in skillet with 2 tablespoons melted butter. Sauté slowly for 10 minutes, then let simmer. Warm milk in double boiler. Thicken with flour and light cream. Add 1 tablespoon butter, the salt and white wine. Take sauce off fire when creamy. Put seafood on toast points and top with cream sauce. Serves 4 to 6.

## OYSTER PAN ROAST (one serving)

8 freshly opened oysters
1 pat of butter
1 tablespoon chili sauce
1 teaspoon Worcestershire sauce
  Few drops of lemon juice
¼ cup of oyster liquor
  Celery salt, to taste
  Paprika
4 ounces cream
1 piece dry toast

Place oysters, butter, chili sauce, Worcestershire sauce, lemon juice, oyster liquor and seasoning in a deep pan. Cook for about 1 minute, stirring continuously. Add cream and when mixture comes to a boiling point pour over toast, placed in a soup plate. Serve immediately.

## BOUILLABAISSE

1 medium carrot, sliced
2 medium onions, sliced
1 clove garlic

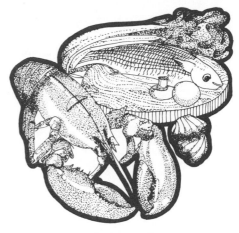

4 tablespoons olive oil
3 pounds fish in season (cod, haddock), precooked if fish has many bones
1 cup tomatoes
1 bay leaf
2 cups fish stock or water
1 dozen oysters, clams or scallops
1 cup shrimp or crab
2 teaspoons salt
½ teaspoon pepper
2 tablespoons lemon juice
¼ cup sherry wine (optional)

Brown carrot, onions and garlic together in hot oil; remove garlic. Add fish, tomatoes, bay leaf and stock. Simmer 15 minutes. Remove bay leaf; add remaining ingredients, except sherry. Continue cooking 5 minutes. Add sherry; serve immediately. Serves 6 to 8.

## BROILED SHAD AND ROE

1 boned shad (3 pounds before boning and cleaning)
1 shad roe
½ pound small mushrooms, sliced
  Salt and pepper
¼ cup butter, melted
1 tablespoon lemon juice
1 to 2 tablespoons white wine
  Parsley, chopped

Preheat broiler 10 minutes. Remove head and tail from shad and cut into 4 or 6 serving pieces. Arrange with skin sides down on lightly greased broiler pan or broiler, with roe and mushrooms around fish. Sprinkle with salt and pepper and brush with half of combined butter and lemon juice. Broil with top of fish two inches below heat for 8 to 10 minutes, basting occasionally. After 4 minutes turn roe and mushrooms and brush with remaining butter mixture. Drizzle on wine, sprinkle with parsley. Serves 4 to 6.

## IMPERIAL CRAB

- 1 pound crab meat
- 2 tablespoons green pepper, chopped
- 1 tablespoon pimento, chopped
- 1 tablespoon onion, chopped
- 1 tablespoon celery, chopped
- 1 egg, beaten
- 2 tablespoons white sauce or mayonnaise
- 1 to 2 teaspoons dry mustard
- 1 teaspoon capers
  Crab shells

Combine green pepper, pimento, onion, celery and sauté slightly. Blend together egg, white sauce, mustard, capers and crab meat. Then stir in sautéed vegetables. Place portions of crab meat mixture on crab shells and bake about 15 to 18 minutes in 350° oven. Serves 4.

## LOBSTER AU GRATIN

- 3 live lobsters, 2 pounds apiece
- 4 celery stalks
- 3 slices lemon
- 3 peppercorns
  Salt and pepper, to taste
- ½ pound butter
- ½ pound cooked mushrooms
- 4 ounces sherry wine
- 4 cups milk
- ½ cup flour
- 1 tablespoon lemon juice

Put live lobsters into boiling water, flavored with celery, lemon, peppercorns, salt and pepper. Boil for 20 to 25 minutes, then cool lobsters, remove and dice meat. Heat ¼ pound butter in

pan and sauté lobster meat and mushrooms. Add wine and simmer for 5 minutes. Make a cream sauce of milk, flour, lemon juice, and ¼ pound butter and add to lobster mixture. Divide into 6 individual dishes and top with mixture of 2 egg yolks and 4 tablespoons whipped cream. Brown under broiler.

## FILET OF SOLE MILTON INN

Take enough filet of sole for 4 generous servings (more if desired) and cover with water in a shallow pan. Then add 2 pieces thyme, a sliced lemon, sliced raw carrot, a dash of pepper, ½ tablespoon salt and 2 tablespoons white wine. Boil the sole gently for about 15 minutes and serve with sauce.

**Sauce:**

Heat to boiling point 1 cup cream, 2 finely chopped hard-boiled eggs, ¼ teaspoon pepper and 4 teaspoons fish broth. Then add 1 well-beaten egg yolk and ½ teaspoon chopped parsley. Stir. Pour sauce over fish while hot.

## BAKED FILET OF SOLE BONNE FEMME

- 2 pounds filet of sole or flounder
- 1 cup water
- 2 tablespoons sauterne
- 1 teaspoon salt
- 1 bay leaf
- 2 ounces butter
- 1 small onion, chopped fine

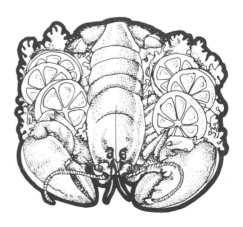

¼ **pound mushrooms, sliced thin**
½ **teaspoon pepper**
1 **cup cream sauce**
1 **tablespoon chopped parsley**

Place filet of sole in pan, add water, 1 tablespoon sauterne, half of salt and bay leaf. Cover with wax paper; bake in oven 350° for 20 minutes. In another pan, place butter, onion, mushrooms and let cook over slow fire until mushrooms are done. Then add remaining sauterne and salt, pepper, cream sauce and the fish bouillon. Let sauce simmer 5 minutes, remove from fire, add parsley. Serve over fish.

## TUNA NOODLE CASSEROLE
1 **small onion, sliced thin**
  **Butter**
1 **can or 2 cups homemade**
  **fried noodles**
1 **can tuna, 13 ounces**
1 **can mushroom soup**
  **Pepper**
¼ **pound potato chips, crushed**

Sauté onion in butter until it is a golden brown. Place half the noodles in a greased casserole dish, spread with layer of onion, tuna and mushroom soup. Top with remaining noodles and sprinkle top with pepper and potato chips. Bake in 325° oven for about a half hour or until thick and brown. Serves 4.

## SWEET-SOUR FISH
Fillet a 3-pound lake trout. Boil fish bones, head and tail with 1 sliced onion; ⅓ cup vinegar; ⅓ cup sugar; pinch of salt; 2 sliced celery stalks; 2 sliced carrots; 1 spray dill; 2 bay leaves; 3 cloves; ¼ teaspoon allspice and a ½ sliced lemon. Add enough water to cover ingredients. To keep broth clear, boil very slowly for 20 minutes and then strain. Cut fish fillets in 3-inch pieces and place in strained broth. Boil slowly until fish is done—about 15 minutes.

Place 1½ cups fish broth in a sauce pan

and add 3 sliced onions; ½ sliced lemon; 1 cup washed raisins; ⅓ cup vinegar and a ⅓ cup sugar. Boil until onions are clear. Add 1 teaspoon cornstarch mixed with water and boil until clear. Cool. Remove fish from broth and place in glass dish, pour raisin sauce over fish and let jell. Sprinkle with parsley and chopped chives. Serve with sliced tomatoes, cucumbers and lemon on crisp lettuce. Makes 6 portions.

## SHRIMP AU GRATIN
2 **pounds shrimp**
  **Dash of lemon juice**
½ **cup butter or margarine**
1 **cup flour**
1 **teaspoon salt**
¼ **teaspoon pepper**
3 **egg yolks**
2 **tablespoons sherry wine**
2 **tablespoons grated cheese**
  **Bread crumbs**

Clean and wash shrimp. Place in saucepan with a quart of water and a dash of lemon juice, then bring to a boil for 10 minutes. In another pan melt butter or margarine; then add flour and stir till smooth. Then add 4 cups shrimp stock, stirring constantly. Stir in seasonings, yolks, wine, cheese. Add shrimp; top with crumbs and more cheese. Bake in buttered casserole at 350° to 375° about 15 minutes. Serves 6 to 8.

## HALIBUT FLORENTINE
2 **pounds halibut steak or filet**
½ **cup white wine**
  **Juice of 3 lemons**
1 **cup heavy cream sauce**
8 **ounces spinach, cooked**
  **and chopped**
3 **green onions, finely chopped**
  **Salt and pepper to taste**
3 **egg yolks**
½ **cup grated Italian cheese**

Place halibut in shallow saucepan. Cover with water; add wine and lemon juice.

Cover and boil 5 to 10 minutes or until liquid is reduced to one third. Remove halibut; place in greased baking dish. Place cream sauce in second saucepan, and add broth from halibut, spinach, onions, salt and pepper. Mix and bring to a boil. Then remove from fire and stir in egg yolks. This gives you a Florentine sauce. Pour this sauce over halibut and sprinkle with grated cheese. Bake at 400° until golden brown. Serve hot from baking dish. Four portions.

## CORONADO CLAM PIE
   2 **cups ground clams**
   ½ **cup cracker crumbs**
   ¼ **cup clam liquor**
   1 **egg, well beaten**
   1 **tablespoon butter**
   1 **cup milk**
   2 **small stalks celery, ground**
   1 **small onion, ground**
     **Salt and pepper, to taste**
   2 **9-inch pie crusts, uncooked**

Mix above ingredients and pour into pie shell. Cover top with pie crust and bake in 350° oven for 1 hour. Serves 4-6.

## SOLE AU CHAMPAGNE
   8 **filets of sole**
     **Soya sauce**
   1½ **cups champagne**
     **Salt, to taste**
   8 **mushroom heads, peeled**
   6 **egg yolks**
   1¼ **cups butter**
   2 **tablespoons sour cream**
     **Pepper, to taste**

Dip filets in soya sauce. Heat enough champagne to cover the filets. Add salt to taste. Poach fish and mushrooms 10 minutes. Remove to hot serving dish, flat oval is the best. Keep hot. Reduce cooking liquid quickly. Place egg yolks in a double boiler over hot, not boiling, water, add butter in small pieces. Then blend in cream, pepper and the reduced cooking liquid. Mix and beat well, with electric beater or wire whisk, until thick. The water must not boil. Correct seasonings. Pour sauce over filets. Serves four.

## CRAB OLD STATION
Add 2 hard-boiled egg yolks to 1 pound of fresh crab meat. Soak ⅓-pound white bread in water, then squeeze dry. Mix bread into crab with hands. Heat 1 pint cream adding: 3 sprigs parsley; 1 sprig thyme; 1 clove garlic and 1 bay leaf. When cream is well seasoned remove herbs. Stir 1 tablespoon butter and 3 tablespoons flour into cream and cook until sauce is thick. Stir in crab mixture. Place the crab mixture in individual oven-proof dishes or large heavy clam shells gathered from the ocean. Sprinkle with buttered bread crumbs and bake 15 minutes or until lightly brown and piping hot. Serves 4-6.

## BAKED OYSTERS HOMESTEAD
   24 **oysters on the half shell**
   2 **medium-size green peppers, diced**
   4 **medium-size mushrooms, diced**
   ¼ **pound crabmeat**
   ½ **cup Parmesan cheese, grated**
     **Salt and pepper**

Take oysters with liquid out of shell and bring to boil. Pinch off hard muscle and place oyster back in shell. Sauté peppers and mushrooms.

**Mornay Sauce:**

Mix together 1 egg yolk, 1 cup hot cream sauce, 1 tablespoon whipped cream, 4 drops yellow food coloring and salt and pepper to taste.

To Mornay sauce add peppers, mushrooms and crabmeat and bring to a boil. Cover oysters with this sauce and sprinkle with grated cheese. Bake in hot oven for 10 minutes. Serves 4.

## NEW ORLEANS JAMBALAYA

½ pound fresh pork, shredded
½ pound raw smoked ham
2 tablespoons shortening
½ pound fresh pork sausage
1 medium onion, chopped
2 cloves garlic, chopped
1 cup tomatoes
1 quart stock
1 teaspoon chili powder
1 tablespoon mixed pickling spices
1 tablespoon parsley, chopped
1½ pounds shrimp, cooked
3 cups cooked rice

Sauté pork and ham 15 minutes in shortening. Add sausage, cook 10 minutes. Stir in onion, garlic and tomatoes. Simmer 10 minutes. Add stock, spices and parsley and cook slowly 30 minutes. Add shrimp and simmer a few minutes. Serve on rice. Makes 6 portions.

## CRAWFISH ÉTOUFFÉE

8 pounds fresh crawfish
    or 8 frozen lobster tails
6 onions, chopped fine
¼ pound margarine or
    1 cup cooking oil
½ cup celery, chopped
¼ cup onion tops and parsley, minced
½ teaspoon tomato paste
½ teaspoon cornstarch
½ cup cold water
    Salt, black pepper and
    red pepper, to taste

Boil crawfish. Peel crawfish tails. Add onions, celery and tomato paste to margarine or oil and cook over medium heat until onions are partially cooked. Add whole crawfish tails. Dissolve

cornstarch in cold water. Add to fish mixture, stirring constantly. Season to taste with salt and peppers. Bring to a boil in uncovered pot over medium heat and cook for 15 minutes. Add green onions and parsley. Mix well. Serve with rice. Makes 8 portions.

## SHRIMP WITH BLACK BEAN SAUCE

1 tablespoon cooking fat
¾ teaspoon salt
    Piece of fresh ginger (size of
    green pea), minced
1 tablespoon black bean sauce
1 pound raw shrimp, cleaned
1½ cups sherry
½ cup stock
    Dash of black pepper
⅓ teaspoon sugar
¼ teaspoon Ac´cent
4 teaspoons cornstarch, mixed with
    ¼ cup of water
4 green onions, chopped

Place fat in hot skillet, add salt, ginger and bean sauce. Stir in raw shrimp until sauce covers them. Pour in wine and stock and cover with tight lid. Boil three minutes. Add pepper, sugar, Ac´cent. Add cornstarch to make light gravy. Mix in onions. Serves 4.

## SHRIMP CURRY CALCUTTA

2 pounds shrimp, boiled
1 cup butter
2 onions, chopped
1 stalk celery, chopped
1 carrot, chopped
1 green pepper, chopped
2 bay leaves
4 cloves
1 tablespoon flour
3 tablespoons curry powder
2 cans chicken broth
½ cup raisins
½ cup cream

Combine butter, onions, celery, carrot, green pepper, bay leaves and cloves and brown slightly. Add flour mixed with curry powder and stir until well blended. Add broth, 4 cups of water, shrimp and raisins. Simmer for about 1 hour. Remove shrimp. Strain mixture and add cream to sauce and then return shrimp and cook for 5 minutes more. Serve with rice and condiments to 6.

## CRABMEAT CAKES

1 pound crabmeat
1 cup extra rich milk
1 cup fresh bread crumbs
½ teaspoon cayenne
1 teaspoon dry mustard
2 teaspoons Worcestershire sauce
3 drops Tabasco sauce
1 egg
  Cracker meal
  Deep fat

Mix ingredients well. Make 8 individual patties and roll in cracker meal. Fry in deep fat until golden brown. Serves 4.

## LOBSTER FRA DIAVOLO

4 1½-pound live lobsters
3 large cloves garlic
1 large onion
  Olive oil, to cover pan bottom
2 No. 2 cans tomatoes
1 small can tomato paste
2 cups white wine

Pinch of leaf oregano
Pinch of dry basil leaves
3 teaspoons salt
2 teaspoons sugar
  Dash of Tabasco sauce
  Pinch of hot pepper seeds
2 ounces Strega (Italian cordial)

Split live lobsters from head to tail. Detach claws and cut into 4 pieces. Cut the rest of the lobster across in 2-inch pieces. Save juice. Chop garlic and onion very fine and sauté in olive oil. Add tomatoes, paste and remaining ingredients, except lobster and Strega. Cook 15 minutes over brisk fire. Add lobster pieces and juice and cook over medium heat for 25 minutes. When done, pour into serving dish and pour Strega over top; serve either plain or flaming. Makes 4 portions.

## SALMON AND TOMATO PIE

2 tablespoons onion, chopped
2 tablespoons green peppers, chopped
1 ounce shortening
½ ounce flour
1¼ cups canned tomatoes
¼ teaspoon salt
  Dash of pepper
½ tablespoon sugar
8 ounces canned salmon, drained
1 ounce American cheese, grated
6½ ounces rich biscuit dough

Sauté onions and green pepper in shortening until tender, but not browned. Add flour. Combine tomatoes, seasonings

and sugar; add to flour mixture. Bring to a boil, stirring constantly. Arrange layer of salmon in shallow greased casserole, cover with tomato mixture and sprinkle with grated cheese. Roll biscuit dough to ⅜-inch thickness; cut to fit top of casserole. Place on top of salmon mixture. Make openings in crust to permit escape of steam. Bake in 400° oven 20-25 minutes, or until crust is done. Serves 4.

## BAKED HALIBUT WITH SAUCE

- 6 halibut steaks
- ¾ pound onions, sliced
- ½ pound mushrooms, sliced
- 2 No. 2½ cans tomatoes
- 1 cup tomato juice
- 1 clove garlic, minced
  Few sprigs parsley, minced
  Pinch of celery salt, nutmeg, cayenne pepper and sweet basil

Sauté onions and mushrooms until soft. Add remaining ingredients, except fish. Simmer 30 minutes. Pour sauce in bottom of 6 casseroles. Place halibut on top of each. Cover with Cheese Sauce.

### Cheese Sauce:

Blend together 2 cups cottage cheese; ¼ pound Parmesan cheese, grated; 3 egg yolks, ¾ cup very thick cream sauce and 1 tablespoon tomato purée. Place on top of halibut and bake 20-25 minutes in 350° oven. Makes 6 servings.

## OYSTER LOAF

Sauté 3 dozen small Pacific oysters in 2 tablespoons butter with 1 cup chopped celery until the oysters are plump, about 8-10 minutes over medium heat. Cut the top crust from 1-pound loaf of French bread (or 6 individual loaves), hollow out the interior and brush the inside and top crust generously with ½ cup melted butter. Brown bread in 450° oven for 4-5 minutes. Add 2 cups medium cream sauce and 1 cup toasted bread crumbs to oysters. Pour mixture into browned loaf

of bread, replace top, and heat in 450° oven for 8-10 minutes. Makes 6-8 portions.

## SALMON PARISIENNE

- 4-5 pounds salmon, sliced thick
- ½ cup vinegar
- 1 large onion, sliced
- 1 large carrot, sliced
- 2 sprigs parsley
- 2 stalks celery
- 2 bay leaves
- ½ teaspoon thyme
- 1 tablespoon salt
- 8 peppercorns
- 1 lemon, sliced

Place salmon in a large saucepan, add remaining ingredients, except lemon slices, with water to cover. Simmer until boiling. Remove from fire and let cool. When cool remove salmon from the pan, take out the bones and remove skin. Place salmon slices on a large platter, then place lemon slices and parsley around the platter for decoration. Serve cold with any kind of vegetable salad. Mayonnaise, tartar sauce or Russian dressing may be served with salmon. Serves 6.

## DOVER SOLE AU VERMOUTH

- 6 Dover sole, 14 ounces per fish
- 6 ounces butter, flaked
- 6 dried shallots, finely chopped
  Salt and pepper, to taste
- 1½ cups French vermouth
- 1½ cups Béchamel Sauce
- 6 ounces whipping cream

In a shallow baking dish place sole, butter, dried shallots, salt, pepper and vermouth. Simmer uncovered in 375° oven for 10-15 minutes. When cooked, take fish from liquid and remove all bones. Place fish on warm service platter. Mix remaining liquid in pan with Béchamel Sauce and whipping cream; pour mixture over sole. Before serving glaze swiftly under broiler. Serve with tossed salad and parsley boiled potatoes. Makes 6 generous portions.

**Béchamel Sauce:**

Make a roux of 3 tablespoons melted butter and 3 tablespoons flour. While beating vigorously add 1½ cups scalded milk, all at once. When it comes to a boil, lower heat and simmer 5 minutes. Season to taste with salt, pepper and pinch of nutmeg.

## PICKLED SHRIMP

Add boiling water to 2½ pounds of shrimp to cover. Then add 6 celery tops, 3½ teaspoons salt and ¼ cup mixed pickling spices. Cook shrimp 10 to 12 minutes. Drain shrimp and cool with cold water. Peel and devein under running water. Alternate shrimp and sliced onions (1 pint) in shallow dish. Add 7 or 8 bay leaves. Cover with sauce.

**Sauce:**

Combine 1¼ cups salad oil, ¾ cup white vinegar, 2 teaspoons salt, ½ teaspoon celery seed and 2½ tablespoons capers with juice, and a dash of Tabasco. Mix well and pour over shrimp dish. Cover and store in refrigerator for at least 24 hours. Will keep for a week. Served as an appetizer, will yield 20 portions.

## ESCARGOTS

(This recipe won the Cordon Bleu Award from the Wine and Food Society of Southern California.)

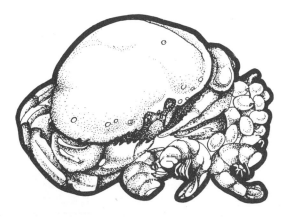

1 pound butter, melted
2 tablespoons parsley, minced
6-8 pieces fresh garlic, minced
⅓ teaspoon nutmeg
1 can (72) escargots (French snails and shells)
1 tablespoon Dijon mustard
1 tablespoon cashew spread
½ cup cracker meal
1 teaspoon dill seed
Thin onion slices, chopped and moistened with Chablis

Combine melted butter with parsley, garlic and nutmeg. Pour this marinade over snails and place in cool place overnight. Then stuff snail meat into shells and place on flat broiler pan. Combine mustard and cashew spread and place on snails. Sprinkle each with ¼ teaspoon cracker meal and a few dill seeds. Top with onion. Put under broiler until piping hot and serve hot with French bread. Serves 12.

## MOULES MARINIÈRES

Scrub 3 pounds closed mussels vigorously to make sure that sand is removed. Cut and discard the "beard." Place cleaned mussels in a large pot. Add 10 ounces water, 10 ounces dry white wine, ½ teaspoon salt, 3 to 4 chives and 1 shallot (both chopped fine). Grind pepper over top, cover pot and put over high heat for about 7 minutes, or until mussels open.

Stir the mussels occasionally if they do not open immediately. After sufficient cooking time (not over 10 minutes), the mussels are ready to serve. Those that have not opened generally are not good and should not be eaten. Divide mussels and broth into 2 portions. Do not strain broth. Serves 2.

## SHRIMP SANTORINI

Peel, devein and clean 24 jumbo shrimp, then dust lightly in flour. Sauté shrimp in 3 tablespoons butter until partly cooked and gold-colored. Place 6 shrimp in each of 4 shallow casseroles. Broil 4 tomato halves, sprinkled with oregano and Parmesan cheese, until partly cooked. Place tomato halves on top of shrimp in each casserole and top each with a slice of feta cheese. Cover with Santorini Sauce; bake at 400° for 5 minutes.

### Santorini Sauce:

Melt 2 ounces butter in a shallow pan; add ½ cup minced onions, 1 teaspoon minced garlic, 1 tablespoon chopped fresh parsley, ¼ teaspoon oregano, ¼ teaspoon basil, 1 tablespoon fresh chopped dill, 2 bay leaves and 1 teaspoon sugar. Bake in preheated 350° oven until golden brown. Then add 3½ cups stewed tomatoes, 1 cup catsup and 4 cups chicken broth; continue baking for 30 minutes.

Place freshly killed 1¼-pound lobster (or equal weight of raw unshelled shrimp) in a large saucepan. Cover lobster or shrimp with baked tomato sauce. Add 6 cups water, cover and simmer over medium heat for 1 hour, or until sauce is reduced by half. Add ½ cup sherry, 1 teaspoon Maggi sauce (or Madeira wine), and salt and pepper to taste. Simmer for a few minutes more.

Remove shells from lobster or shrimp, clean and cut seafood into small pieces. Return to sauce and press all through a medium food strainer.

## DOVER SOLE À LA VERONIQUE

4 **whole Dover sole, dressed**
  **Salt and pepper to taste**
½ **cup dry white wine**
4 **tablespoons flour**
½ **cup water**
5 **tablespoons butter**
2 **tablespoons whipped cream**
2 **tablespoons hollandaise sauce**
¼ **cup seedless white grapes,**
  **fresh or canned**

Arrange fish in shallow pan and sprinkle with salt and pepper. Add water and wine and simmer gently about 10 minutes. Remove fish to serving dish and keep warm. Make a medium-thick sauce of butter, flour and liquid left from cooking sole; correct seasonings. Blend in whipped cream and hollandaise sauce. Spread over fish, garnish with grapes and place under broiler until lightly tanned. (If fresh grapes are used, simmer them 3 minutes, then drain.) Serves 4.

## LOBSTER DIEN BIEN

2 **pounds fresh lobster meat**
6 **ounces butter**
⅔ **cup chopped scallions**
1 **green pepper, diced**
1¼ **cups fresh mushrooms**
½ **cup Uncle Ben's converted rice**
3 **ripe tomatoes**
⅔ **cup chicken consommé**
1 **teaspoon powdered tarragon**
1 **teaspoon pepper**

Cut lobster in small pieces, season with ½ teaspoon pepper and ⅓ teaspoon salt, then brown in 4 ounces of butter in pan. Partly brown lobster in butter, making sure that butter is hot enough so lobster will not lose juice. Chop scallions, green pepper and mushrooms and add to lobster.

Simmer 5 minutes. Add rice, stirring continuously, until rice is loose. Add tomatoes, chopped fine, and consommé. Stir once and cover. Cook about 25 minutes, then remove from heat. Put remaining 2 ounces butter in a pan and brown evenly, then add tarragon and pepper. Pour over lobster and mix well. Serves 3.

## TROUT SOUFFLÉ

Remove meat from skin of four 6-ounce boned trout, leaving head, tail and skin intact. Put fish meat through grinder or chop very fine. Combine 4 egg whites, 2 teaspoons salt, ¼ teaspoon pepper and ¼ teaspoon nutmeg with fish and beat mixture at high speed until thickened to a paste. Add 2 cups whipping cream; whip at highest speed until mixture resembles dough. Stuff into trout skins. Refrigerate 30 minutes to 24 hours.

Place fish on buttered pan, brush with butter, sprinkle lightly with paprika and bake at 450° for 15 minutes. Trout will puff up. Remove from oven, garnish with parsley and lemon, and pour sauce over top.

**Sauce:**

Clarify 1 cup of sweet butter and brown it slowly, add ¼ cup tomato juice and the juice of 1 lemon. Simmer 5 minutes.

## POACHED FISH DE PESCA

Boil 1 quart water in a deep, heavy pan. Place in it four 10-ounce pieces of whitefish (or halibut, snapper or salmon). Then add 2 medium-sized potatoes, peeled and cut in 1-inch slices; 2 bay leaves; 1 teaspoon pickling spices; ¼ teaspoon salt and ¼ teaspoon Ac´cent (MSG). Simmer for 10 minutes.

Remove fish and potatoes to 4 individual casseroles (or 1 large shallow dish). Pour 3 ounces olive oil over all. Sprinkle with 1 teaspoon chopped parsley, the juice of 1 lemon and freshly ground pepper. Serve with melted butter and 4 lemon halves wrapped in cheesecloth. Serves 4.

## SHRIMP CABRILLO

Peel, clean and wash 36 large raw shrimp. On a skewer place 1 shrimp, 3 pieces of bacon, a piece of green pepper and a mushroom cap. Continue in this order until there are 6 shrimp on each of 6 skewers. Baste skewered shrimp with melted butter and season with salt and pepper to taste, then broil on both sides 8 inches from hot fire until shrimp are pink. Serve with sauce. Serves 6.

**Sauce Cabrillo:**

Combine 1 teaspoon Coleman mustard, 10 dashes Worcestershire sauce, 5 dashes Tabasco and juice of ½ lemon. Add 14 ounces catsup. Simmer for 20 minutes.

Remove from fire, add 4 ounces butter a little at a time, using a wire whip.

## ARCTIC CHAR À LA MEUNIÈRE

 **8 thick arctic char steaks
   (or salmon or lake trout)**
 **1 cup white wine**
 **1 cup court bouillon
   Bouquet garni**
 **2 bay leaves**
 **8 peppercorns**
 **1 clove garlic, mashed**
 **1 lemon, juice and rind**
 **1 teaspoon Worcestershire sauce**
 **1 leek (white part only)**
 **1 small onion**
 **2 anchovy fillets**
 **½ cup butter**

Cut the fish into steaks, wipe and salt. Boil in white wine combined with court bouillon (the liquid must cover the fish). Add to the liquid a bouquet garni, bay leaves, peppercorns, garlic, juice of the lemon and Worcestershire sauce. Simmer until fish is tender, about 15 minutes.

Chop the leek, onion, anchovies and lemon rind. Add butter. Heat the mixture, stirring constantly, and cook until golden brown. Place fish on platter, remove center bone and skin. Cover with the above mixture and serve with sour cream sauce.

**Sour Cream Sauce:**

Melt 3 tablespoons butter over low heat, stir in 4 tablespoons flour, mix until smooth. Add 2½ cups milk gradually, stirring well. Add 3 tablespoons butter, ½ cup sour cream, ½ teaspoon sugar and salt to taste. Boil a few minutes, then add 2 tablespoons sherry. Serve hot over char steaks.

# SOUPS

## CHEESE SOUP

- 4 tablespoons butter
- ½ cup diced carrot
- ½ cup diced green pepper
- ½ cup minced onion
- ½ cup minced celery
- ⅓ cup flour
- 1 quart well-seasoned chicken stock
- 6 ounces young Cheddar, grated
- 6 ounces well-cured Cheddar, grated
- 3-4 cups fresh milk
  Salt and white pepper

Melt butter in double boiler top. Add vegetables. Braise till tender, not brown. Blend in flour. Cook 1 minute, stirring constantly. Add stock and cook; stir till thick. Add cheese; stir till it melts. Thin with milk to creamy consistency. Season with salt, pepper. Strain. Reheat in double boiler. Serve hot — or in warm weather, very cold. Makes 2 quarts.

## NEW ENGLAND CLAM CHOWDER

- 1 quart soft clams
- ¼ cup diced salt pork
- 3 small onions, sliced
- 4 cups diced potatoes
- 2 tablespoons flour
- 2 teaspoons salt
- ⅛ teaspoon pepper
- 2½ cups boiling water
- 1 quart milk, scalded
- 2 tablespoons butter

Separate clams from liquor, discard dark stomach contents, and mince clams. Fry pork to a golden brown, then add sliced onions, and fry these to a light golden color. Add a layer of potatoes and sprinkle with flour, salt, and pepper. Add clams, then another layer of potatoes sprinkled with remainder of flour, and with salt and pepper. Add boiling water and simmer until potatoes are done. Combine milk, clam liquor, and butter before adding to clam mixture. Simmer for 5 minutes. Serve with crackers.

## WILLIAMSBURG CLAM CHOWDER

- 1 cup large chowder clams
- 1 cup cold water
- 3 ounces salt pork, diced
- ½ cup celery strips
- 1 medium-size onion
- 1 large-size potato
- 1 tablespoon green pepper
- ½ teaspoon thyme
- 1 cup tomatoes
  Salt and pepper
- ½ tablespoon sherry
  Parsley to taste

Put clams in boiler; cover with water. Simmer 15 minutes, remove from fire, and strain through cheese cloth. Pick and wash clams; put through a food chopper. Fry salt pork until crisp; add celery, onion, potatoes, and pepper, all chopped. Add clams and stock, thyme, tomatoes, salt and pepper. Cook on a slow fire, stirring very often for an hour. Remove from fire, add sherry, and finish with chopped parsley. Makes 6 generous servings.

## CREAM OF TURNIP SOUP
- 1 quart milk
- 1 onion
- 1 tablespoon flour
- 2 tablespoons butter, melted
- 2 cups grated raw turnip
- 1 teaspoon salt
- Parsley, chopped

Heat milk in double boiler with the onion, halved. Add flour and butter well blended, then the turnip and salt. Cook until the turnip is tender — about 10 minutes — then remove onion. Sprinkle chopped parsley over the soup just before serving. A giant bowl makes a hearty winter lunch.

## SOUPE A L'OIGNON GRATINÉE
- 4-5 pounds short ribs of beef
- 15-20 large onions
- ¼ cup olive oil
- 4 tablespoons butter
- Salt and pepper
- 2 tablespoons sugar
- French bread or Dutch rusk
- Grated Parmesan cheese
- Red wine

Simmer beef short ribs in water slowly for 1 hour. Slice onions on the bias — no rings — and sauté in skillet with olive oil. When tender and golden, add butter, salt, pepper, sugar. Remove short

ribs from stock and add onions; allow soup to simmer until ready to serve. Cover slice of French bread toast or Dutch rusk with grated Parmesan cheese, and melt under broiler. In each bowl of soup put 1 slice toast and add 1 tablespoon red wine.

## CALDO DE FRIJOLES
## (Mexican Bean Soup)
- 1 cup frijoles (pinto beans)
- 1 cup cold water, or beef or chicken broth
- Seasonings: 2 green onions with tops, chopped; 1 clove garlic; 5 sprigs chopped parsley; 1 tablespoon chopped green chili; pulp of 1 red hot chili pepper (or 1½ teaspoons chili powder); 1 teaspoon oregano; ½ teaspoon salt
- 1 cup beef broth

Wash frijoles and soak overnight in cold water. Drain, add to quart of water or broth. Simmer 4 to 6 hours (adding boiling water as needed) till beans are tender. Add seasonings; simmer till tender. Then rub soup through colander and reheat. Add cup beef broth if necessary (soup should be consistency of thin puree). Serve with small rounds of toast, rolled in finely grated sharp cheese. This recipe serves 6 to 8.

## SPLIT PEA SOUP
- 2 quarts soft water
- 2 cups green split peas
- 1 stalk celery, chopped
- 1 large carrot, chopped
- 1 small onion, chopped
- ¼ teaspoon thyme
- 1 pinch cayenne pepper
- 1 bay leaf
- Salt and pepper

Boil ingredients vigorously for 20 minutes, then slowly until the peas are done. Strain this mixture through a colander. This recipe will make 8

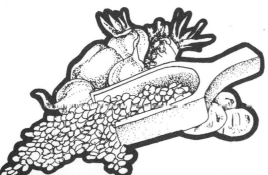

servings of a soup that is noted all over California for its excellence. If you are a connoisseur of soups, you will make a meal of this one.

## MELON SOUP
    1-pound Chinese melon
1 quart chicken stock
¼ pound raw pork, diced
3 Chinese water chestnuts, peeled
1 egg

Pour stock into a 2-quart saucepan and bring to a rapid boil. Add pork and sliced water chestnuts; cook until pork is done. Then add salt and melon, cut into bite size; boil 10 minutes. *Do not cover pan after adding melon.* Break egg into soup. *Do not stir,* as the egg is supposed to remain whole. Serve immediately. Some Chinese prefer to break egg into serving bowl, then pour hot soup onto raw egg.

## MAINE FISH CHOWDER
3 pounds haddock
6 slices salt pork
2 onions, diced
4 large potatoes, cubed
1 quart milk, scalded
1 teaspoon salt
⅛ teaspoon pepper
    Common crackers

Boil haddock and bone it. Fry salt pork and cook onions in the fat. Cook cubed potatoes in just enough salted water to cover. When potatoes are cooked, add salt pork, fat, onions, fish and scalded milk to potatoes and water. Salt and pepper to taste. Float crackers on chowder before serving.

## CHEESE SOUP
¼ pound butter
1 cup flour
½ teaspoon salt
1½ pints milk
7 ounces Cheddar cheese
¼ cup finely diced celery
¼ cup finely diced onions
¼ cup finely diced peppers
¼ cup finely chopped carrots
1 pint chicken stock
    Paprika to color

Melt butter and blend in flour, salt and milk. Cook until thickened. Melt cheese in double boiler, parboil vegetables in chicken stock and then combine all ingredients. Bring to a boil, stirring constantly. Serve piping hot. Makes 8 generous helpings.

## JELLIED CUCUMBER CONSOMMÉ
4 cups chopped cucumber
1 onion, sliced
1 tablespoon chopped parsley
1 teaspoon pickle spice
    Salt and pepper, to taste
2 tablespoons gelatin
1 tablespoon lemon juice
    Sour cream
    Celery salt
    Paprika

Put cucumber in saucepan with 3 pints of water, onion, half of parsley and pickle spice. Bring to a boil and simmer 1 hour. Strain and season. Soak gelatin in ½ cup of cold water 5 minutes, then add to hot consommé. Cool, add lemon juice and pour into shallow pan. Chill in refrigerator until firm. Serve topped with sour cream, celery salt, paprika and rest of parsley. Serves 6.

## NEW ENGLAND FISH CHOWDER
1 pound halibut or haddock
    Bones from a whitefish
1 onion, cut fine
½ cup celery, chopped
½ pound butter
¼ teaspoon salt
¼ teaspoon curry powder
    Few grains pepper
1½ tablespoons flour
½ pint milk
½ pint cream
2 cups raw potatoes, diced

Wash fish and fish bones and cover with salted water, bring slowly to a boil,

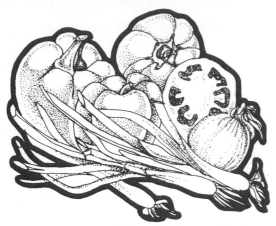

simmer covered for 15 minutes. Drain, reserving stock. Sauté onion and celery in ¼ pound butter. Add salt, curry powder and pepper. Then melt ¼ pound butter in a large saucepan, and blend the flour into this, stirring to make a smooth paste. Heat and combine milk and cream and slowly blend this into mixture. Add 1 quart fish stock, fish, celery, onions and potatoes. Bring to a boil and simmer 5 minutes.

## SOUTHERN BISQUE
1⅓ cups tomato soup mixed
    with ½ cup water
¼ cup each, butter and flour
¼ cup each, cream and milk
¾ cup cream-style corn
1 tablespoon sugar

Bring tomato-soup mixture to a boil. Melt butter, stir in flour, and add cream and milk, stirring constantly. When creamed, add this mixture, corn and sugar to soup. Stir till blended. Serves 6.

## VIRGINIA PEANUT SOUP
¼ pound butter
1 small onion, diced
2 stalks celery, diced
3 tablespoons flour
2 quarts chicken broth
1 pint peanut butter
⅓ teaspoon celery salt
1 teaspoon salt
1 tablespoon lemon juice
½ cup unroasted peanuts, ground

Melt butter in pan, then add onion and celery. Sauté for 5 minutes (don't brown). Add flour and mix well; blend in hot chicken broth and cook for 30 minutes. Remove from stove, strain and add peanut butter, celery salt, salt and lemon juice. Sprinkle ground peanuts on soup just before serving. Makes 15 average servings.

## SNAPPER SOUP
1 small snapping turtle or ¾ pound
    boiled turtle meat
3 ounces butter
3 ounces flour
½ scant teaspoon each: mace, thyme,
    allspice, ground cloves and dry
    mustard
  Salt and pepper, to taste
2 cups turtle stock
2 hard-boiled eggs, chopped fine
3 ounces sherry

Boil turtle until meat falls off bones. Separate meat from broth. Make a smooth paste of butter and flour and cook until dry, then add seasonings. Stir this mixture into turtle stock and simmer for 1½ hours. Add turtle meat in small pieces, eggs and sherry. Simmer for ½ hour. Serve hot. Makes 1 quart.

## BLACKIE'S BEEF VEGETABLE SOUP
Place a 4-pound meaty soup bone in large pot. Add 1 large chopped onion, ½ bunch chopped celery and cover with water. Cook slowly for four hours. Skim off top of beef stock occasionally. Sauté in ¼ pound butter: 2 large chopped onions, ½ bunch chopped celery, 3 large sliced carrots and 3 green peppers. Add 2 cups stewed tomatoes, 4 ounces tomato puree and 3 large diced potatoes. Cook 30 minutes over medium heat. Add beef stock, 4 teaspoons salt and ½ teaspoon pepper. Remove meat from beef bone, chop in small pieces and add to soup. Then add ¼ pound frozen green peas, ¼

pound frozen baby lima beans and 4 drops of Tabasco. Cook 30 minutes over low heat. Makes 10-12 hearty main-dish portions.

## CRÈME OF TOMATO SOUP WITH ALMONDS

2 cups milk
1 cup light cream
1 medium can tomato paste, or 1 No. 2 can tomato puree
1 tablespoon sugar
1 teaspoon salt
2 tablespoons Parmesan cheese
2 ounces butter
2 tablespoons flour
1 cup whipping cream
2 dozen almonds, toasted and sliced

Bring milk and light cream to a boil, then add tomato paste or puree and stir briskly. Stir in sugar, salt and cheese. Melt butter and blend in flour to make a smooth paste, then add to the soup and beat until it is smooth and thick as heavy cream. Whip the whipping cream and top each bowl of soup with a generous tablespoon of it. Sprinkle with almonds and serve. Serves 6.

## WESTERN POTATO SOUP

1 gallon fresh, rich beef stock
1 small bunch green onions, chopped fine
½ green pepper, chopped fine
¼ teaspoon black pepper
1 teaspoon salt
1 teaspoon Aċ cent
3 freshly boiled potatoes, mashed
1 generous tablespoon butter
1 tablespoon flour
1 cup milk

Simmer onions and green pepper and seasonings in beef stock until vegetables become soft. Add freshly mashed potatoes and butter and simmer. Combine milk with flour to a smooth mixture and blend into soup. Serve with golden brown toast or your favorite cracker.

## GAZPACHO ANDALUZ

Liquefy 1 garlic clove and 1 medium onion in a blender. Add: 5 very ripe tomatoes; 2 sprigs parsley; 2 tablespoons vinegar; 3 tablespoons olive oil; ¼ teaspoon paprika; 1 cup beef stock or consommé. Run blender at high speed for 2-3 minutes. Season to taste with salt and pepper. Place in soup tureen and refrigerate. Then serve in chilled bowls with separately chopped cucumber, tomato, green pepper, green onions and croutons. Serves 6.

## WATERCRESS SOUP

In 3 tablespoons of butter sauté together: 1 cup celery, diced, 1 cup chopped white onion, and finely diced stems from 2 bunches of watercress. Add 4 cups chicken broth and simmer until celery is tender. Season to taste with salt and pepper. Add watercress leaves to broth. Simmer for 2 minutes. Stir in 2 eggs until they separate into shreds. Serve with toasted French bread sprinkled with Parmesan cheese. Serves 5.

## TIFFANY'S BEAN POT SOUP

2 cups dried pinto beans
1 pound ham, cubed
1 quart water
22- ounce can tomato juice
2 cups chicken stock
3 onions, chopped
3 cloves garlic, minced
3 tablespoons parsley, minced
¼ cup green pepper, chopped
2 tablespoons brown sugar
1 tablespoon chili powder
1 teaspoon each: salt, crushed bay leaves, monosodium glutamate and oregano
¼ teaspoon each: crushed rosemary leaves, celery seed, ground thyme, ground marjoram and sweet basil
1 cup sherry

Cover beans with water and soak

overnight. Add remaining ingredients,
except sherry. Bring to a slow boil and
simmer for 3 hours or until beans are
tender. Add sherry. Serve in generous
soup bowls, topped with chopped green
onions. Six generous servings.

## HOTEL UTAH BORSCHT
To 1 quart of beet juice add 2 cups of
chicken stock, 1 teaspoon salt, 1 teaspoon
monosodium glutamate and 2 teaspoons
fresh lemon juice. Bring to a boil.
Dissolve 2 tablespoons cornstarch in a
little cold water and add to hot liquid.
Boil slowly for 5 minutes. Then combine
2 cups sour cream with 4 egg yolks; mix
well. Beat this with 1 cup of the hot
beet-juice mixture. Then add sour-cream
mixture to soup. Bring to a boil *but do
not boil.* Garnish with unsweetened
whipped cream, chopped egg yolk and
parsley. Serves 8.

## SWISS ONION SOUP
- ½ **cup butter**
- 2 **pounds onions, thinly sliced**
- 1½ **teaspoon paprika**
- ¾ **cup flour**
- ½ **cup vegetable oil**
- ¾ **teaspoon celery salt**
  **Salt and pepper, to taste**
- 6 **cups beef stock**
- 8 **ounces dark beer**
- ½ **cup Parmesan cheese**
- 12 **slices of bread, buttered, sprinkled
  with the cheese and paprika,
  then toasted.**

Cook onions in butter until soft. Add
paprika. Make a roux by browning oil
and flour, add roux, celery salt, pepper
and salt to beef stock and simmer for at
least 2 hours. Add beer; bring to serving
temperature. Pour into soup bowls; add a
slice of toast to each and sprinkle with
Parmesan cheese. Serves 12.

## BLACK MUSHROOM SOUP
Soak 1½ cups dried, smoked, black
mushrooms overnight in cold water.
Rinse, then boil in slightly salted water
to cover until just tender. In a separate
pan bring to a boil 3 quarts of strong
chicken stock, then add ⅜ teaspoon garlic
powder, ¾ teaspoon onion powder, ¾ cup
chopped onions and 2 stalks of celery,
finely sliced. Simmer for half an hour.

Meanwhile drain mushrooms, saving the
cooking water. Cut mushrooms into bite-
size pieces and add to stock. Strain
mushroom cooking water through a towel
or cheesecloth; add to simmering stock.
Cook 30 to 45 minutes. Serve with thick
slices of sourdough bread and butter.

## NAVY BEAN AND CABBAGE SOUP
Soak 1 pound navy beans overnight.
Next day, add water to cover, bring to a
boil, reduce heat and simmer, covered,
for 2½ hours.

Drain beans; combine with 3 quarts
chicken stock, 1 pound pork bone, 1
small chopped cabbage, 1½ cups chopped
onion, 3 chopped carrots and 1 scant
teaspoon marjoram.

Simmer for 2½ hours. Remove and
discard bones, and skim off surface fat.
Season to taste with salt and pepper. Just
before serving stir in ½ cup chopped
parsley. Makes 3 quarts.

## FRESH CREAM OF HERRING
## SOUP
- 1 **leek**
- 2 **large onions**
- 1 **carrot**

2 pieces of celery
2 tablespoons cooking oil
5 fresh herrings, cleaned
2 cloves garlic, mashed
   Pinch of saffron
   Pinch of cloves
   Salt and pepper, to taste
10 cups water
4 tablespoons butter
4 tablespoons flour
2 egg yolks
½ cup whipping cream
   Croutons

Cut leek, onions, carrot and celery in large pieces and sauté in hot oil, stirring, until golden. Add herrings, garlic, spices and salt and pepper to taste. Add water and bring to a boil. Cook 15 to 20 minutes on high heat. Strain, reserving bouillon and herrings.

Prepare a roux by melting butter and gradually adding flour while stirring. Add bouillon to roux gradually, stirring constantly until mixture thickens.

Just before serving, beat egg yolks into cream and pour into a tureen. Add herrings and thickened bouillon, then stir. Serve with croutons. Makes 8 portions.

## CRÈME VICHYSSOISE

4 leeks
1 medium onion
2 ounces sweet butter
4 medium-sized Idaho potatoes
1 quart chicken broth
4 cups 18% cream
   Salt and pepper
1 cup sour cream
   Chopped chives

Slice the white part of the leeks and finely chop onion; then cook together in butter. Then add quartered potatoes and chicken broth. Boil fast for 30 minutes. Mash, then strain through fine cheese cloth and add 18% cream. Season to taste and bring to boil. Cool and strain again through fine muslin cloth and add sour cream and chill. Serve this soup ice cold, topped with chives.

## DARTMOUTH CHEDDAR CHEESE SOUP

2 ounces butter
2 tablespoons whites of leeks or mild onion
¼ cup carrots
¼ cup celery hearts or yellow heart leaves
1 lemon, grated rind
¼ inch bay leaf
¼ teaspoon white pepper
½ teaspoon dry mustard
1 quart rich chicken stock, boiling
6 ounces grated sharp Cheddar
1½ teaspoons Worchestershire
   Salt and Tabasco, to taste

Melt 2 ounces butter in top of double boiler. Add leeks, carrots, celery and lemon rind and smother until transparent. Add bay leaf, pepper and mustard. Pour in stock and simmer for 20 minutes. Place pan over double boiler bottom that is filled with water just under boiling point and whip in cheese. Combine 2 tablespoons butter, 2 tablespoons flour and 1 pint of hot milk into a cream sauce and whip into mixture. Let stand 10 minutes. Strain through cheese cloth. Add remaining seasonings. Serves 6.

## BLACK BEAN SOUP, PRINCETONIAN

½ pound salt pork
½ Spanish onion, chopped
  A few celery leaves
2 bay leaves
3 cloves garlic
1½ cups flour
3 quarts water
1½ pounds black beans, soaked
    overnight
6-8 potatoes, sliced
  Salt and pepper to taste
1 cup sherry
1½ cups hard boiled eggs, chopped
1 lemon, sliced very thin

Heat pork in heavy pan, then add onion, celery, bay leaves and garlic and fry for 5-8 minutes. Blend flour into mixture until it is smooth. Then add water and soaked beans. Bring to a boil and add potatoes to soup. Simmer uncovered for 3-4 hours. Remove from fire and strain through fine sieve. Season to taste and add sherry just before serving. Garnish individual bowls with chopped eggs and sliced lemon. Serves 10-12 portions.

## VEGETABLE SOUP

1 2-pound soup bone
½ cup each: diced potatoes, carrots,
    celery and onions
½ cup lima beans
½ cup corn niblets
½ cup peas
½ cup string beans
1 No. 2 can tomatoes, mashed
3 bay leaves
¼ teaspoon thyme

Cover soup bone with 2 quarts cold water and add all ingredients. Fresh vegetables are preferred. Cook slowly for three hours with cover on. Remove bone. Makes 8 portions.

## SHE-CRAB SOUP

1 cup white crab meat
2 tablespoons butter
1 small onion, grated
  Salt and pepper to taste
½ teaspoon mace
3 stalks celery, grated
2 cups milk
½ cup cream
2 tablespoons Worcestershire sauce
2 teaspoons flour
1 tablespoon water
3 tablespoons sherry

Simmer crab, butter, onion, salt, pepper, mace and celery in double boiler for 5 minutes. Heat milk, add crab mixture to it. Stir, adding cream and Worcestershire. Thicken with paste made of flour and water. Add sherry. Cook over low heat for ½ hour. Serves 4.

## MOM'S MINESTRONE SOUP

2 pounds pinto beans, soaked
    overnight
2 pounds fresh pork hocks, cut
1 large onion, cubed
1 cup celery, sliced
1 medium sized carrot, cubed
¼ head medium cabbage, shredded
1 teaspoon rosemary
2 medium size potatoes, cubed
2 tablespoons salt
1 teaspoon pepper
¾ cup noodles
1 small onion, chopped very fine
1 clove garlic, chopped fine
3 ounces olive oil

Boil pinto beans in 8 quarts of water over low flame for 1 hour. Add pork and cook another hour. Then add all of the vegetables (except small onion and garlic) and the spices and cook slowly until vegetables are tender. Sauté onion and garlic in olive oil and add with noodles to soup about 15 minutes before serving. Serves 12-14.

# STUFFINGS & DRESSINGS

## TAVERN CHESTNUT DRESSING

1 pound chestnuts, chopped
½ loaf white bread
3 cups water
½ cup chopped Virginia ham
½ stalk celery, chopped
2 medium onions, chopped
1 tablespoon parsley

Soak bread in 3 cups water. Add chopped ham. Brown celery and onions lightly; add bread and ham together with chestnuts, freshly boiled. Stir thoroughly. Bake at 300° for 15 minutes. Serve with your holiday turkey which has been roasted separately after having been stuffed with a stalk of celery and chopped onions and carrots. Top with parsley.

## WILD RICE DRESSING

1½ cups wild rice
1 large onion, well minced
1 cup bacon drippings or butter
1½ loaves stale cracked wheat
    bread
1 cup cooked celery, chopped
2 teaspoons parsley, chopped
1 level teaspoon curry powder
    (optional)
    Sage, if desired
    Salt and pepper to taste
2 eggs, well beaten

Boil rice about 20 minutes in 3 quarts of water, drain well and cool. Fry onion in

fat until clear. Break bread into fine crumbs. Mix all ingredients, folding in beaten eggs last and toss dressing lightly. This recipe makes enough to stuff a 12- to 15-pound turkey. Delicious also with any other type of fowl or with veal and pork.

## CHESTNUT DRESSING

⅓ cup pork sausage
1 cup ground chestnuts
3 cups bread crumbs
1 apple, cut in small pieces
1 tablespoon onion, chopped
1 tablespoon parsley, chopped
    Salt and pepper, to taste

Fry pork sausage, then mix all ingredients together. This recipe makes enough to stuff a 10-pound turkey.

## SWEDISH STUFFING

Toss the following ingredients together lightly: 4 cups cubed bread (half rye and half white); ¼ cup raisins; 1 small apple, chopped; ½ tablespoon onion, chopped; 1 teaspoon sage; ½ cup fat, melted; and a little water if a more moist dressing is desired.

## BROWN RICE DRESSING

2 cups brown rice
½ teaspoon salt
2½ cups broth from boiled giblets
1 cup onions, chopped
2 tablespoons celery, chopped

2 tablespoons green pepper,
    chopped
¼ teaspoon pepper
¼ teaspoon ground sage, scant
¼ pound butter
1 cup pineapple, crushed

Pour broth over rice and salt in sauce pan; add water, if necessary to raise liquid to ½-inch above rice. Boil vigorously, uncovered, until liquid evaporates to rice level. Remove from heat, cover and allow to steam 15 minutes. Sauté onion, celery and green pepper in butter. Season. Combine vegetables, rice and pineapple. Stuff 4½ to 5-pound roasting hen.

## BREAD STUFFING BALLS

  2 cups chicken stock
22 ounces stale white bread,
    cubed
  3 eggs
¼ cup chopped parsley
1½ teaspoon salt
½ cup chopped green pepper

½ teaspoon pepper
½ cup chopped onion
½ cup chopped celery
⅓ cup lightly browned,
    melted butter

Mix one cup of the stock into other ingredients; form into loose 2-inch balls. Arrange on pan and add remaining chicken stock. Bake in 350° oven for 15 minutes or until lightly browned. Serves 4 to 5.

## TURKEY DRESSING CASSEROLE

Crumble 2 cups cornbread and 2 yeast rolls in a bowl. Soften with 2 cups warm, seasoned, rich turkey broth.

Blend ½ cup buttermilk, 2 medium-sized onions (quartered) and ¼ teaspoon soda in blender. Add to crumb mixture, stir in 4 well-beaten eggs, ½ cup melted turkey fat (or butter) and 1 tablespoon celery seed. Pour into well-greased 9x12-inch pan and bake at 350° until brown, about 1 hour. Serve hot with giblet gravy.

# VEGETABLES

## POTATO DUMPLINGS

3½ cups mashed potatoes
¼ teaspoon nutmeg
1½ teaspoons salt
¼ teaspoon white pepper
  2 egg yolks
½ cup flour
  4 quarts boiling, salted water

Mix potatoes, nutmeg, salt, pepper, and egg yolks. Form into small balls 1½ inches in diameter; then roll in flour to keep the outside from sticking. Drop carefully into boiling, salted water. When the dumplings rise to the top, simmer for 25 minutes. Remove and serve. Excellent served with sauerbraten. Makes 6 portions.

## NEW ENGLAND BAKED BEANS

1½ cups dried beans, kidney or
      California pea
2 tablespoons finely chopped
      onion
¼ pound salt pork
⅓ cup molasses
¼ teaspoon mustard
1½ tablespoons brown sugar
2 tablespoons catsup
1 teaspoon salt
⅛ teaspoon pepper
1 tablespoon butter

Pick over beans and rinse with cold water. Cover with water and soak overnight. Drain and cover with fresh water; simmer about ½ hour until skins burst when blown on; drain. Together with chopped onion put in a greased bean pot with salt pork cut in chunks. Mix remaining ingredients with 2 cups hot water and pour over beans. Add enough water to cover beans and dot with butter. Cover pot and bake in slow oven about 6 hours. Add water as needed.

## BEETS IN ORANGE SAUCE

8-10 beets, sliced and cooked
1 small onion, grated
1 tablespoon vinegar
3 tablespoons sugar
1 tablespoon melted butter
1 orange — juice and grated rind
      Salt to taste

Mix all ingredients and place in a sauce pan. Cover tightly and simmer for 15 minutes. This unusual vegetable dish is often ordered with baked Western ham or fried chicken dinners.

## ASPARAGUS SOUFFLÉ

1 cup asparagus, cut
1 tablespoon flour
1 egg, beaten
1½ cups milk
1 tablespoon sugar
½ teaspoon salt
1 tablespoon butter, melted

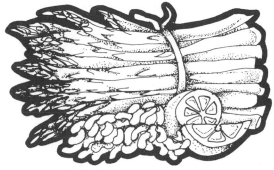

Mix asparagus and flour; then combine with mixture of beaten egg and milk. Stir well. Add sugar, seasonings, and butter. Bake in ungreased casserole in moderate oven, stirring occasionally until mixture begins to thicken. Bake until firm but not long enough to bake dry.

## CORN PUDDING

2½ cups cream-style corn
3 eggs, beaten slightly
2 cups milk
1 teaspoon salt
¼ teaspoon pepper
1 tablespoon minced onion
1 pimento, chopped
½ green pepper, chopped
2 tablespoons butter

Mix ingredients together and bake in a 325° oven for an hour. This makes an interesting and colorful way to serve part of the vegetable course for either holiday meals or party fare.

## SWEET POTATO SOUFFLÉ

6 cups cooked sweet potato
1 cup sugar
¼ cup butter
½ teaspoon vanilla
⅛ teaspoon nutmeg
3 whole eggs

Have all ingredients whipped well in an electric mixer. Then put mixture in an ungreased casserole and bake in 400° oven until light brown. Serve immediately.

## CANDIED SWEET POTATOES WITH PEANUTS

6 medium-sized sweet potatoes
½ cup brown sugar
1 cup boiling water
4 tablespoons butter
½ teaspoon salt
2 teaspoons chopped peanuts

Pare and slice sweet potatoes. Make a syrup of sugar, water, butter and salt. Put in a greased shallow baking dish with potatoes. Bake in slow oven for 1 hour or until candied. When nearly done, sprinkle with chopped peanuts and brown lightly.

## ESCALLOPED TOMATOES

1 No. 2½ can tomatoes
1 small onion, chopped fine
¼ cup butter
1¼ cups dry bread cubes
½ cup brown sugar
1 teaspoon salt
⅛ teaspoon pepper

Sauté onion in butter, using an iron frying pan. Add bread cubes and sugar; cook slowly. Stir in tomatoes and seasoning. Place mixture in buttered shallow pan and bake 45 minutes in medium oven.

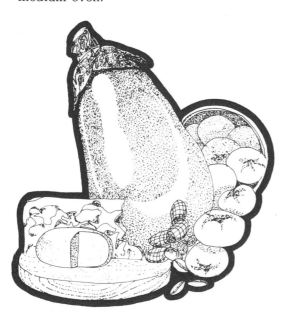

## SPINACH LOAF WITH HORSERADISH SAUCE

1 quart spinach, cooked
1 cup cream sauce
1 cup bread crumbs
3 eggs, separated
2 teaspoons chopped onion
1 tablespoon butter, melted
½ teaspoon salt
⅛ teaspoon pepper

Chop spinach. Mix in other ingredients, folding in beaten egg whites last. Place in pan of hot water and bake in 350° oven for 45 minutes. Excellent for a main course or a vegetable dish.

**Sauce:**

Fold ¼ cup drained horseradish into ½ pint cream, whipped and sweetened. Add dash of salt.

## CHEESE BEAN À LA FALLHALL

2 cans cut yellow wax beans
Butter
Brown sugar
White sauce
½ cup grated cheese
½ cup aged cheese

Drain some juice from beans and cook in a little butter and brown sugar until dry. Combine with a white sauce flavored with ½ cup grated cheese. Place in a buttered casserole dish and cover the top with ½ cup ground aged cheese. Bake 20 minutes in a moderate oven. (To age cheese: dry cheese, grate it until very fine, and pack in glass jars. It keeps indefinitely and has a fine tang.)

## EGGPLANT PROVENÇALE

1 medium-size eggplant, peeled and sliced
4 large tomatoes, peeled and chopped
½ cup olive oil
2 cloves garlic, crushed
½ cup bread crumbs
½ cup Parmesan cheese
Salt and pepper, to taste

Simmer tomatoes with 3 tablespoons olive oil in a skillet until it thickens. Heat remaining olive oil in another skillet before mixing in combined garlic, crumbs, and cheese. Dredge salted eggplant slices in crumb mixture and fry until tender in oil; then remove to casserole. Put tomato sauce and crumb mixture between layers, and spread on top also. Bake for 30 minutes at 375°. Good hot or cold.

## CELERY AU GRATIN WITH ALMONDS
- 2 tablespoons butter
- 2 tablespoons flour
- 1 cup chicken stock
- ¼ cup light cream
  Salt and pepper, to taste
- 2 cups celery, parboiled and cut
- ¼ cup blanched almonds
  American cheese, grated
  Bread crumbs, buttered

Make a cream sauce of the butter, flour, chicken stock, cream, salt and pepper. Add celery and chopped almonds. Bake in a buttered casserole, topped with cheese and crumbs, until brown.

## CREAM-STYLE FRESH CORN
- 2 quarts fresh corn, grated
- 8 tablespoons butter
  2 to 3 cups whole milk
  Salt, to taste

Grate fresh sweet corn a little older than desired for eating on the cob. Melt butter in large deep skillet, then add corn. Cook over medium or low heat, stirring constantly to keep from sticking. Add milk to prevent too much thickening. When corn tastes as if starch is cooked remove from stove. Season to taste. Serves 6.

## RESIN BAKED POTATOES
Renowned chefs cook these special potatoes over a fire in a cast-iron cauldron with a tight cast-iron cover. A large chunk of naval stores resin is melted in it (about an hour), and Idaho potatoes dropped in. After about 1 hour, potatoes rise to the surface and are cooked 15 minutes more. Then they are removed with iron tongs and each one placed on a piece of heavy butcher paper, which is twisted around it to form a jacket. Waiters cut through paper and potato to serve it topped with butter and hickory salt. (Show this recipe to the amateur chef in the family at your own risk!)

## CREAMED SWEET POTATOES IN ORANGE CUPS
- 6 large sweet potatoes, boiled
- 1 cup sugar
- 2 whole eggs, well beaten
- ½ cup raisins
- ½ cup coconut
- 1 cup milk
- ⅓ cup butter, melted
  Pinch of salt
- ⅛ teaspoon ginger
- 8 oranges
- ⅓ cup pecans or black walnuts, broken
  Maraschino cherries

Peel the cooked potatoes, then beat until all lumps have disappeared. Add all the remaining ingredients, except the oranges, nuts, and cherries. Halve the oranges; remove fruit; stuff shells with potato filling. Cook 20 minutes in medium oven. Top with nuts and cherries. Serve hot. Serves 12 to 16.

## SWEET POTATO DELIGHT

- 6 large yams
- ½ pound butter
- 1½ cups sugar
- 3 cups orange juice
- 1½ cups chopped black walnuts
  Marshmallows

Peel potatoes and slice crosswise. Cook until tender in as little water as possible. Drain water and whip potatoes until creamy. Add other ingredients (except marshmallows) and mix well. Place in greased baking dish and top with marshmallows. Brown in oven for about 10 minutes. Serve piping hot. Serves 12.

## TOMATO PUDDING

- 1 cup brown sugar
- ¾ cup boiling water
- ½ teaspoon salt
- 1 10-ounce can of tomato puree
- 1 cup bread, diced
- ½ cup melted butter

Add sugar, water and salt to tomato puree. Boil 5 minutes. Place bread squares in a greased casserole and pour melted butter over them. Add hot tomato mixture and place cover on casserole. Bake in a moderate oven, about 350°, for 30 minutes. Serve as an entrée side dish, not as a dessert.

## BAKED SPINACH SOUFFLÉ

- 2 pounds fresh, cooked spinach, finely chopped
- 3 tablespoons chopped onion
- 1 teaspoon salt
- ½ teaspoon pepper
- 6 egg whites
- 2 cups cooked chestnuts, chopped
- ¼ cup melted butter
  Hard-boiled eggs, to garnish

Add onion, salt, pepper and egg whites to spinach. Beat together with wire whip until smooth. Have ready a 3-pint mold ring greased with butter. Fill mold with spinach mixture and bake in 375° oven for 20 minutes. Remove from mold and turn out on platter. Fill center with chestnuts and melted butter. Surround with hard-boiled eggs cut in quarters. Serves 12.

## FRESH VEGETABLE CASSEROLE

- 8 small new potatoes
- 8 baby carrots
- 1 small cauliflower, broken in flowerlets
- 1 cup fresh peas
- 1 cup baby lima beans
- ½ pound process cheese, sliced
- 2 cups medium cream sauce
  Several celery stalks and onions
- 1 tablespoon cheese, grated

Cook vegetables separately (except celery and onions). Drain well; place in casserole. Add sliced cheese to hot cream sauce and stir until melted. Chop a few stalks of celery and a couple of small onions together and add water to them. Simmer until a broth is obtained. Mix this broth into sauce and pour over vegetables. Place casserole in 350° oven, about 30 minutes, until well heated. Sprinkle with grated cheese and garnish with parsley. Serves 8.

## BAKED KIDNEY BEANS

- 1 pound dry red kidney beans
- ½ pound salt pork, cut in strips
- 3 tablespoons onion, chopped
- 2 tablespoons brown sugar
- 1 tablespoon dry mustard
- 2 bay leaves
- 1 tablespoon cider vinegar
- ½ clove garlic, minced
- 2½ tablespoons molasses

Soak beans overnight. Parboil for a half hour. Fry pork until golden brown. Add salt pork and fat with rest of ingredients to beans. Bake in a slow 250° oven for 6 to 7 hours or until tender. Add additional water during baking as needed. Makes 1½ quarts of beans.

## ITALIAN EGGPLANT

Cut 1 medium-size eggplant into half-inch slices and peel. Beat 1 egg with 1 tablespoon milk. Dip slices in egg mixture and then dredge in cracker crumbs. Fry in small amount of fat until golden brown on both sides. Place slices in shallow baking pan. Brown 1 diced onion in fat and add 2 cups tomatoes, 1 teaspoon salt, ⅛ teaspoon pepper and 1 teaspoon sugar. Simmer for 30 minutes, then add ⅔ cup grated Cheddar cheese. Pour tomato mixture over eggplant and sprinkle top with ⅓ cup grated cheese. Bake in 350° oven for 1 hour or until eggplant is tender. Serves 6.

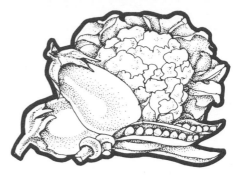

## DRAMBUIE YAMS

  4-6 yams or sweet potatoes
  ⅛ pound butter
  3 tablespoons honey
  2 tablespoons brown sugar
  2 ounces Drambuie

Steam the potatoes until tender, but not soft. Cool slightly and peel. Arrange whole potatoes in a baking dish. Spread honey, brown sugar, chunks of butter and 1 ounce Drambuie over potatoes. Bake in 350° to 375° oven for 15-20 minutes. Approximately 5 minutes before removing from oven, pour remaining Drambuie over potatoes. Cut potatoes in half for serving. Makes 4-6 portions.

## PEAS EPICUREAN

  1 No. 2 can peas
  1 cup heavy cream
  4 strips bacon
  ½ large Bermuda onion, chopped
  1 cup canned or fresh mushrooms
  1 tablespoon flour
    Salt and freshly ground pepper
    Worcestershire sauce and
      Ac´cent
  ¼ cup sherry

Chop raw bacon into pieces and sauté with onion until brown. If fresh mushrooms are used, these may be sautéed at this time. Add flour and cream, stirring constantly over low flame. After sauce has thickened and is

smooth, add seasonings, sherry and canned mushrooms. Add peas last and fold gently into mixture. Serves 8.

## BAKED EGGPLANT

  2 medium eggplants
  5 eggs, unbeaten
  1¼ cups milk
    Salt and pepper, to taste
  3 cups American cheese, grated
  3½ cups saltine crackers, crushed
  1½ cups margarine, melted

Peel, slice and boil eggplant until tender. Drain in colander 10 minutes. Pour into a bowl and add eggs, milk, seasonings, half of crumbs, half of cheese and half of margarine. Mix well. Pour into a baking dish, having mixture about 1 inch thick. Sprinkle top with remaining cheese, crumbs and margarine. Bake in 450° oven 20 minutes, until firm. Serves 8-10.

## ONIONS VIENNESE

  2½ pounds medium-size Bermuda
      onions
  2 tablespoons sherry wine
  ½ cup celery, chopped
  ¼ cup pimentos, chopped
  1 cup mushrooms
  ½ teaspoon marjoram
    Pinch of thyme
  1 tablespoon Alamo Zestful
      Seasoning
  2 cups medium cream sauce
  1 cup Cheddar cheese pieces
  1 cup cracker crumbs

Peel onions and quarter. Cover with cold water and bring to a boil. Drain juice and add ingredients listed above except cream sauce, cheese and crumbs. Combine cream sauce with onion mixture. Put a layer of this mixture into a buttered casserole and sprinkle with cracker crumbs and dot liberally with Cheddar cheese. Continue to build up casserole with additional layers. Sprinkle top with paprika and bake for 1 hour in 325° oven. Serves 10.

## CRÉOLE CABBAGE
- **1 pint cured ham drippings with fat**
- **3 cups tomatoes, mashed**
- **1 medium size cabbage, shredded**
- **6 pods tender okra, cut**
- **1 bell pepper, diced**
- **1 small onion, diced**
- **1 cup ham, diced**
  - **Salt, white pepper, Worcestershire sauce, Tabasco sauce, wine vinegar and sugar to taste**
- **⅔ stick butter**
- **½ cup flour**

Add tomatoes to ham drippings and bring to boil. Add cabbage, pepper, onion and okra. Bring to a boil and add seasonings. Reduce heat and simmer 20-30 minutes or until cabbage is tender. Add diced ham. Blend butter and flour and stir into cabbage to thicken. Serves 8 to 10.

## SWEDISH BAKED BEANS
Grind together: 1 apple, ¼ cup raisins, ½ cup onion and a small piece of ham. Mix well with ¾ cup catsup, 1 tablespoon prepared mustard, ¼ cup sweet relish, ¾ cup brown sugar. Then blend into 1 quart baked beans. Bake in bean pot in a 225° oven for 1½ hours. Serves 8.

## SOUFFLED SQUASH
- **2 eggs, separated**
- **2 cups cooked squash**
- **¼ cup onion, cut fine**
- **¼ cup celery, cut fine**
- **⅛ cup green pepper, cut fine**
- **1 teaspoon sugar**
- **1 teaspoon baking powder**
- **1 tablespoon flour**
- **⅓ cup milk**
  - **Salt and pepper, to taste**
- **3 tablespoons butter**
- **⅛ cup cracker crumbs**

Beat eggs separately, adding 1 tablespoon of water to both egg whites and yolks. Slice squash and cook until tender. Mash squash, then add celery, green pepper, onion, sugar, baking powder, flour, milk and salt and pepper. Add egg yolks and whites separately. Pour into greased glass or aluminum cups. Top with cracker crumbs and dot with butter. Cook until lightly brown in 350° oven. (Grated cheese is good on top.) Serve hot. Makes 8 generous portions.

## SPINACH PUDDING
- **3 cups cooked fresh spinach**
- **½ small onion**
- **½ green pepper**
- **1½ garlic buds**
- **2 eggs**
- **1 teaspoon salt**
- **¼ teaspoon pepper**
  - **Dash of nutmeg**
- **1½ cups finely ground bread crumbs**
- **½ cup softened butter or margarine**

Put spinach, onion, green pepper and garlic through a grinder, using a fine blade. Add eggs and seasonings, mixing well. Mix in 1 cup of the bread crumbs. Take a clean dish towel and spread the butter onto it, forming a 9- to 10-inch square. Sprinkle butter with remaining bread crumbs. Drop spinach mixture in center of crumbed area and form into a roll about 1½ inches thick. Wrap cloth loosely around roll. Tie ends and middle loosely with string. Steam 20 minutes. Makes 10 to 12 portions.

## CREAMED HOMINY

2 No. 2½ cans white hominy
1 medium onion, minced and
    sautéed
1 4-ounce can pimentos, minced
6 strips bacon
1 quart white sauce

Fry bacon until crisp and drain. Add hominy, onion and pimentos to warm white sauce. Simmer until well heated. Mince crisp bacon over top and serve. Makes 6-8 portions. Excellent with baked ham.

## WESTERN SUMMER SQUASH

3 pounds summer squash
1 medium onion, grated
1 4-ounce can green chili peppers
3 tablespoons butter
¼ pound American cheese

Clean squash and cover with water, simmer until soft. Drain and whip squash, then add onion and minced green pepper. Add butter and salt to taste, pour into greased casserole and grate cheese over top. Bake in warm oven until cheese is melted. Serves 6-8.

## POIS CASSÉ PARISIENNE À LA TAIX

¾ pound dried split peas
1 gallon beef shank stock
1 medium onion, chopped
1 leek, chopped
¼ head cabbage, chopped

3 celery hearts, chopped
1 medium carrot, diced
1 medium potato, diced
1½ teaspoons pepper
1⅓ teaspoons salt
1 bay leaf
1 pinch thyme
1 ounce ham grease

Soak peas for 6 hours. In a 1½ gallon pot heat 1 ounce ham grease, then add onion and cook until golden brown. Add leek, celery, carrot and cook until reduced. Mix all other ingredients, except peas and 1 quart of stock. Bring to a fast boil. Reduce temperature and simmer 2 hours. The split peas are cooked in 1 quart of beef stock, and are started an hour after the other ingredients have been cooking. When vegetables are cooked, split peas are added. Serves 8-10.

## STUFFED ONION COLORADO

6 large onions
2 tablespoons fat
2 tablespoons green pepper
1 clove garlic
1 tablespoon parsley, chopped
¾ teaspoon salt
½ teaspoon celery salt
¼ teaspoon pepper
¾ pound ground beef
¼ pound ground pork sausage
1 egg, slightly beaten
¼ cup cracker crumbs, fine
¼ cup tomato sauce
¼ cup grated cheese
    Paprika

Boil onions 20 minutes; drain, cool, and remove centers. Chop centers and green pepper and brown in fat with garlic. Add to meat with parsley and seasonings. Mix in egg, crumbs and tomato sauce. Fill onion shells with this mixture, then sprinkle with cheese and paprika. Bake at 350° for 45 minutes. Baste often. Serves 6.

## BOSTON BAKED BEANS

2 pounds navy beans
1 teaspoon soda
1 pound salt pork
1 medium-size onion
$\frac{2}{3}$ cup molasses
2 teaspoons dry mustard
4 teaspoons salt
$\frac{1}{2}$ teaspoon pepper

Soak beans overnight. In morning parboil for 10 minutes with soda. Run cold water through the beans in a colander. Dice rind of salt pork in 1-inch squares, cut each in half. Place half of pork on bottom of 2-quart bean pot with whole onion. Pour beans into pot and top with the rest of the pork. Mix other seasonings with hot water. Pour over beans. Bake in 300° oven for 6 hours. Add water as necessary to keep beans moist. Makes 10 portions.

## STUFFED EGGPLANT ON THE HALF SHELL

1 medium eggplant, split lengthwise
  Salt and pepper, to taste
1 cup celery, chopped
1 teaspoon onion, chopped
3 ounces butter
2 eggs, well beaten
1 cup milk
2 tablespoons grated cheese
1 cup Ritz crackers, rolled

Scoop insides from eggplant and cook in salt water until tender. Drain and season with salt and pepper. Cook celery and onion until tender. Add with remaining ingredients to mixture. Return mixture to shells and place in baking dish. Sprinkle top with additional cracker crumbs. Bake 1 hour in 350° oven, or until a silver knife inserted comes out clean. Serves 4.

## LOWELL INN RED CABBAGE

1 medium head red cabbage
1 medium sweet onion
2 large apples
1 heaping tablespoon bacon fat
1 teaspoon salt
$\frac{1}{2}$ cup sugar
1 cup vinegar
$1\frac{1}{2}$ cups water
1 bay leaf
2 whole allspice
2 cloves (heads removed)
6 peppercorns

Remove outer leaves from cabbage and wash the head. Core cabbage and slice. Peel onion and apples and slice. Toss cabbage, onion and apple together. Add remaining ingredients to cabbage mixture and simmer $1\frac{1}{2}$ hours in a covered pan. Thicken slightly with about 2 tablespoons of cornstarch blended with cold water. This dish is especially good with wild game of any kind and is excellent reheated. Makes 6 servings.

## ENDIVES MEUNIÈRES

Wash 12 small Belgian endives well and place in buttered casserole. Add juice of 2 lemons, let them boil over a flame, then cover with foil and a lid. Bake in 300° oven for 1 hour, then drain them and cook slowly in a pan of melted butter until brown.

## CRUZAN POTATOES

$\frac{1}{2}$ cup butter
1 cup chopped onions
1 cup chopped sweet green peppers
1 cup chopped celery
1 cup raisins
2 tablespoons thyme
1 small can tomato paste
1 tablespoon Tabasco
6 eggs
6 cups mashed potatoes (instant potatoes may be used)

For 10 minutes sauté in butter the onions, peppers, celery, raisins and spices, well mixed with the tomato paste. Beat eggs and mix well with potatoes. Combine both mixtures and bake in 350° oven for 25-30 minutes until firm. Serves 8.

## TOMATOES ORIENTAL

Hollow out 6 fresh tomatoes slightly. In 2 tablespoons of butter sauté 2 tablespoons finely chopped onions until golden brown. Add 2 cups clear chicken broth and 1 cup raw rice. Season with salt, 1 bay leaf and pinch of Spanish saffron. Cover, simmer until liquid is absorbed. Remove bay leaf and stuff tomatoes with rice mixture. Bake in 350° oven for 15 minutes. Makes 6 portions.

## BRAISED ROMAINE LETTUCE

- 2 heads medium-size romaine lettuce
- 8 slices bacon
- ½ cup onions, sliced
- ¼ cup celery leaves
- 1 carrot, peeled, cut lengthwise
- 1 teaspoon salt
- ¼ teaspoon pepper
- 1 cup pot roast sauce or roast beef natural juice
- 1 cup beef broth

Wash romaine well and carefully without cutting. Parboil lettuce, then drain. Place bacon slices, onions, celery leaves and carrot in pan. Top with lettuce. Add remaining ingredients. Cover. Braise in a 350° oven for an hour. Remove. Cut off ends of lettuce and flatten leaves by gliding flat side of knife over them. Fold lettuce and place on plate. Garnish with vegetables and juice. Serves 4.

## CELERY CASSEROLE

- 3 cups celery, diced
- ¼ cup almonds, slivered
- ½ cup water chestnuts
- 5 tablespoons butter
- 3 tablespoons flour
- 1 cup chicken broth
- ¾ cup half-and-half
- ½ cup mushrooms
- ½ cup Parmesan cheese
- ½ cup bread crumbs

Parboil diced celery for 5 minutes. Drain and put in casserole with almonds and water chestnuts. Heat 3 tablespoons butter and make smooth paste with flour. Slowly stir in broth and half-and-half. Simmer over slow fire for 5 minutes. Add mushrooms to sauce just before pouring over celery. Sprinkle with cheese, butter dots and bread crumbs. Bake in 350° oven until bubbly. Serves 6. (This recipe can be used with green or lima beans as the main ingredient.)

## BEETS AND PRUNES

Cut 3 cups of canned beets into strips. Place beets and liquid in a pan with 1 pound prunes. Season with ½ teaspoon salt, 4 tablespoons sugar and 2 teaspoons vinegar. Mix well, cover and steam over low heat until prunes are just done. Serve hot.

## MUSHROOMS EN CASSEROLE

Sauté 24 whole, fresh mushrooms using the following seasoned butter: Soften ½ pound butter in a bowl; add 1 tablespoon chopped shallots, ½ teaspoon black pepper, juice of 1 lemon, ½ teaspoon salt, 1 tablespoon Worcestershire sauce and 4 sprigs of freshly chopped parsley; blend together. Sauté mushrooms until brown, remove from pan.

Add 2 cups burgundy and 2 cups water to saucepan. Add juice of 1 lemon, ½ teaspoon salt, ¼ teaspoon white pepper and a pinch of rosemary leaves. When mixture comes to slow boil add ½ cup cornstarch blended with a small amount of water until desired thickness is achieved. Pour over mushrooms.

# EGGPLANT MUSHROOM CASEROLE

Peel and slice 3 eggplants; soak in salted water 1 hour; pour off water. Boil until tender, drain; set aside in mixing bowl.

Sauté 1 cup finely minced onions slowly in 1½ tablespoons olive oil or butter for about 10 minutes until tender but not browned.

Season lightly with salt and pepper and add to eggplant.

Twist 1 pound finely minced fresh mushrooms, a handful at a time, in a towel to extract juice. (Or use canned mushrooms.) Sauté them in 3 tablespoons butter and 1 tablespoon olive oil until very lightly browned (5 to 6 minutes). Season with salt and pepper; add to eggplant.

Mash 4½ ounces cream cheese, then beat it into eggplant mixture. Beat in 4 tablespoons minced parsley and ½ teaspoon basil or ¼ teaspoon thyme. Put eggplant mixture in casserole, top with 3 tablespoons grated Swiss cheese mixed with 3 tablespoons fine dry bread crumbs; baste with 2 to 3 tablespoons melted butter.

Place casserole in pan with ⅛ inch water; bake at 375° for 25 to 30 minutes to heat thoroughly and to brown topping. Serves 8.

## STUFFED ARTICHOKES

- 6 fresh artichokes
- 2 quarts boiling water
  Freshly squeezed lemon juice
- 2 teaspoons salt
- ½ cup olive oil
- 1 cup chopped mushrooms
- 2 cloves garlic, crushed
- 1 small onion, minced
- ½ cup melted butter
- ¼ cup chopped parsley
- ½ pound ground cooked ham
- 2 cups bread crumbs
- 1 cup grated Parmesan cheese

Cut tips from artichokes and brush with lemon juice. Cook until tender in boiling water, to which salt and olive oil have been added. Drain artichokes and remove centers.

Sauté mushrooms, garlic, and onion in butter until browned. Stir in parsley, ham, cheese and bread crumbs and mix well. Spoon into artichoke shells and heat at 325° about 15 minutes. Serve hot. Serves 6.

## ZUCCHINI SOUFFLÉ

- 1 pound zucchini
- 2 ounces butter
- 1 clove garlic, mashed
- 3 scallions, chopped fine
- ⅔ cup sauterne
  Juice of ½ lemon
- 1 tablespoon chopped parsley
  Pinch of nutmeg
  Salt and pepper, to taste
- 2 pimentos, diced fine
- 6 eggs, separated and beaten
- 2 tablespoons Parmesan cheese

Pare the tops and bottoms of the zucchini and cut it into strips about as big around as a pencil and about 1 inch long.

Heat butter in a skillet, add garlic and scallions, and sauté until half done. Add zucchini pieces and cook for 2 minutes, stirring several times.

Add sauterne, lemon juice, parsley, nutmeg and salt and pepper to taste. Cook briskly until the pan is almost dry and zucchini is tender but firm. Add pimentos, mix well. Remove from pan and put aside to cool.

In a bowl combine the beaten egg yolks with the Parmesan cheese. Add zucchini mixture and fold in stiffly beaten egg whites with a wooden spoon. Pour into a deep 2-quart baking dish which has been coated with butter and chilled. Place baking dish in a pan of cold water and bake in 400° oven for about 25 minutes, or until firm and fluffy. Serves 6.

# FOOD STORIES

## Camp Cook Tells All

*by E. W. Smith*

Old Wingy Jones used to say: "My idea of heaven is a kitchen with no one in it but me and the cook stove." Wingy was against companionship. He craved privacy in which to cook.

One spring four of us were tenting on a trout river, and Wingy slipped on a boulder and sprained his ankle. I was elected to stay in camp and do his bidding. It was a privilege to watch him at work.

Wingy's effortlessness around a campfire was the result of planning. Every pot, dish and utensil was laid out in advance within easy reach. His pile of selected firewood lay to the left of the fire. In front of the fire, the wind at his back, Wingy sat or kneeled, producing his simple masterpieces without once standing up, moving nothing but his hands.

When the party was on the move, Wingy's knapsack or pack basket showed the same fascinating organization. If lunch called for potatoes, canned string beans, broiled trout and tea, those items — except the trout, which we were obliged to provide on the spot — were on top of his pack, together with utensils required for their preparation.

The traditional tool of most camp cooks is the frying pan. Wingy *never* used a frying pan except for very small trout, breakfast eggs, or his Olympian hashes. He used a grill. Boil, bake or broil. That was his law, and the cases of indigestion it has saved are uncounted. Greasy foods infuriated him, offending his finer sensibilities.

Some great simplifier has remarked that cooking is the application of heat to edible raw materials. He does not say how to create this heat. How do you build a broiling fire? And what woods make the best coals?

If you don't have charcoal, use dry hardwood. Hickory, apple, ash, maple, beech, birch and oak are all good, with hickory first choice. These woods will burn to coals, and when the coals are a little brighter than cherry red, it's broiling time.

But if there's no hardwood, you can broil with softwood — not *over* it, but vertically against its flame. White pine burns with a bright flame, down to a feathery white ash. So does poplar. Most cedars and spruces snap and throw sparks. The pitchy pines burn with an orange flame and throw off oily smoke. Stand your broiler vertically, or leaning a little toward the flame, and about eight inches from it. The result is far better than the frying pan.

Wingy's fire was never larger than his minimum requirement. If it were noon, a hot tea and sandwich meal, his fire would be exactly the size of the bottom of his tea boiler — or about six inches across. The wind would be away from him, which is to say toward the back side of the fire.

If his meal required space for two pots and a broiler for meat or fish, he cut his wood sixteen inches long, and his fire would be only six or eight inches wide, at the base. It hurt his pride to waste any heat, or wood. More important, he could get right snug to his cook fires without frying his knuckles or singeing his eyebrows.

One of our most revered meat-packing houses (Swift & Co.) has come out definitely for seasoning broiled meats *after* cooking, *not before*. Wingy knew this all the time. His arguments: salt makes the juice run out of meat, and it also cooks away while the meat is cooking. Sometimes he spread prepared mustard on meat before cooking, and sometimes he touched it up with a sliver of garlic. But he believed generally that good meat had its own flavor and that heavy or bizarre seasoning wasn't right. Salt, pepper, a little butter, after the meat came off the fire.

There is a way to tenderize tough meat, and even improve its flavor. South Sea Islanders have used it on fish and meat for generations. You can buy their ingredient in the larger grocery stores — it's papaya juice. Put your meat in a pan or dish, pour over it some of the papaya juice, just enough to cover the bottom of the dish, and leave for a few hours before cooking. I have read recently that the juice of any citrus fruit will have a similar effect.

Wingy was a wizard with game and fish. Did you know that the fishy ducks, coot and shelldrake (Merganser), can — this is no gag! — be made to taste second only to mallard, canvasback and black duck? The fishy taste is mainly in the oil sacks in the skin of these birds. Skin off the breasts, section them from the breast bone with a sharp boning knife, soak for an hour or two in lukewarm water to which a tablespoonful of soda has been added, and broil with thin strips of salt pork cross-hatched over the flesh. Or pan-fry with a minimum amount of oil or grease.

One of our most memorable meals in the cabin came about two days after we'd had hard luck on partridge. There were six of us to feed, and only two birds. Wingy dressed the birds, cut them up as you would a frying chicken, and baked them — deeply within, and surrounded by, a pot of baking beans! We liked it so well that we asked for and got it each hunting season.

Here's his tried recipe for a sauce for partridge, ducks, woodcock or venison. Into a hot frying pan in which a tablespoon of stock is smoking very slightly, dump about four ounces of red currant jelly. As the jelly melts down, add a dash or two of water to get the desired consistency. When the jelly is blended, add a tablespoon of red wine, claret preferred. Squeeze in about a quarter of the juice of a lemon. Spoon this in small quantities over the bird or venison at serving time. Grape jelly is on the same plane. A teaspoonful of soy sauce, or about ⅓ that much of Kitchen Bouquet, is also a good added touch.

But on the whole, Wingy was against sauces, as well as companionship. Both cloyed the appetite, he felt, except on rare occasions. He was a skillful and simple man, and the seasons we couldn't hire him on as cook were generally sorrowful. ■

---

# Everybody's Kentucky Derby Party *by Jonnie Vatter*

Kentuckian Irvin S. Cobb once said it all: "Until you go to Kentucky and with your own eyes behold the Derby, you ain't been nowhere and you ain't seen nothin'!"

Kentuckians all agree. We would like for everyone to come to Louisville, hear the beat of the horses' hooves thundering down the stretch at Churchill Downs, smell the fragrance of thousands of red and yellow tulips, and whiff the aroma of a good mint julep.

But perhaps you can't get a seat for the Derby, find a baby-sitter or arrange for motel reservations. In that case, how about having a "Run for the Roses"

party at your own house? You can have all the color and tradition of gracious Derbytime entertaining in Louisville, you can do it simply, even without help in the kitchen, and the race can be taken care of by your television set.

All over the United States, transplanted Kentuckians try, on Derby Day, to pretend they never left home—and their parties develop distinctive traditions. Some hosts buy the Racing Form for their guests. Others hang out the Kentucky flag. Many import mint for their juleps from Kentucky—"I wouldn't feed this local mint to a horse" — and there's a good deal of emotional argument over the question of whether it should be bruised, with no definite answer in sight. On one subject, however, all agree: guests who have never been to a Derby party before, and lack mint julep orientation, should be warned to proceed with caution. "But this is so *good!*" the innocent newcomer is likely to say, draining the cup in a few gulps—and the next thing he knows, he's trying on lampshades and singing "My Old Kentucky Home."

We live in Louisville, but on Saturday, May 2, we won't be at the track. We'll be having our Derby party at home.

We'll send written invitations about two weeks in advance—attractive printed ones are now available with a horse's head, or the twin-spired Churchill Downs. The race is run about 5:30 Eastern Standard Time, but we'll ask our guests to come an hour earlier. We'll greet them with a frosty mint julep and let them select their favorite horse by drawing at random from folded slips of paper, each with the name of a Derby entry, in a jockey's cap. At the same time, each guest throws a dollar or two into the cap and there's the winner's prize, ready and waiting. By the time the announcer is saying, "The horses are coming onto the track," we are all settled in front of the television.

After the Derby, there will be much discussion about which horse should have won, and why. Did one jockey ride the rail too closely in the stretch? Was another jockey too high in the irons? Time for another julep—and then the buffet.

We'll use an arrangement of yellow and pink tulips, or red roses, on a brightly-colored linen cloth covering the serving table. The traditional Kentucky menu which follows contains guest-tested recipes for 12 hungry people:

**DERBY BUFFET**
**Frosty Mint Juleps**
**Baked Country Ham, Sliced**
**Grits Soufflé Casserole**
**Fresh Asparagus with Pimentos**
**Assorted Fruit Platter**
**Derby Pie**
**Hot Coffee and Iced Tea**

**Frosty Mint Juleps:** My husband makes the best mint julep in the state of Kentucky and this is his secret recipe:
**Crushed ice**
**6 sprigs of mint for each julep**
**100 proof bourbon**
**Simple syrup**
Remove the leaves from 4 sprigs of mint and place in silver julep cup or glass. Add a small amount of crushed ice and gently bruise the leaves with a large spoon or wooden pestle. Add 1½ ounces of good bourbon, ¼ ounce of simple syrup, and stir gently until outside is frosty. Place two whole mint sprigs into the cup, and dust with confectioners'

sugar. Cut a straw in half, and place both halves in the julep so that when you sip the drink, your nose is in the mint. Most important!

**Baked, Sliced Country Ham:** Several good brands of country ham are now available nationally, but a Kentucky ham is the obvious choice. Our ham will soak in cold water for 24 hours, then go to a local bakery to be baked and glazed. (If you do not care for the peppery and unusual flavor of country or Kentucky ham, smoked "city" ham straight from the supermarket would do perfectly well.) Slice and arrange the ham on a large platter early Saturday morning, cover with plastic wrap and refrigerate until buffet time.

**Grits Soufflé:** This is my favorite make-ahead casserole. It keeps well under refrigeration for hours.
**1½ cups uncooked white grits**
**6 cups cold water**
**1 pound very sharp grated cheese**
**2 sticks margarine or butter**
**3 eggs, beaten slightly**
**4 teaspoons seasoned salt**
**½ teaspoon cayenne pepper**
**Tabasco sauce to taste**
Bring the water to a full boil and add the grits slowly. Cook and stir over medium heat until the grits have thickened (3 to 5 minutes). Add the remaining ingredients while the mixture is hot. Pour into a well-greased two quart casserole and refrigerate, covered, until buffet-time. About the time the race starts, put the casserole into the oven and bake for one hour at 350 degrees.

**Fresh Asparagus with Pimento Slices:** This vegetable "comes into its own" in Louisville in the spring. However, another green vegetable may be substituted. Be sure to serve it piping hot, but NOT overcooked. Add a dash of paprika, thin pimento strips, butter, salt and pepper.

**Assorted Fresh Fruit Salad:** Another make-ahead! The arrangement of fresh fruits may be prepared in the morning and covered and refrigerated until serving time. Melon balls, fresh pineapple wedges, orange sections and strawberries with the caps left on would be a tasty selection. In keeping with the Derby theme, tuck a few mint sprigs around the fruit.

**Derby Pie:** This is a delicious way to end your Kentucky Buffet. It is also a make-ahead, and freezes well.

- **4 eggs, slightly beaten**
- **2 cups sugar**
- **1 cup flour**
- **2 sticks melted butter or margarine**
- **2 teaspoons vanilla**
- **2 cups chopped pecans or walnuts**
- **2 cups chocolate chips melted over hot water**

Combine the eggs, sugar, melted butter, vanilla, nuts and melted chocolate chips in large bowl. Mix well, add flour, and mix again. Spread into two unbaked 9-inch pie shells. Bake at 350 degrees for 30 minutes. Serve with a small fluff of whipped cream. Very rich!

It's too soon to know which one of the three-year-old colts or fillies will wear the traditional blanket of roses in the winner's circle May 2 at Churchill Downs. But if you have a Derby party at your home that Saturday, your guests will put *you* in the winner's circle—for sure! ∎

# Cuisine for the Hearty Eater

*by Nancy Kennedy*

Sometimes when talk of low cholesterol diets, 85-calorie meals and the beauty of Twiggy's bones becomes too much for me, I like to luxuriate in thoughts of the feasting, past and present, in Philadelphia and the rolling fertile farmlands of the Pennsylvania Dutch which radiate from this city.

Philadelphia is a good place to start. The Quaker City has a long history of being one of the food-lovingest of all U.S. cities. The Philadelphians' special fare is traditional . . . snapper and oyster stew served with hard water crackers, pepper hash, sticky cinnamon buns, scrapple, pepperpot soup and Philadelphia ice cream, that golden creamy confection deliciously flecked with tiny fragments of vanilla bean.

One often-suggested reason for the very early concern with excellent cuisine in these parts was the character of the early Quaker settler, who had a natural aptitude for making compensation to the appetite for the rigors imposed on the spirit. Perhaps a more important reason, however, is the city's location and climate that have made the surrounding Pennsylvania Dutch farm world famous.

Early visitors to Philadelphia, although forewarned, seemed never to be prepared for the lavishness of its tables and its concentration on epicurean pleasures. John Adams wrote in his diary while in Philadelphia, "a most sinful feast again, everything that would delight the eye or allure the taste—meats, turtle and every other thing—flummery, jellies, sweetmeats of twenty sorts, trifles, whipped syllabubs, floating islands, Parmesan cheese, punch, wine and porter. Not refreshments served by weight-watchers!"

Even the seemingly ubiquitous George Washington added to the food lore of the City of Brotherly Love, for it was during the siege of Valley Forge that the famous Philadelphia pepperpot soup was created by a Pennsylvania Dutch cook in General Washington's army.

The American soldiers were in rags, and there never was enough food. So to stop desertions and boost morale the General called his cook and begged him to prepare a hot tasty meal. When a caldron of fragrant soup was produced the following night made with tripe, peppercorns, and all the kitchen scraps the cook could find, it was so excellent that the men were soon in high spirits and ready to face the Red Coats. The present day version of this soup is much less Spartan but retains its distinctive peppery flavor. There is so much work involved in making the soup that most people buy it prepared. It's a complete meal in itself, usually served with crusty bread on a cold winter day.

Fish House Punch has become world famous but its home is the Fishing Company of the State, a club in Schuylkill, founded in Philadelphia in 1732. Claiming to be the oldest club in the country, its membership of 30 fishermen-gourmets meets every two weeks and serves the renowned punch, a delectable and potent drink made with cognac, rum and peach brandy. The clubmen also insist that they invented planked shad, or at least their special gourmet version of it.

As early as Penn's time, the Philadelphians began developing the unique combination of town and country life for which the Philadelphia area is famous. Penn and many of his friends had not only their houses in town but their estates in the country as well, to which fact many of the beautiful old roads through the countryside still testify.

At any rate, the early settlers of the city were soon enjoying the life of the country for holidays and vacations and they quickly learned to relish the food specialties of their Pennsylvania Dutch neighbors. This cooking at its best is still found in the ample farmhouses of Lancaster County. Some delicacies can still be bought in the markets which twice weekly become treasure stores of everything the nearby farmers produce. Even in this era of instant mixes and frozen TV dinners people in the city of Lancaster still get up at dawn and tote old-fashioned market baskets down to the food-filled stalls of their favorite market.

The farmers arriving before the sun include many plain people from the Amish and Mennonite districts, who believe it frivolous to be late. That is why so many clocks in Pennsylvania Dutch farmhouses are set a half hour fast.

Eating is—and always has been—serious business to people in this part of the country. On market mornings a successful businessman will apply all of his talents to choosing a shoofly pie of gingerbread spiciness, yet pie consistency, a requirement to be understood only when you bite into the almost-black molasses-rich interior of this crumb pie, so aptly named because its sticky sweetness compels the cook to keep shooing off flies.

Your knowing marketer will head unerringly for the stand of a farmer whose butchering he respects and whose sausage and bologna are his favorites. For each farm family cherishes their own secret blend of herbs and seasonings for their meat products. There they will choose links of a peculiar smoked sausage which later will be browned slowly in an iron skillet and put on the table with potatoes fried so that they are crisp outside, mealy inside. At the same stand he may have the farmer slice up a stack of Lebanon bologna. He may select a pan of scrapple, that imaginative Pennsylvania Dutch creation born of thrift, which is made from pork scraps saved from butchering, plus cornmeal and seasonings. This comes to the breakfast table golden brown, hot and crisp, on a frost-nipped morning, ready to be doused with maple syrup, ketchup or applesauce.

## Scrapple goes world-wide

Until fifty years ago scrapple was made only by butchers in the Philadelphia area and, of course, on the Pennsylvania Dutch farms where it originated. Because of a lack of refrigeration, the scrapple season was the same as that of the oyster. Then modern packing plants were opened which produced canned scrapple so that it could be enjoyed year around. Fresh scrapple is still available from local butchers and in the farmers markets but the canned variety makes it a food item which can, and does, go around the world. (If you'd like to try this regional specialty write to: The Conestoga Trading Company, P. O. Box 527, Valley Forge, Pa. 19481.)

## Other delicacies

The shopper also knows which stall has his favorite dried corn, to be soaked, cooked, drained and served with nothing but salt, butter and ground pepper. He seeks out the hand cheese made exactly as it was in Germany 300 years ago.

The kitchen is truly the heart of the homes in this green and fertile southeastern corner of Pennsylvania. And the tables they set! The traditional seven sweets and seven sours sit in the center of the table in old-fashioned cut-glass bowls. The sours may include a corn salad that has the zing of dry mustard, vinegar and celery seed; beets spiced with ginger; and watermelon pickles. Among the sweets are such treats as pickled peaches, yellow tomato preserve, spiced crabapple and the most delicate of red raspberry jam. So it takes restraint if justice is to be done to the ensuing tureens of golden chicken-corn soup, the roast chicken bursting with sage and breadcrumb stuffing, the fried country ham, the assortment of pies and cakes.

Tomorrow I diet! ∎

# Dinner Over an Open Fire

*by Bradford Angier*

The fact that snow was hissing off river ice, to glisten into steam among the birch coals of my cooking fire, may have had something to do with the savor of the best meal I've ever eaten. Then, too, there was an aquamarine sky tremulous with aurora borealis, and the company of my sorrel saddle horse pawing snowballs nearby.

Ordinarily, I'd have settled for the liver of the Stone sheep I had just shot. Tonight, though, the fat-sheathed back steaks were just too tempting. I cut off three juicy slabs, scoured my hands with snow, heaped ice in the tea pail, got a bannock browning in one frypan, and then started the backstrap sizzling.

What I do in pan broiling all such game meat is cut it thick, quickly sear both sides in a hot and preferably heavy frypan, and then cook with slightly less heat until done to taste. Salt the metal well before putting the meat in and have it really hot. No grease at all is used, and that sputtering from the meat is tipped out. Salt and pepper if you want and daub with butter after cooking. Serve on preheated plates, or, if alone, the frypan itself.

Augmented with butter-dripping chunks of steaming bannock, and washed down by cup after cup of hot black tea, these steaks were delicious even though not aged. I happen to think that sheep provide the finest of all animal meat.

Just as fat rams shot before the rut are the big game kings of the dining table, the subtly flavored white meat of the large, plump, blue grouse is about the best you're going to sit down to in the game bird realm. The way I like these is cut into serving pieces, well rubbed with cooking oil, liberally salted, dusted with a few flakes of pepper, and then slowly broiled over hot coals. Start with the bony side toward the heat. Turn after about ten minutes, again basting and seasoning. When a fork slips in easily and there's no gushing of red juices the grouse is done.

You sometimes get a coat full of blue grouse, though, in high, windy country where no satisfactory hardwood is at hand for coals. One way around is just to use the legs and breasts, saving the giblets and the rest for soup. Dredge the legs and breasts in salted and peppered flour. Then bring six slices of bacon slowly to a sputter in a heavy frypan, starting with the pan cold. Remove the bacon to a hot dish when it is crisp. Quickly brown the grouse on both sides in the hot fat. Salt and pepper, then remove to more moderate heat. Cover and cook 15 minutes.

Put the grouse on the hot dish with the bacon. Now stir two tablespoons of flour into the fat and juices. Still stirring, add one and one-half cups of rich milk. When this has thickened the way you like it, season it to taste. Let everyone spoon his share over the grouse, bacon, and any vegetables. This is grub you're never going to forget.

When I was recently writing a book on survival, *Living Off the Country*, I tasted every kind of wild meat I could come by handily—lynx, wolf, cougar, muskrat, beaver, moose, caribou and antelope. I also sampled opinions. Those who dine on bear fairly often, I found, are almost unanimously agreed that the North American wilderness affords no more delicious game, with the single exeption of mountain sheep.

Many people who have never tasted bear meat or smelled it cooking are prejudiced against blackies and grizzlies for one reason or another. One complaint often heard concerns the animals' eating habits. Yet the most ravenous bear is a finicky diner when compared to lobster and chicken.

It's true that not even a plump young yearling furnishes really good steaks, which is where many culinary attempts end. But even oldsters large enough to carpet a cabin will cook up into roasts and stews so moist and savory that you have to eat them to believe them. The meat then so resembles top grade beef that you can serve it as such to individuals who have vowed they'd never touch bear meat and actually have them coming back for more.

And the stews? Well, if bear weren't

such good eating, I'd have given up hunting them after collecting my first two or three.

Any excess fat should be trimmed off before the meat is cooked. This fat may then be heated in open pans to extract the grease. Strained into jars, that of the black bear hardens into a clear white solid that makes the best shortening that any user I've talked to has ever come across.

What applies to grizzlies and blackies, however, doesn't go for polar bear, which, because of their diet, taste fishy. Matter of fact, the flavor of all game is pretty much determined by diet. Deer are a common example. I've eaten a lot of them in the Canadian Rockies that have kept alive by gnawing poplars, and their meat has the same bitter overtones that predominate the bark. Deer I've shot in Southern California, that keep fat on wild oats, taste just about like the range cattle that graze along with them.

But all wild game that's taken and handled as it should be, and which isn't subject to arson or other culinary crimes, is good eating. Whether or not some people immediately like a game meat, though, largely depends on their taste prejudices. In other words, some individuals sit down for the first time to deer that stayed sassy on willow shoots, and they expect it to taste like corn-fattened beef. It doesn't.

Such taste prejudices can work themselves out in a while, when repeated servings begin to assume a familiar taste. There are better ways around, however. One is to present the meat in as favorable an aspect as possible, surrounded with familiar and favorite side dishes, especially the impressionable first time.

What too many well-meaning cooks do to game meat shouldn't happen in a nightmare. The result? The sportsman is crestfallen. The cook feels unappreciated. A lot of topnotch grub is wasted.

More game is ruined by overcooking than by any other misadventure. The major reasons for this are (1) the cook has the mistaken opinion than an abundance of heat is the way to assure tenderness, and (2) the erroneous notion that high temperatures will burn away the wild flavor.

If your game tastes best to you rare, that's fine. If not, there's still a way around. Overcooking is ordinarily fatal to most big game, with the exception of bear, because of its general lack of the layers of fat common to comparable domestic meat. Such wild meat dries out under heat, and the fibers quickly tend to harden and toughen. An antidote? A nonseasoned meat tenderizer. For best results with game, use more than the instructions suggest and let it stand a shorter time. ∎

# Recipe
# for a Cookout

*by Nancy Kennedy*

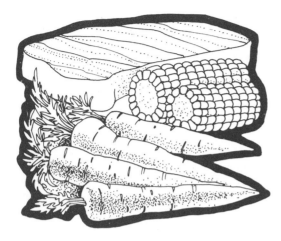

It was a snowy day in February when I visited Charles Virion and his wife, Ethel, in their lovely 1790 home, Monblason, in the rolling countryside of the Berkshires, about 100 miles north of New York City. The purpose of the call was to talk about outdoor cooking and to gather some tips for *Ford Times* readers from this master chef, former innkeeper and author of the recently published "Charles Virion's French Country Cookbook" (Hawthorn Books Inc., 260 Madison Avenue, New York City, $12.95).

His philosophy of cuisine — simplicity without complicated equipment — is found in his book, which is not just another French cookbook reserved for armchair perusal, although it does make fascinating reading.

On many of the book's pages are reminiscences of meals past, lovingly prepared six decades ago over the huge open fireplace in his grandparents' bustling kitchen in the French province of Lorraine. This area of France has turned out superb cooks. The men,

mostly farmers, cooked as well as their wives. The heart of the home was the eternally burning open kitchen fire.

The blue of the sky could be seen at the end of the chimney flues. On these smoke-darkened walls hung dozens of hams and a half dozen varieties of aromatic sausages slowly curing over a constantly burning smoky wood fire.

In Virion's youth, there were always a couple of cauldrons simmering over the hearth, filling the entire house with the heavenly fragrance of country vegetable soup, smoked sausage, boiled dinners, baked beans and pot-au-feu.

Using simple utensils and abundant farm products Virion became an exponent of the country version of French cuisine and to this day he remains especially fond of outdoor cooking.

"Cooking outdoors makes the day seem very special," says Virion. "The beauty of the scenery, perhaps a roaring brook and pure country air give a lighthearted, holiday air to the whole proceedings. Outdoor meals should be relaxed and informal and kept simple in menu and service.

"When you start preparing the fire, you know it will be hot but don't worry about the exact temperature as you might in your indoor oven. You'll not be preparing soufflés that require exact temperature and timing.

"Here are a few favorite recipes from my kitchen and cookbook which should be fun to try outdoors. *Bon appétit.*"

## SALMON CUTLETS WITH MAÎTRE D'HÔTEL BUTTER

  **6 ¾-inch-thick salmon slices**
     **(trout or other fish steaks)**
     **Vegetable oil**
     **Salt and freshly ground black**
      **pepper**
  **½ cup Maître d'Hôtel Butter (see**
     **recipe opposite)**

Dry salmon slices between paper towels. Brush lightly with oil and sprinkle each side with some salt and pepper and let stand for 15 minutes. Set the salmon in a broiler pan or on an outdoor grill. Place the pan under preheated 500° broiler and broil for 3 to 4 minutes on each side or broil same length of time over high heat on outdoor grill. The fish, when ready, should flake when tested with a fork and separate from the bones. Do not overcook the salmon, or it will be dry. Pour Maître d'Hôtel Butter over each salmon slice. Serves 6.

## MAÎTRE D'HÔTEL BUTTER

*Mix ½ cup sweet butter, soft but not melted, with ½ cup minced parsley and 1 tablespoon lemon juice. Add ¼ teaspoon black pepper and ¼ teaspoon salt. Taste for additional seasoning. Makes ½ cup.*

## FRESH VEGETABLES COOKED IN FOIL

*Center 2 or 3 servings of cleaned prepared vegetables on a 10- or 12-inch double thick square of heavy-duty aluminum foil. Lift foil edges slightly. Season as desired with salt and pepper. Dot with 1 tablespoon butter or Maître d'Hôtel Butter. Add 1 tablespoon water. Close package securely with a double fold on top and ends, leaving a little space for steam expansion. Place on grill and cook until tender, turning package once.*

## PAN-SAUTÉED STEAK WITH MAÎTRE D'HÔTEL BUTTER

Before the modern broiler was invented, the French housewife cooked on top of a wood, coal or gas stove. So, of course, she pan-broiled all of her steaks.

- **4 Delmonico steaks, cut ¾-inch thick**
  **Seasoned salt**
  **Freshly ground black pepper**
- **½ cup vegetable or olive oil**
- **2 tablespoons rendered fresh beef suet, or fat**
- **½ cup Maître d'Hôtel Butter**

Trim any excess fat off the steaks. If there is a layer of gristle around the steak, cut incisions into it to prevent the steak from curling. If the steak is moist, dry it thoroughly with paper towels. Season the steaks with the salt and pepper. Pour 2 tablespoons of the oil over each steak. Cover them with wax paper and marinate at room temperature for 1 hour. *Note:* It is most important to have the steaks at room temperature before you start cooking. If you attempt to prepare a steak medium rare when it has just come out of the refrigerator, the center will invariably be ice-cold when you serve it. Place the suet or fat in a heavy skillet over moderately high heat. When the fat starts smoking, it will be hot enough to sear the meat. Sauté the steaks on one side 2½ to 4 minutes, turn over, and sauté the other side the same amount of time. If you are fast enough in cooking and serving pan-broiled steaks, none of the juice essences will be lost. When your steaks are ready, put them on a hot platter and divide the Maître d'Hôtel Butter among the four steaks. Serve with French-fried potatoes and buttered string beans. Makes 4 servings.

## COTRIADE, OR BRITTANY BOUILLABAISSE

Cotriade is the Brittany fisherman's favorite soup. The secret of this soup is good fresh fish.

"It is great fun to cook this recipe outdoors in the authentic way, over a wood fire," says Virion. "When I was a child, I used to see fishermen's wives cooking fresh vegetables over a fire on the beach. When the sail boats came in they would clean the fresh fish and add them to the pot. The soup was a meal of celebration for the fishermen's safe return and for a good catch.

"In place of the fish used in Brittany, you can use cod, red snapper, mackerel or lobster."

6 tablespoons sweet butter
6 large yellow onions, sliced
3 quarts water
6 large potatoes, peeled and cut in
   quarters
¼ teaspoon thyme
1 clove garlic, minced
2 bay leaves
4 sprigs fresh parsley
   Fish of your choice, cleaned (5 to 6
     pounds, cut in large chunks)
   Salt and freshly ground
     black pepper
   French bread, sliced and toasted

Heat butter in a large kettle over a wood fire and in it sauté the onions. When the onions turn a pale gold, add water, potatoes, thyme, garlic, bay leaves and parsley. Bring the mixture to a boil. Cook until the potatoes are nearly done. Add the fish and boil rapidly for 5 to 10 minutes or until just done. Do not overcook. To serve, put all the liquid in a tureen with the slices of toasted French bread and place the fish on a large platter surrounded by the potatoes. Serves 6-8. ∎

# Wisconsin's Wonderful Fish Boil

*by Vern Sneider*

One of the pleasures of traveling, for me at least, is to sample what the French call *la cuisine regionale*.

*La cuisine regionale* simply means, to all intents and purposes, the cooking of the region; and America abounds in regional cooking. There are the New England clambakes, the creole dishes of New Orleans, the savory foods of the Pennsylvania Dutch country. The list is long and extensive.

So whenever I drive around this country, whenever I stop at an inn or restaurant, I always ask the waiter or waitress if there are any regional dishes on the menu. Often they can be found, sometimes in the form of fried catfish and corn bread, abalone, crayfish gumbo, or ham and red eye gravy.

Recently, however, while in Wisconsin I had cause for hesitation. Was there a regional dish on the menu, I questioned. Indeed there was, came the reply. They had boiled fish. Boiled fish! It conjured up thoughts of a soggy mass, dripping with water. But then I tried the Wisconsin fish boil, and as a fish lover from way back, I can testify that it is some of the best fish I have ever eaten.

Like most regional dishes, the Wisconsin fish boil goes back in time, in this case 100 years or so. And like all regional dishes, it is based on the foods readily available in the area. It is believed that the early Scandinavian settlers, who established the sawmill villages of Wisconsin, brought the custom to this country. Whitefish and lake trout were plentiful. So were potatoes and onions. It was an easy matter to prepare a meal by boiling these ingredients together in a large pot outdoors. And today this simple dish has become not only famous in its region but also a tradition.

The first thing needed for a Wisconsin fish boil is a kettle. Specially made aluminum kettles can be purchased in the state. They are of 12½-quart capacity and consist of three parts: a large outer container, a metal basket insert and a cover with adjustable vents. This is specialty equipment, to be sure, but a fish boiler can be improvised out of any large kettle, provided you have some sort of insert basket that can be removed. The lid need only be left slightly ajar, replacing the vents.

Any large, soft-finned food fish is suitable. In Wisconsin, whitefish, lake trout, steelheads and coho salmon are most frequently used. The fish is cleaned, then cut into cross sectional steaks 1½" thick, allowing one pound of steak per person when only men are being served; one-half pound of steak when it is a mixed group.

The potatoes should be new and uniform in size to insure even cooking. The normal allowance is two potatoes for men and one for women. Do not peel, but scrub thoroughly and cut a thin slice from each end.

One onion is allowed per person. It is merely peeled.

Here is the method of cooking, using the special fish boiler:

Remove the basket and place the potatoes plus eight quarts of water in the kettle. Cover with vents open. Over high heat, bring the water to a boil.

When the water boils, add the onions and one cup of salt, pouring slowly. As soon as the water starts reboiling, begin timing. Time for 20 minutes with the cover on and vents open.

At the end of 20 minutes, lower the fish steaks in the basket into the boiling water. Slowly add one more cup of salt. Cover, with vents open, and cook, at a rolling boil, for 12 minutes longer.

To test, spear a potato with a fork. If done, the fork will penetrate it easily. When cooked, the fish, also tested with the fork, will flake. The cooking time may vary two or three minutes either way, depending on the size of the potatoes and the fish steaks.

Drain the fish, potatoes and onions. Serve with melted butter, chopped parsley and sliced lemon.

The consensus is that fish prepared this way tastes like lobster. And in spite of the great amount of salt used, the fish, potatoes and onions don't have a salty flavor.

Of course, it isn't necessary to go to Wisconsin to try the wonderful boiled fish. Actually, the fish boil is an ideal way to prepare a one-dish meal for a group of any size, in a simple operation. It is perfect for camping, the specially made kettles have a rack (available at a slightly higher price) for use over an outdoor fire. It is ideal for a fishing trip, boiled fish offering a welcome change from the usual fried fish.

Boiled fish has always been a gourmet's delight in Europe. For those on a camping or fishing trip (or even those at home with frozen fish from the supermarket) who wish to try boiling or poaching methods other than the Wisconsin fish boil, here are some variations:

In Europe fish prepared by these methods is cooked in what is called a *court-bouillon. Larousse Gastronomique,* sometimes called the bible of French cooking, lists several kinds of *court-bouillon.* One is a simple salt water type, prepared by adding 1½ teaspoons of salt to each quart of water. This is recommended for poaching fish such as sea perch, cod, whitefish and haddock. For crustaceans add bay leaf and thyme to the above.

Another type of *court-bouillon* is made by adding 2 teaspoons of salt and 2 tablespoons of lemon juice to each quart of water. This is good for any small food fish.

In the usual method of poaching or

boiling using a *court-bouillon*, the cleaned fish is placed in the cold or tepid liquid, rapidly brought to a boil, then the heat is reduced and the fish simmered. At all times the fish should be submerged. Small fish, of a pound or less, require about one quart of *court-bouillon*. Fish weighing four pounds or more require six or more quarts.

The cooking timetable varies according to the variety of fish, but the following serves as a guide, the timing beginning when the *court-bouillon* begins to boil:

| | |
|---|---|
| Thin fillets............................ | 5 minutes |
| Two-pound fish..................... | 15 minutes |
| Six-pound fish ...................... | 40 minutes |
| Six to ten-pound.................. | 50 minutes |

The Wisconsin fish boil is a bit of regional America, but it is a bit of Americana for all to enjoy, wherever we live. ■

# Dinner with Mr. Jefferson

*by Marshall Fishwick*

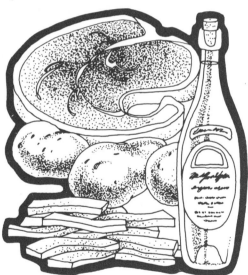

There was no greater social prize in the early days of the United States than an invitation to have dinner with Thomas Jefferson at the White House. It wasn't only that he was President. It wasn't only the assurance of dining well—dining magnificently, as a matter of fact. It wasn't only the beautiful surroundings. The pleasure centered on the man himself. He was wonderful. He was surrounded by an aura of charm, and he charmed all those around him. He was an inventor, a diplomat, a philosopher, a musician, an architect, a gardener, a scientist, an aristocrat, a democrat—and a gourmet.

An invitation went to the Rev. Mr. Manasseh Cutler to have dinner at the White House on February 6, 1802. He was asked not by the "President" but by Mr. Jefferson. The author of the Declaration of Independence abhorred titles and snobbery. He believed all men were created equal.

When Mr. Cutler arrived at 4 p.m.—the usual dinner hour—other guests were on hand, 15 others, and the lively talk, which was as delectable as the food and wine, had begun. So had the music, which Mr. Jefferson called "the passion of my life." Among the six musicians was a violinist; Mr. Jefferson played a violin himself, though never when he was host. We don't know what music he chose that night, but can guess that "the Italian mode" was favored, as on other evenings.

And we can guess that, as on many other mornings, Jefferson had been up before dawn to go with his steward Lamar to the Georgetown market. "He often took 50 dollars to pay the marketing used in a day," Lamar recorded. "Mr. Jefferson's salary did not support him while he was President." This is borne out by the meticulous figures Jefferson kept; so is the relative importance of wine in his overall budget.

Included in "Analysis of Expenditures from March 4, 1801 to March 4, 1802" are these items:

Groceries (not wine)................$2,003.71
Wines..........................................$2,797.28

In viniculture, as in many things, Mr. Jefferson had a scientific passion for testing, classifying, excelling. A few months earlier he had placed a wine order for five pipes (630 gallons) of Madeira, 540 bottles of sauterne, and 400 bottles of claret. He was already well supplied with two other favorites, white Burgundy and champagne.

While Jefferson greeted his guests, the eleven servants he had brought up from Monticello (his Virginia manor house) were preparing to serve the elaborate dinner "in the French style." This means there were separate "covers" (we say courses) for soup, salad, meats and vegetables, desserts, cheeses and fruits.

That night rice soup was served. The salad contained whatever vegetables his dawn trip to Georgetown could produce: he favored "cucumbers, cress, endive, lettuce, chives, cabbage, and peppergrass." But especially in the winter months, when greens were hard to come by, the gastronomic weight fell heavily on the meats: beef, turkey, mutton (always a particular Jeffersonian favorite), ham, loin of veal and cutlets of veal.

To assure such range and variety of meat, Jefferson had not only to spend liberally for available stores but also to plan ahead for future dinners. Hence a letter to his Monticello overseer contained these instructions: "Keep it in deer, rabbits, guinea, pigeons, etc. Let it be an asylum for hares, squirrels, pheasants, and partridges."

Such lists should not lead today's reader, who seldom has such choices of food even at banquets, to conclude that the Sage of Monticello was a glutton. "He was never a great eater," his steward, Edmund Bacon, wrote, "but what he did eat he wanted to be very choice. He often told me that the meat I gave one servant for a week would be more than he would use in six months." Bacon also recalled that peas were Jefferson's favorite vegetable; he raised 30 varieties and took special pride in serving the first dish of green peas each spring.

## MACARONI PIE

The unusual item that caught the guests' eyes on that February 6 was "a pie called macaroni." This was one of the items Mr. Jefferson discovered in Europe, and brought back after making careful notes of ingredients and recipes. On other nights he served "French fries" with beefsteak—a novelty which invariably brought comments from the guests. Desserts were another area in which the ingenious Mr. Jefferson loved to experiment. Here Mr. Cutler's account is so revealing that we might best quote him exactly:

"Ice cream very good, crust wholly dried, crumbled into thin flakes; a dish somewhat like a pudding—inside white as milk or curd, very light and porous, covered with cream sauce—very fine. Many other jim cracks, a great variety of fruit, plenty of wine, and good."

The group sat at the table until about six. Then the ladies retired, leaving the men to their cigars and men's talk. (Jefferson might have complained, as he did often in 1801, that Mr. Hamilton had made government finances so complicated that neither Congress nor President understood them. He had plans to straighten this out.) The ladies returned about seven, when the tea tray was brought in. There was laughter and more good talk until about 10, when the guests left the warm, friendly atmosphere for the streets of Washington.

The next day, in all probability, there would be another dinner party. "Jefferson dines a dozen every day," said his predecessor, John Adams. If that was meant as criticism, Mr. Jefferson didn't take it that way. He was a Virginia gentleman, and hospitality was in his heritage. He himself said, "Man was destined for society."

No wonder those who went to dinner at the White House with Mr. Jefferson remembered and commented on it. So did another President, 160 years later. Dining with a group of leading twentieth century minds, John F. Kennedy said: "This is the most extraordinary group of intellectuals that has sat at this table—with the possible exception of when Mr. Jefferson had dinner alone!"

■

# Food Surprises in Canada

*by Gertrude B. Fiertz*

Those who travel north of the border are likely to return home with a long list of fond recollections, but seldom is Canadian food mentioned near the top of that list. Nonetheless, tucked off in unexpected and often unpublicized corners of the Maritimes, Ontario and Newfoundland, gourmet specialties do exist. Sometimes they prove to be old stand-bys like chowder, sometimes offbeat and regional favorites like cloudberries and cods' tongues.

In Newfoundland we tried our first cods' tongues, which proved to be delicious morsels dipped in egg batter, then in crumbs, and fried golden. The Canadian National Railway, which runs across the "Great Island," often serves them, but cods' tongues are not often found on restaurant menus. The cod fishermen routinely split their catch, toss the livers into a pail for separate sale, spread the flesh to dry on long, open-air "flakes," and usually keep the more perishable tongues for themselves.

Almost all along the Maritime coasts fresh fish comes in daily—hake, halibut, mackerel, tuna and, of course, cod. Up here chowder comes as it does in Maine—creamy, with no nonsense about tomatoes. Cod steaks, a *plat du jour* in the Gaspé, are served hardly an hour from deep water, and preferably not overcooked. In season there is superb Atlantic salmon, perhaps your own, river-caught and cooked over driftwood.

Clams, oysters and lobsters follow the Nova Scotia, Prince Edward and New Brunswick shores. Clambakes and picnics with lobsters cooked over beach fires are something to remember, but the seafood is equally sea-fresh and flavorful when served in local inns with white linen and silver tableware.

Over in Fredericton, the elm-shaded capital and university town of New Brunswick, our lobster came accompanied with fiddlehead ferns. Princess Margaret was served the same dinner when she visited Fredericton in 1958. These ferns are cut just before the "fiddle" uncurls, are boiled briefly, dipped in butter, and look like asparagus (just as good, too).

There is fine fruit country up the St. John's River in New Brunswick, and miles of apple orchards in Nova Scotia just across Fundy Bay. Once, early in June, we crossed the Annapolis Valley, all abloom with lilac and apple blossom. At a roadstand we bought apple blossom honey, and drank freshly pressed cider, fragrant and innocent of preservative even at that time of year. Huckleberries grow over much of eastern Canada—big patches in Newfoundland and Nova Scotia, between St. John and Moncton in New Brunswick, through much of the Gaspé, and again Ontario.

Once we were served baked apple pie in a Maritime village, and found it was not apple at all but northern "cloudberry," a juicy relative of the raspberry. Later on we picked cloudberries ourselves on the rugged "barrens" of Newfoundland and ate them as breakfast fruit.

On Grand Manan Island, right at the mouth of the Bay of Fundy, we heard of another specialty. At a church sale we lingered over the food table. "Did you know," one woman asked me, "that sea gulls' eggs make the best sponge cake?" I did not, though I had heard of experiments which have shown that the eggs of all birds are edible, and almost all are highly palatable.

Along these Maritime shores, and south into Maine, certain greens may be served that are neither spinach nor broccoli. In fact, any of several wild plants may appear. "Scurvy-grass," for instance, a crisp green of the mustard family, may come to table, or one of the burdocks, or coltsfoot, and of course the better known young leaves of dandelions wilted with bacon. Small sage fritters sometimes appear in Quebec, and full-flavored jelly made from black or "rum" cherries—delicious with red meats—local tansy cheese, and crusty home-made

bread baked in outdoor ovens.

West of the Maritimes, and out from Niagara Falls, Ontario, the Queen Elizabeth Highway leads northeast through another fruit area. Roadstands open in June with strawberries and cherries, and continue later with plums—purple, scarlet, and golden Mirabelles—tree-ripe peaches, grapes, and the whole family of berries.

Fifty miles northwest of the Falls, in southern Ontario's heartland, comes a cluster of towns. One of the largest is Kitchener. Here we reached the center of fertile, Mennonite country much like Lancaster County in Pennsylvania. This region was in fact largely settled by our own Pennsylvania Dutch after the American Revolution. Here in Kitchener a weekly market is held that is famous through Ontario. Saturday mornings see the country people—many of the women in plain Mennonite dress with crisp white caps—set up long stands in a central square, as in Old World markets, and heap them with bright red and white radishes, crisp salad greens, snap beans, asparagus and cabbages.

Other stands hold plump, meticulously plucked poultry, and sometimes homechopped, delicately seasoned goose liver spread. Nearby are German and Swiss varieties of "wurst" (sausage) that even Yorkville cannot supply. Golden wheels of Canadian cheddar cheese stand ready for cutting, and tubs of home-prepared "spreading cheese" (Schmierkäse) for ladling into containers that will be sprinkled with home-grown caraway. One finds even a type of "cottage cheese" made from sheep's milk—a bit strong alone, but blending well with dark bread, sweet butter and a sprig of watercress. European cuts of meat, like Kasseler Rippchen (smoked pork ribs) appear, and suddenly we came upon what we had taken only for a joke—pigs' tails for sale! That evening at a local grill we ordered pigs' tails for dinner, and found them delicious tender strips cut along the backbone, grilled, and served with a barbecue sauce.

North of the Mennonite country, north even of North Bay, comes a surprisingly fertile "Little Clay Belt" where we picked up a pale golden clover honey. Up in this remote rock-and-lake country that forms the Canadian Shield, we found wall-eyed pike for dinner, or rainbow, speckled, or perhaps the big lake trout. In season there is game—wild goose or duck, venison, even moose and bear. (A bear's paw is a hearty helping, can even serve two, we found.) Wild rice grows in Ontario, too, and sugar maples. Try crumbling maple sugar over cooked wild rice—as explorers and *voyageurs* learned from the Indians—for a new old-fashioned favorite, rice pudding. With breakfast pancakes one may even run across the light, delicate syrup made from the sugar birch, or the heavier, almost pungent syrup from the wild black cherry.. In such casual encounters lies the fun of unheralded discovery! ∎

# The Jelly Lover's Friend *by Marilyn Mills*

It was a soft spring day when I drove into Union Church, Mississippi. State Highway 28 is a two-lane road with little traffic and plenty of opportunities to pull over and inspect the wild flowers that abound on both sides of the road. Picturesque small farms with cattle can be seen all along the route, and occasionally a modern brick suburban-type home presents itself surprisingly to view.

The town of Union Church, first settled in 1806, is a tiny, pleasant community between Jackson and Natchez. The first settlers were Scottish Presbyterians, and it was their church, established in 1817, that gave the village its name. At first glance there seems very little to distinguish this town from dozens of others in the South—or even in the North. What makes it worth a visit are the fine antique shops, several historic buildings and, of course, the gustatory delights of Alyne Stroud's Restaurant.

Union Church is there before you know it, and Stroud's Restaurant is easy to find, just inside the town limits. I parked my car and went in late on a Saturday afternoon. The lady behind the counter smiled a greeting and continued folding napkins around silverware. I told her I wanted to buy some jelly and she indicated the shelves in front of the window where row after row of brightly colored jars were stacked.

I looked at the labels: persimmon butter, tomato jam, corn cob jelly, cauliflower mixed pickles, rose petal jelly, pear honey, "ole fashion" chow chow, quince jam, camellia jelly, azalea jelly, cantaloupe conserve, and other scrumptious sounding delicacies. I chose a jar each of pyracantha jelly, quince jam, and rose petal jelly and brought her my selections. "Will that be all?" she asked, her tone indicating that rarely if ever did anyone purchase just three kinds of jelly. I found myself seated at the counter ordering coffee and homemade apple pie.

Behind me the door opened and a man came in with his little boy. "Howdy, Miss Alyne!" he said.

"Hello, Mr. Smith," she beamed, "you're all red in the face. You must have been mowing somebody's lawn!"

"No, ma'am," he grinned, sitting down at the counter. "I just been playin' some handball with this boy here."

I looked at the boy, some seven or eight years of age, who kept wiping the moisture from his forehead with a grimy hand.

"Yessum," his father was continuing, "we could sure use something tall and cold about now."

Mrs. Stroud placed two gigantic soft drinks where they could be easily reached, and she and Mr. Smith began talking politics and religion, happily oblivious to the rule that says you don't discuss such things in public. The boy gulped down his drink and had finished his second glass of water when his father rose to leave.

"Guess you'd better give me some hot pepper jelly, Miss Alyne," Mr. Smith said.

She reached briskly towards the shelf over the coffee pot. "You want a large one or a small one?" she asked.

"Now, you know better'n that," he replied, "I can't afford a big one. You better give me the smallest one you have."

She quickly added up the amount, and held out her hand for the money. He gave her, among other coins, three half dollars. "Look at that," she exclaimed, fingering them. "You don't see too many of them all at once. You must've broken into that boy's gumball

bank this mornin'."

The boy spoke up for the first time. "I don't have half dollars in my bank." He was serious, determined that Mrs. Stroud be set straight on this important subject.

She waved them out the door, then returned her attention to me. Did a lot of out-of-town people come here? Oh yes, she said, they come from all over the country and some foreign places. And they always order more jams and jellies after they get home. Some days, she said, she and her helpers cook as many as 300 jars of jelly.

It was in 1955 when it all started, during a fund drive for one of the town churches. She was chairman of the drive and began selling her pickles, jellies, and preserves to meet her goal. After the successful fund raising, people kept on coming back for more of her goodies. Many of the ingredients come from her garden; and others—such as azaleas, roses and pyracanthas—come from her neighbors'. Some of the recipes are her own, others were contributed by friends, and still others are clipped from newspapers and magazines.

She has two helpers in the preparation of the jellies, but she does the major cooking herself. Assisting in the restaurant is a long-time faithful friend, Mrs. Leota Smith, who was not there the day I dropped in. Preparation of all the unusual goodies is a complicated matter, Mrs. Stroud said, and finding the necessary ingredients can be a problem. Her storeroom is nearly always stacked with jars of vegetables and fruits and crates of fresh produce. The workroom is also packed with ingredients and jars of concoctions ready for sale. She has seven freezers in the room filled with frozen fruits and vegetables and homemade pies.

A guest register reveals names of customers from Paris, London, South America, Mexico and most states in the nation. During a year's duration, it is not unusual for Mrs. Stroud to ship 1,500 dozen or more jars of jellies, jams and pickles to people all over the country who have either stopped at her restaurant or have heard about it.

I asked whether she had lived there all her life. No, she said, she is a native of Clarksdale, Mississippi, and first came to Union Church in 1945 with her husband. "The Lord directed us here," she said. It was a hot summer day when they arrived, and "we drove up under this big old tree in the yard—the storms have gotten it since—and I told him, 'We're moving down here.'" Mr. Stroud, who since has died, operated a service station. His wife began her restaurant business not too long afterward and has been cooking up friends ever since.

A warm, friendly, thoroughly likable person who makes delectable jellies and jams, that's Alyne Stroud. And it seems that the only way you will be able to taste any of them is to go by there; or drop her a letter. She has watermelon pickles, fresh mint jelly, crisp pickled squash, tart plum jelly, hot pepper sauce, peach jam . . .

**Something Special from Mrs. Stroud's Kitchen**

## SMOTHERED CHICKEN

1 **large frying chicken**
  **Salt and pepper**
1 **can cream of chicken soup, undiluted**
½ **cup canned broken mushroom pieces and liquid**
½ **cup water**
2 **tablespoons parsley flakes**
1 **teaspoon lemon juice**
1 **tablespoon soy sauce**

Cut up fryer and season with salt and pepper. Combine remaining ingredients and pour over chicken pieces. Cover pan with foil and bake at 350° until tender. Remove foil, drain gravy. Return chicken to the oven for a few minutes. Thicken gravy by adding a little cornstarch dissolved in water.

## MARINATED CARROTS

1 **can bisque of tomato soup, undiluted**
½ **cup cider vinegar**
1 **cup sugar**
¾ **cup salad oil**
1 **tablespoon dry mustard**
2 **tablespoons Worcestershire sauce**
5 **cups sliced, cooked carrots**
1 **raw onion, sliced in rings**
2 **green peppers, sliced**

Combine soup, vinegar, sugar, oil, mustard and Worcestershire. Bring to a boil and pour over carrots. Add sliced onion and peppers, stir well. Keep covered in refrigerator overnight before serving. Drain to serve cold as a relish, or heat for a vegetable course.

## NEVER-FAIL BISCUITS

*Mix together 1 cup warm water, 2 packages of yeast and 3 tablespoons sugar. When yeast dissolves, add 3/4 cup salad oil, 2 cups buttermilk and 1 teaspoon soda and mix well. Add 5 cups self-rising flour. Put in a covered bowl for a few hours or overnight. Stir slightly and dip out with a spoon onto a floured board. Work with hand to form a biscuit. Bake at 450° for 10-12 minutes or until golden brown. Remaining dough can be kept, covered, in refrigerator for a week.*

## HOT PEPPER JELLY

¾ **cup finely ground green pepper**
¼ **cup finely ground hot, red chili or jalapeño pepper**
  **6-ounce bottle of Certo**
1¼ **cups apple cider vinegar**
6½ **cups sugar**
  **Few drops green food coloring**

Combine peppers, vinegar and sugar and bring to a rolling boil. Add Certo and bring back to boiling for about 3-4 minutes. Add a few drops of food coloring. Take off stove and continue to stir for several minutes. Seal in jars. ■

# The Worldwide Cuisine of Our Northeast

*by Evan Jones*

Traveling through Yankee country in 1789, George Washington was disappointed when he stopped at a tavern in Milford, Connecticut. He found his New England boiled dinner "too poor to eat," so he sent it back and settled for bread and milk. Things are far better than that today. In fact, eating out in New England is an experience more rewarding than it has been for most the last two centuries, not only because the food is more edible than Washington's beef and vegetables proved to be, but because there is greater variety. Today's restaurant menus from Connecticut to Maine offer the good tastes of many cuisines.

Take, for example, the many-storied Wayside Inn at South Sudbury, Massachusetts, which may be the country's oldest roadside tavern. It started in the pre-stagecoach days of 1686 as an ale house owned by the Howe family and later was known as the Red Horse, an inn where a traveler might get a meal of salt beef and shell beans, along with a whortleberry pudding. The Red Horse's Yankee flavor inspired Henry Wadsworth Longfellow to write the classic *Tale of a Wayside Inn,* which in turn caused its proprietor to adopt its fictional name. Restored in the 20th century, it has the look of Colonial America and a menu that reflects changing times: It is not unusual to find a guest at the Wayside Inn enjoying beef Stroganoff, a dish created in Paris for an emigré Russian count.

Migrating restaurateurs have transformed the face of New England. Eighteenth century Yankee hostelries — like the Jed Prouty Inn at Bucksport, Maine, or the pre-Revolution Publick House at Sturbridge, Massachusetts — still welcome wayfarers. In addition, however, there are splendid Italian, French, Chinese and other restaurants. Once dismissed as "foreign," they thrive in the same areas that then were meccas for those in search of shore dinners or for the Yankee cooking that earned no greater praise than that it was plain and substantial.

Those were Down East meals that could be monotonous. The courses of a single New Hampshire shore dinner ran a gamut from clam chowder through four kinds of fish to corn on the cob and hot rolls. A typical meal at an inn deep in the country was in its own way equally redundant; whatever the pièce de résistance, it was never without a "relish tray" bearing cottage cheese, chow chow, piccalilli, conserves and vegetable relishes.

Nevertheless, the Yankee penchant for plain and substantial eating-out prevailed for generations. The European immigrants who started coming to the Northeast in the middle of the 19th century soon had their own neighborhood eating places with ethnic bills of fare. Yet such bistros were not easily found by outsiders. It took the Jet Age, which made world travelers of millions of Americans, to create a demand for epicurean meals; many came home with enthusiasm for the food of countries they had visited. And it is in the last decade or so that masters of other cuisines have made such gastronomic discoveries a possibility for the average diner-out in New England.

I like to think that *haute cuisine* came to the Green Mountains when René Chardain pioneered the new trend with his arrival in Vermont's still-Colonial-looking village of Newfane. (His *truite au bleu* may be the next best thing to a trip to France.) Now there are dozens of Frenchmen presiding over New England kitchens, including the staff of Pierre's, a well-known restaurant recently moved from mid-Manhattan to Manchester Center, Vermont.

The acceptance of a Parisian emphasis by Yankee restaurant-goers, however, has not been the only change. Other menus are influenced by the Alpine character of many of the ski areas in New England. A molten *raclette* of Swiss cheese is a natural and flavorsome antidote to Yankee winter. And — equally comforting — there are high-style, sophisticated meals prepared these days by German cooks in such places as Londonderry, Vermont, and Brewster, on Cape Cod.

"Continental" menus may have become ubiquitous, but genuine Italian restaurants — some specializing in delicate Milan and northern Italy nuances, some effulgent with Neopolitan sauces — are pervasive. They are numerous in and around Boston, in other towns where Italians have settled and, in fact, are scattered across the six states. There now are many places where one can order a subtly flavored veal *picatta* or *saltimbocca*. I know a small one in Brattleboro that bears the portentous name of Rome's Via Condotti.

For their part, Greek restaurateurs no longer hide the dishes of their ancestors but proudly serve many specialities of the Mediterranean islands. So with other Middle Eastern cooks. One of the fine restaurants of Worcester, Massachusetts, is El Morocco, on Turk Hill, specializing in kebabs. Japanese restaurants have moved out into the country, and so have "genuine" Chinese dining places that no longer emphasize chop suey and chow mein but concentrate on one or another of China's superb regional cooking styles. A Fukien restaurant, highly recommended, is strategically close to the Yale campus in New Haven.

Come to think of it, young people are probably as responsible as any for the trend so evident among New England hostelries. They are the most traveled generation in the history of public eating places. Lots of them have settled down in Yankee country in an effort to circumvent the vicissitudes of cities. Some of them have fostered the austerities of health-food diets, it is true. But some have taken over old inns and brought them back to life. Still others, showing another kind of creativity, have made great changes in the Yankee look. They believe that connoisseurs of good food should find the ambience as attractive as the meals themselves.

Both ambience and menu are remarkable at a remote Vermont inn at Montgomery Center, not far from the Canadian border. Called On the Rocks, in jaunty salute to the terrain on which the timbered stucco cottage was erected, its menu ranges from buckwheat groats to *tournedos béarnaise* and gazpacho. A sunken "conversation pit" arcs out from the warming fireplace, and pillared candelabra are placed at diners' elbows when they are seated.

On the Rocks is a personal restaurant, the creation of Chef Jon Zachadnyck, who perfected the basics of his classic repertoire at New England's famed

Culinary Institute of America. Driving away from his cottage through the rugged beauty of Hazen's Notch, where Jay Peak rises majestically in the background, a well-fed traveler reflected once more on the rewards to be found in Yankee country.

Unlike George Washington after his long-ago trip, I know the chances are remote that I will ever have to settle for bread and milk at the end of a day of travel. ∎

# The Infinite Variety of American Sandwiches

*by Nancy Kennedy*

The odyssey of the sandwich is as old as the history of the world. It goes back to ancient times and varied with ethnic groups and geographic locations, just as it does today. The origin of the sandwich cannot be definitely established, although there are many theories about its beginning. Some believe that sandwiches are as old as bread itself. The Greeks and Romans enjoyed a wedge of meat between two slabs of bread, and so, without a doubt, the Babylonians, Danes, Saxons and Normans probably ate their version of a hero, too. Another school of history traces the origin of the sandwich to the great Jewish teacher, Rabbi Hillel, in 50 A.D.

During the Passover feast ritual, Jewish people still follow Hillel's custom of eating a sandwich made of two pieces of matzo containing bitter herbs, chopped nuts and apple.

Whoever invented the sandwich, it was the Fourth Earl of Sandwich who gave his name to this great American favorite. According to legend, it came about during the late 18th century and over the gaming table. The Earl, an avid gambler, disliked interrupting his cards and dice while he ate. For convenience sake, he ordered meat between slices of bread. The meal required no elaborate place setting and left a hand free for gambling.

Others saw these advantages and soon all were having "the same as Sandwich." It wasn't long before "sandwich" was an accepted word in the dictionary of foods.

The Earl had captured the restless, eat-in-a-hurry spirit of the new country, America. The sandwich became a cross-country favorite. The ingredients vary from region to region and usually are created from the simple, homely foods that are in bountiful supply.

In New England, for example, the lobster roll, a mouth-watering combination of chunks of fresh lobster meat with a little celery and mayonnaise on a long egg roll, is a longtime favorite. In my youth when I visited relatives in Maine, this was one of the treats that I looked forward to. Then it was almost as prevalent and inexpensive as the hot dog.

Another New England and Midwestern farm favorite, the baked-bean sandwich, has become a menu star in some areas. Out of big-city Italian neighborhoods in the East emerged the dazzling and creative sandwiches with robust fillings: submarines, heroes or heroines.

In the bayou country, the New Orleans' Po' Boy reigns. This snack is supposed to have originated with a kindhearted owner of one of the best coffee stalls of the Old French Market, who used to make up those hefty sandwiches and hand them out to hungry little boys who would beg: "Mister, please, sir, give a sandwich to a po' boy." They are now standard fare in nearly every city in the United States, and when you come down to it, are just a Southern and French-accented cousin of the Northern heroes.

Down Florida way, the shrimp sandwich, in dozens of variations, appears on roadside stands and in all kinds of restaurants. This sandwich is just a good excuse to enjoy some of the wonderful flavor of the fresh Gulf shrimp which go from fishing trawler to table in shoreside communities.

On the bill-of-fare at a Colonial restaurant in Virginia is a Colonial-style ham sandwich. Very thin slices of Virginia ham are served between two slices of buttered French bread. Another version of this is served on the area's beaten biscuits.

A little farther south and west, the barbecue was born as a regional sandwich that now is at home everywhere. Succulent roast pork, beef or ham slices are heated in spicy barbecue sauce and then placed on buttered, toasted split buns. A great meal-in-a-mouthful.

A Midwestern cousin of the barbecue is the breaded pork tenderloin sandwich that Hoosiers eat with great gusto. An associate of mine gets a dreamy look on his face when he thinks of this Indiana delicacy and says that Sam's Subway Restaurant in Indianapolis is one of

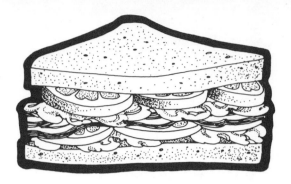

many places that serve the tasty fried pork loin on a warm egg roll bun. He confesses that when he and his family cross the border into the state, they make a stop immediately for this sandwich.

Traveling west, the same regional reasons for sandwiches crop up. In Alaska and northern California, the king-crab sandwich on sourdough bread is one of many seafood sandwiches that abound. Another West Coast invention is the California club sandwich that adds generous slices of avocado to the traditional three-decker sandwich.

Back in New York, where the American deli first became an institution, the corned beef sandwich is king. Served either on a chewy piece of corn rye or pumpernickel—breads with real character that are sliced from loaves as the sandwich is made—it has provided millions of eminently satisfying meals.

A more elegant cousin of the plain corned beef sandwich is the Reuben, which bears the name—wherever it is served—of the Manhattan emporium that invented it.

The Western, or Denver, supposedly was whipped together by hungry Western railroad men who wanted a hearty meal and wanted it fast. What could be simpler and more nourishing than eggs, ham, onions and green pepper cooked and popped onto buttered toast?

So it goes with the history of the sandwich and America's regional favorites. They were born in one neighborhood of a big city or a region and then were adopted by Americans everywhere. No longer are these creations limited by state and regional boundaries. Good cooks and scouting restaurateurs continually see that the food frontier is broken. Long live the sandwich!

## GRINDER, SUBMARINE, TORPEDO, HOAGY, HERO

The variations of this Italian American sandwich are endless. One of the names, "hero," supposedly derived from the saying that you've got to be a hero or heroine to eat one.

- 4 small Italian loaves,
  12 inches long or
- 8 small Italian rolls, 6 inches long
  Mayonnaise
- 2½ cups shredded lettuce
  Italian dressing or oil and
  vinegar dressing
  Salt and pepper, to taste
- 8 ounces sliced salami
- 8 ounces sliced bologna or
  Lebanon sausage
- 8 ounces sliced provolone cheese
- 2 tomatoes, sliced thin
- 8 paper-thin slices onion
  Green pepper strips

Slit loaves lengthwise and spread cut surfaces generously with mayonnaise. Combine lettuce, 3 tablespoons dressing, salt and pepper and spoon onto loaves (drain slightly to avoid dripping when eating). On lettuce arrange remaining ingredients in layers down length of loaves. Cut loaves in half crosswise and serve with additional mayonnaise or dressing. Serves 8.

## FLORIDA SHRIMP SALAD SANDWICH

- 2 cups cooked small or
  medium shrimps,
  cleaned
- ½ cup diced celery
- ¼ cup diced green pepper
- 2 tablespoons mayonnaise
- 1 tablespoon chili sauce
- 1 tablespoon chopped onion
- 1½ teaspoons diced pimento
- 1½ teaspoons capers
  Salt and pepper, to taste
- 4 pita loaves, halved
  Romaine lettuce

Combine shrimp, celery, green pepper, mayonnaise, chili sauce, onion, pimento and capers. Chill well. Season with salt and pepper. Open pockets of pita, line with romaine and spoon in shrimp mixture. Serves 4.

## NEW ORLEANS PO' BOY

*Take a long loaf of French bread, slit it in half, lengthwise, and butter both sides. Then slice the loaf in thirds or fourths (not cutting quite through bottom crust), and put a different filling in each section. Fried oysters almost invariably go in one part, and the other sections can be filled with French sausage, ham, chicken salad, or dressed greens—any appetizing tidbit at hand.*

## MIDWEST AND NEW ENGLAND FARM BEAN SANDWICH

*Spread a slice of whole wheat bread with butter. Spread a second slice with tomato ketchup. Add ¼ teaspoon onion, which has been diced very fine, to enough cold baked beans to spread on the bread.*

## CALIFORNIA CLUB SANDWICH

- 18 slices toasted white bread
- ¼ pound butter
- 1 avocado, peeled and sliced
- ½ lemon juice
  Lettuce
- 12 slices crisp bacon
- 12 slices tomato
  Mayonnaise

Butter 6 slices of toast and arrange avocado slices on them. Sprinkle with lemon juice. Top with lettuce. Butter both sides of 6 slices of toast and place on top of lettuce. Top with bacon and tomato. Spread remaining slices of toast with mayonnaise and place on tomato. Makes 6 sandwiches.

# The Best Bread in the World

*by William E. Pauli*

On Costa Zmay's first visit to San Francisco he took his wife to Fisherman's Wharf for lunch.

"Our waiter brought a basket of bread to the table," he recalls. "It was the best looking French bread I'd ever seen. I couldn't wait to try it, so I pulled off a hunk, buttered it and took a big bite.

"Then I told my wife, 'Blanche, watch out for the bread — it bites.'"

And, like most novice sourdough samplers, once bitten, Zmay couldn't get enough of the bread. It wasn't long before he sold his home in the East to pursue a baking career in San Francisco. Today, as vice president of Parisian, San Francisco's largest sourdough bread producer, he praises this city's famous, tart staff of life.

"Give slices of sourdough to 10 people and you'll get 10 different reactions," says Zmay. But more important to Parisian and the 10 other major sourdough bread bakers in the Bay area, they'll have made at least a half dozen converts.

What's so special about a hard-crusted bread that showers crumbs all over anyone who eats it?

"Taste," booms Zmay. "San Francisco sourdough can't be duplicated. Nobody can copy it. They can't come up with the flavor."

Zmay credits the tongue-tingling taste to atmospheric conditions. Whatever the cause, the bread, according to San Francisco's Convention and Visitors Bureau, rates in popularity with the cable car, the Golden Gate Bridge and Chinatown.

Many gourmets consider San Francisco sourdough the best bread in the world — ranking it ahead of the brioche of Paris, the pumpernickels, ryes and black bread of Eastern Europe, and, would you believe, New York City's bagel.

Even the French, who have been known to look with disdain on American cuisine, bow to sourdough. After a visit, the co-publisher of France's influential travel and gastronomical magazine, *Gault-Millau*, had this to say: "San Francisco is the only big city in the United States where a Frenchman can live happily. Even the bread — well-baked, well-leavened and well-salted — reminds him of his motherland."

Sourdough, shaped in long slender loaves, fat ovals and plump rounds, is turned out at the rate of 400,000 pounds a day in the city (except when the bakeries close on Wednesday and Sunday). And area bakers admit they're having a hard time keeping up with the bulging demand.

It wasn't always so. When Parisian and other bakeries started as "mom and pop" operations in the late 1850s, the bread was baked at home and sold door-to-door. Some credit these early enterprises with introducing French sourdough to San Francisco residents. They say the bakers brought the bread with them from their native Basque region of France. Others claim the bread got its start and name from prospectors called "sourdoughs" who rushed to the Yukon and Alaska in the gold strikes at the turn of the century. With them came the legendary leather pouches of bread "starter" they wore around their necks. This food source was guarded as closely as gold. The starter — a form of natural dry yeast — resulted from mixing flour, salt and water. When it was exposed to the San Francisco elements, "it went wild and sourdough bread was born."

Bakers say a microorganism they've named "lacto bacillus San Franciscus" is what gives the Bay bread its zest. And, they boast, the organism thrives only in the San Francisco area. Adds Zmay, "We set up a sourdough bread bakery in Tokyo. Although we used our starter, the Japanese loaves don't have the exact San Francisco flavor."

This mysterious bacterium has even managed to elude modern science. Zmay enjoys telling how the Department of Agriculture spent several thousand dollars looking for the organism. "After two years a researcher claimed to have isolated a 'bug' he said was responsible. He told the press that he'd be able to ship test tubes of the flavor all over the world. So far nothing has happened. I think he bit off more than he could chew."

Of course, some of sourdough's country-wide popularity is due to former San Francisco residents who miss their daily ration. However, sales experts believe it's the tourist who is spreading the good news. "He brings his family here and they discover the bread," says Zmay. "It's only natural they want to take a couple of loaves home to share with relatives."

Area bakers make it easy for out-of-towners to find the bread. For example, loaves in all shapes and sizes are stacked sky-high on stands along Fisherman's Wharf. Boudin, the oldest

sourdough bakery in the city, even operates a branch on the wharf where visitors watch the bread being made behind large glass display windows.

All major West Coast airports market sourdough. It isn't unusual to spot an Easterner or Midwesterner struggling to board a 747 — his or her shopping bag filled with fresh loaves.

The bread's ingredients — flour, water and salt — prove the value of simplicity. Each morning, long before the first cable car begins to climb Nob Hill, sourdough bakers all over the city don their aprons to turn this simple-sounding formula into award-winning bread.

At the heart of every loaf is the starter. It was first added to Parisian dough back in 1856. Since then it has been passed on by saving a portion of each day's dough for use in the following day's batch. Two of the bakeries — Parisian and Larrabura — not only keep their bread formulas secret, but have a second starter stashed in a hideaway.

Every loaf of sourdough is hand-shaped, and slow-baked in a hearth oven at nearly 500°. During the baking, a huge amount of steam is injected into the oven, causing the natural sugar in the high-protein flour to carmelize and form the familiar crisp, golden-brown crust.

A loaf of sourdough will stay fresh for a week. Some have lasted a lot longer, according to Zmay. "We received a letter from a New Jersey housewife who bought two loaves to take back east. When she got home she and her husband ate one loaf and put the other in the freezer. They forgot about it until seven months later when they were ready to drive to Colorado on vacation. So they tossed it into a cooler along with some other food. After several nights, the couple took the bread out and let it warm up in the sun most of the day. They ate it that evening and she swears it was still good."

Zmay and his bakery are working to make certain that the New Jersey housewife and other sourdough fanciers don't have to trek to San Francisco everytime they yearn for a slice of their favorite bread. His company recently began marketing frozen loaves in several large cities.

Frozen sourdough is great. But there's nothing like eating sourdough in San Francisco. How can anything equal sitting down to an elegant dinner on Nob Hill in your finest attire and covering yourself with bread crumbs? ■

# Pioneer Christmas Fare

by Nancy Kennedy

A Christmas visit to Conner Prairie, an imaginative re-creation of an Indiana pioneer community in the 1830s, is really taking a giant step backward in time. This is no static, dusty collection of buildings and antiques accompanied by canned speeches from bored guides . . . this is a town that lives, breathes, talks, cooks and chats with the visitors as though they were neighbors who just stopped in for a visit. It delights young and old and literally transplants them to another, almost fogotten era.

Conner Prairie Pioneer Settlement is not a restoration; it is not a reconstruction. It is a re-creation of life-styles as they existed in 19th century Indiana. A museum program of Earlham College, the Conner Prairie research and education departments created the roles of the "real people" who now inhabit the town. (Each "resident" has a 104-page book of authentic historical background to draw from for his or her character's daily conversation.) The old barns, buildings, homes, store and covered bridge were brought from all over Indiana and rebuilt to create the town.

From the first Tuesday in April through the first Sunday in November, the village offers a fascinating look at Indiana of the 1830s, and there are occasionally special projects focusing on particular aspects of pioneer life. One of these is "Pioneer Craft Days" during the second weekend of June. Probably the most popular, however, is the "Traditional Christmas at Conner Prairie" (this year December 9-12 and 16-19) when the village is reopened briefly to show how pioneers celebrated the holidays. Let's visit the Conner residence, the grand mansion of the small community.

The housekeeper opens the door with a cheery greeting and tells us that Mr. Conner is off to pick up some holiday treats which were shipped from the east. Further she relates that even though it is Christmas day, the children are in school; the men are working regular hours but there will be a special festive meal in the evening. She lets us peek at the dining room table which they are setting for the family meal. There is a dessert table laden with a dozen different sweets for the last course of the family dinner. There is a stack cake, chocolate cookies and lemon and pumpkin-squash pies, to name a few. (Recipes for some of these old fashioned desserts will be found at the end of the article.)

The housekeeper then points out the new hall rug which Mrs. Conner had woven by the village weaver in time for the holiday season. Seconds later we move to the kitchen as she cautions us about the lighted candles in the hall. The 20th century seems to fade into the mists.

The Conner kitchen is the scene of bustling activity. The cook and hired girl are hard at work—as they have been for days. Bread baked in the brick beehive-shaped oven is being cooled as are the pies and cakes which were baked with the bread. Since today is Christmas, the turkey is slowly being revolved on the spit and is carefully basted. While the meat is cooking, vegetables are cut and boiled in cast iron pots over the open fire. Jars of canned preserves, pickles and jams are brought out of the fruit cellar. Visitors see the actual preparation of the meal.

When we reluctantly take our leave of the Conner kitchen, we amble over to another large and comfortable house, that of the newly arrived town physician Doctor Campbell and his wife. Because the Campbells are new in town they are having an open house to meet all of their new neighbors. In this kitchen last minute touches are being made on the array of desserts which the townspeople will sample later in the day.

There are fudge cookies, a coconut pound cake and a Bourbon cake. Spiced tea and hot chocolate will be served with the rich, high calorie sweets.

One of the educational aspects of Conner Prairie is that the visitor learns that all families did not live in the same manner just because they lived in the same place at the same time.

When we arrive at the blacksmith's house, his wife—not a servant—is alone in the kitchen preparing a much simpler meal than those in the two large homes of the town.

There is a wild turkey, which her husband shot that morning, rotating on a new-fangled spit which doesn't need constant manual operation. After all, she explains, because of his profession her husband likes new things. "Why he even eats tomatoes," she says. Another of his ideas is a hearth oven where squash and spicy gingerbread are baking. He is ahead of his time and his wife obviously is pleased with all of the labor-saving devices in her house.

The last kitchen is the simplest of all. It is the hearth in the log cabin of a struggling family. To save gun-shot—which is expensive—this rugged pioneer snared a rabbit which is in a black pot hung over the roaring fire. Squash, turnips, corn and bread made on the hearth will round out this humble Christmas dinner. Because candles are also expensive, the hard-working wife tells us that they will snuff out their lights right after dinner and will not sit and visit for hours as people do in the wealthy homes of the town. Also, when breakfast is served at 4 a.m., bedtimes are early.

Following is a collection of authentic 19th century recipes prepared at Conner Prairie during the holiday season. All have been adapted for today's cooks.

## COCONUT POUND CAKE

- 3 **cups sifted flour**
- ¼ **teaspoon salt**
- 2 **teaspoons baking powder**
- 1 **cup softened butter**
- 3½ **cups powdered sugar**
- 2 **teaspoons vanilla**
- 1 **drop of lemon extract**

4 eggs, well beaten
½ cup milk
4 ounce can grated coconut
1 lemon, grated rind only

Sift flour, salt and baking powder together. Set aside. Cream butter, then add sugar a little at a time, beating until smooth. Add vanilla and lemon extract and the well beaten eggs. Mix in flour and milk alternating them—starting with flour and ending with flour. Finally, stir in coconut and lemon rind. Pour batter into a buttered and lightly floured 10-inch tube pan. Bake in preheated 350° oven for 35 minutes. Reduce oven heat to 325° and continue baking 35 minutes longer or until cake pulls away from the sides of the pan. Cool about 10 minutes, then remove from pan, and cool completely on a cake rack. Serve cake without frosting, cut in very thin slices. This cake keeps well if wrapped in foil.

### FUDGE FANCIES
1 cup light brown sugar
1 cup white sugar
½ cup butter
1 6-ounce package of chocolate bits, melted
3 eggs, beaten
2 cups sifted flour
1 teaspoon soda

1 teaspoon salt
1 tablespoon vanilla
1 cup chopped walnuts

Cream butter and sugars together. Add cooled melted chocolate bits and eggs. Beat well. Sift together flour, soda and salt. Stir in and beat until well blended. Add vanilla and nuts. Place on greased cookie sheet in small balls about 3 inches apart. Bake at 375° for about 12 minutes. Makes about 5 dozen small cookies.

### STACK CAKE
1 cup butter
1 cup sugar
1 cup molasses
1 teaspoon soda
3 eggs
1 cup milk
4 cups flour
1 teaspoon each: salt, cinnamon, nutmeg and allspice
    Spicy applesauce or cooked dried apricots, for filling

Cream butter and sugar together, add molasses, mix well. Beat eggs into mixture, add milk alternately with combined dry ingredients. Mix well. Pour batter 1/2 inch deep in 6 eight-inch layer pans. Bake for 20 minutes in a 375° oven. When cool fill layers with spicy applesauce, cooked dry apricots, or canned apricot filling. Do not ice.

### OHIO LEMON PIE
*Slice two lemons, rind and all, as thin as paper. Place them in a bowl and mix with 2 cups of sugar. Let stand for 2 hours or more. Line a 9-inch pie plate with lower crust. Add 4 beaten eggs to lemon mixture and mix well. Pour into crust. Add top crust with small vents cut to let out steam. Place in 450° oven for 15 minutes and then cut down heat to 350° and bake until a silver knife comes out clean.* ■

# �A𝖭𝖣EX